Community Economic Development

The role of economic development in communities is multi-faceted, having an array of antecedents, impacts, and implications. This volume explores the relationships between economic development and community development, focusing on the aspects that impact communities such as social capital, participation, and business development. It discusses the need for aligning the goals of community betterment more closely with economic improvement and finding ways to enhance leadership and other resources. Including both current contributions and "classics," the evolution of the relationship between, and roles of, the two kinds of development is explored.

The articles in the volume present several theoretical perspectives of development. Most common among them are sustainable economic development and social capital theories. Utilizing these theories and data from various sources, the authors are able to suggest specific development strategies for improving community economic and quality of life outcomes. The volume offers an exploration of directions for future research, including the need for more theoretical and empirical work on the role of amenity development on rural community economic and quality-of-life outcomes. Practitioners of community and economic development, along with researchers and students will find this volume useful and relevant for both theory and application.

This book is a compilation of articles published in the *Journal of the Community Development Society*.

Rhonda G. Phillips, Ph.D., AICP, CEcD is a professor, a planner and community economic developer whose work fosters innovative development approaches. Her research and service outreach includes assessing community well-being and quality-of-life outcomes. She holds professional certifications in both economic development and planning.

Terry L. Besser, Ph.D. is a professor of rural sociology. Her research focuses on rural economic vitality, social capital, business networks, and business social responsibility. Most recently she has examined these topics for rural prairie towns experiencing dramatic increases in Hispanic immigration.

Community Development – Current Issues Series
Series Editor: Rhonda G. Phillips

The Community Development Society (CDS) in conjunction with Routledge/Taylor & Francis is pleased to present this series of volumes on current issues in community development. The series is designed to present books organized around special topics or themes, promoting exploration of timely and relevant issues impacting both community development practice and research. Building on a rich history of over 40 years of publishing the journal, *Community Development,* the series will provide reprints of special issues and collections from the journal. Each volume is updated with the editor's introductory chapter, bringing together current applications around the topical theme.

Founded in 1970, the Community Development Society is a professional association serving both researchers and practitioners. CDS actively promotes the continued advancement of the practice and knowledge base of community development. For additional information about CDS, visit www.comm-dev.org

Tourism, Planning, and Community Development
Edited by Rhonda G. Phillips and Sherma Roberts

Community Development Approaches to Improving Public Health
Edited by Robert Ogilvie

Community Economic Development
Edited by Rhonda G. Phillips and Terry L. Besser

Community Leadership Development
Theory, Research and Application
Edited by Mark A. Brennan

Cooperatives and Community Development
Edited by Vanna Gonzales and Rhonda G. Phillips

Local Food and Community Development
Edited by Gary Paul Green and Rhonda G. Phillips

Developing Sustainable Agriculture and Community
Edited by Jeffrey Jordan and Lionel J. Beaulieu

Community Economic Development

Edited by
Rhonda G. Phillips and Terry L. Besser

LONDON AND NEW YORK

First published 2013
by Routledge
2 Park Square, Milton Park, Abingdon, Oxon, OX14 4RN

Simultaneously published in the USA and Canada
by Routledge
711 Third Avenue, New York, NY 10017

Routledge is an imprint of the Taylor & Francis Group, an informa business

British Library Cataloguing in Publication Data
A catalogue record for this book is available from the British Library

ISBN13: 978-0-415-63409-0

Typeset in Times New Roman
by Taylor & Francis Books

Publisher's Note
The publisher would like to make readers aware that the chapters in this book may be referred to as articles as they are identical to the articles published in the special issue. The publisher accepts responsibility for any inconsistencies that may have arisen in the course of preparing this volume for print.

Contents

Citation Information

The following chapters were originally published in *Community Development*. When citing this material, please use the original page numbering for each article, as follows:

Chapter 2
Achieving Sustainable Economic Development in Communities
Ron Shaffer
Community Development, volume 26, issue 2 (1995) pp. 145-154

Chapter 3
Gleaners, Do-Gooders, and Balers: Options for Linking Sustainability and Economic Development
Ted K. Bradshaw and Karri Winn
Community Development, volume 31, issue 1 (2000) pp. 112-129

Chapter 4
The Community and Economic Development Chain: Validating the Links Between Processes and Outcomes
Robert Pittman, Evan Pittman, Rhonda Phillips and Joe Canglelosi
Community Development, volume 40, issue 1 (2009) pp. 80-93

Chapter 5
Economic Development in the Nonmetropolitan West: The Influence of Built, Natural, and Social Capital
Jessica Crowe
Community Development, Vol. 39, No. 4 (2008) pp. 51-70

Chapter 6
Development of Last Resort: The Impact of New State Prisons on Small Town Economies in the United States
Terry L. Besser and Margaret M. Hanson
Community Development, volume 35, issue 2 (2004) pp. 1-16

Chapter 7
Chain stores and local economies: a case study of a rural county in New York
Stephen Halebsky
Community Development, Vol. 41, No. 4 (Oct-Dec 2010) pp.431-452

INTRODUCTION

Rhonda Phillips and Terry L. Besser

The role of economic development in communities is multi-faceted, having an array of antecedents, impacts, and implications. This volume explores the relationships between economic development and community development, focusing on the aspects that impact communities such as social capital, participation, and business development. It discusses the need for more closely aligning the goals of community betterment and economic improvement and finding ways to enhance leadership and other resources. Both current contributions and "classics" are used to explore the evolution of the roles and relationships between these two kinds of development.

The chapters included here present several theoretical and applied perspectives of development. Most common among them are sustainable economic development and social capital theories. Utilizing these foundations and data from various sources, specific development strategies are suggested for improving community economic and quality of life outcomes.

THE RELATIONSHIP BETWEEN COMMUNITY DEVELOPMENT AND ECONOMIC DEVELOPMENT

Community development and economic development have both evolved from a wide variety of fields and perspectives. The need for both types of development and the attention paid to them through the years has increased, especially as economies decline and social systems are stressed. And while each is distinct, there is an overlap in the areas of community improvement and economic betterment that has given rise to approaches and practices of *community economic development*. In other words, this is economic development at the community level with a healthy dose of community development included.

We begin to explore these relationships by defining the key terms involved.

Phillips and Pittman provide a working definition of community development as the following:

> A *process*: developing and increasing the ability to act collectively, and an *outcome*: (1) taking collective action and (2) the result of that action for improvement in a community in any or all realms: physical, environmental, cultural, social, political, economic, etc. (2009, p. 6)

It is implied that capacity, commonly referred to as social capital, fuels the community development process, fostering desirable outcomes. A definition of social capital is:

> the extent to which members of a community can work together effectively to develop and sustain strong relationships, solve problems and make group decisions; and collaborate effectively to plan, set goals, and get things done. (Phillips & Pittman, 2009, p. 6)

Of course, there are other forms of capital that are important in community development. These include physical, financial, natural, and built resources as well as others. Emery and Flora describe "seven different components of community capital: natural, cultural, human, social, political, financial, and built capitals" (2006, p. 20). While all of these are important and even essential, without social capital it would be hard to actualize effective community development because it represents the capacity to get things done.

Community development has a rich history originating in late nineteenth-century social movements concerned with collective action and civil society and later reenergized by the social movements of the 1960s. These movements in the 1960s coupled with the leadership provided by development professionals and disciplines concerned with urban planning, policy, and rural sociology prompted thousands of community development corporations to emerge in response to the severe challenges facing urban communities as well as rural and small towns. The needs of the newly created community development corporations and the enthusiasm of practitioners and scholars alike led to the founding of the Community Development Society (CDS) in 1970 in North America. The goals of this society are expressed in its core Principles of Good Practice:

- Promote active and representative participation toward enabling all community members to meaningfully influence the decisions that affect their lives.
- Engage community members in learning about and understanding community issues, and the economic, social, environmental, political, psychological, and other impacts associated with alternative courses of action.
- Incorporate the diverse interests and cultures of the community in the community development process; and disengage from support of any effort that is likely to adversely affect the disadvantaged members of a community.
- Work actively to enhance the leadership capacity of community members, leaders, and groups within the community.
- Be open to using the full range of action strategies to work toward the long-term sustainability and well-being of the community. (CDS, 2012)

The International Association for Community Development (IACD), with members from across the globe, put forth their current strategic priorities as the following:

- Promote community development as a key method for addressing challenges, opportunities, and priority issues in rural and urban areas locally, regionally, and internationally.

- Facilitate quality practice exchange, education, training, research, and publications in support of practitioners, educators, researchers, policy analysts, activists, and other community workers and organizers.
- Engage practitioners, educators, researchers, policy analysts, activists, and other community workers and organizers at country and regional levels and thereby promote their community-based planning and development work. (IACD, 2012)

One can quickly see that the values of social justice, equity, and participation are central to the ethos of community development.

Let us now turn our attention to economic development. Economic development, as a practice and profession, grew from a focus on industrial recruitment. Modern practices of industrial recruitment in the U.S. originated in the twentieth century when southern states attempted to recruit northern manufacturers to move south. In the more recent past, myriad programs, strenuous efforts, and huge expenditures have been devoted to attracting companies to relocate or open in a particular community, county, or region. As just one of many examples, in September 2012 various Iowa government agencies agreed to provide approximately $240 million to an Egyptian fertilizer company to build a plant in southeast Iowa (Eller, 2012). Terry Branstad, Governor of Iowa, indicated that an additional $50 million in loans and grants was necessary to top Illinois' tax, grant, and loan package. The competition between locations to attract employers illustrated by this example has fostered what Gary Green and Anna Haines (2007) call the "race to the bottom."

The rationale for industrial recruitment activities can be found in two theories summarized here, economic base theory and market failure theory. The central premise of economic base theory is that development requires enticing external monies into the local or regional economy. Especially attractive are employers that provide products or services to be sold outside the community. These "exporters" will bring in more external monies resulting in a larger multiplier effect compared to other kinds of economic activity. According to this reasoning, the initial investment to lure an exporting employer will provide a greater return to the location than other kinds of economic investments.

The logic of economic base theory has been used to justify recruiting non-export-oriented employers as well. Even though the expected multiplier effect is lower, communities defend providing generous start up packages to retail firms (see Halebsky in Chapter 7) and prisons (see Besser and Hanson in Chapter 6) with the belief that new jobs of any kind will generate wealth for the area. Economic base theory has generated a host of tools and techniques to gauge and assess the strength of a local economy. These include location quotients, cluster/targeted industry, and shift-share analysis.

Another theory used to support the intense and expensive marketing efforts involved in industrial recruitment is market failure theory. Proponents of this theory maintain that the allocation of goods and services in the marketplace is not always efficient. The inaccessibility of information prevents an optimum match between those seeking to invest and build productive capacity and communities that represent a good location for that investment. Thus the marketing efforts of communities and states to recruit new employers is intended to remedy this market failing.

So, why hasn't industrial recruitment been more successful in generating new economic activity especially in rural areas? And even when a new employer is recruited to a location, too often the community at large, or significant sections of the community, do not gain economically. One of the reasons is that state and local governments have not always been successful at picking and choosing "winners" in which to invest. As Haughton describes, "years of experience have shown the futility of pouring large amounts of state and private sector investments into projects which lack a long-term, community-based perspective" (1999, p. 1). Yet this does not serve as a deterrent as states and localities (at least in the U.S.) continue to pump significant funds into industrial recruitment. Over the last decade, Michigan spent between $100 million and $250 million per year; in 2011, Florida spent $11 million, Indiana $37 million, and a major effort by Ohio surpassed them all: $1.4 billion proposed to be spent in one year (Cauchon, 2011). While not all this is for industrial recruitment, a significant portion appears to be; other spending plans include for new industrial parks, loan programs, and speculative industrial sites.

Despite state agencies' continued investment in industrial recruitment, many local governments and community leaders realize the difficulty of pursuing a finite number of corporate and employment opportunities. Consequently they have shifted their economic development efforts toward the creation of location-specific opportunities instead of relying predominately on recruiting external ones. Especially common are activities such as small business development, programs to encourage and support entrepreneurship, and local business retention and expansion efforts. The idea behind expanding the kinds of economic development strategies utilized is that it will take more than industrial recruitment to create wealth in communities and regions. Economic development should be goal-oriented change, not change for change's sake, and reflective of *development* instead of just economic growth (Shaffer, Deller, & Marcouiller, 2004, p. 4). The American Economic Development Council (now the International Economic Development Council) defined economic development along these lines nearly thirty years ago as:

> the process of creating wealth through the mobilization of human, financial, capital, physical and natural resources to generate marketable goods and services. The economic developer's role is to influence the process for the benefit of the community through expanding job opportunities and the tax base. (AEDC, 1984, p. 181)

What's missing from this definition? While the focus on wealth creation continues to be front and center, newer approaches include the need to consider quality of life dimensions as well. Rangarajan et al. elaborate this perspective, "When quality of life is viewed from an economic development perspective, it refers to the economic well-being of the region, the lifestyle that people lead, and the environment that a region has to offer" (2012, p. 321). Beauregard (1993) long ago pointed out that in economic development there is a tendency to lose sight of broader political and social issues impacting community quality of life. Rangarajan et al. and others have encouraged practitioners and scholars to expand definitions and indicators (both quantitative and qualitative) of economic development to include community well-being. This is very similar to the definition of community development, and we will soon see how the paths cross more explicitly.

The merging of economic and community development is evident among the new generation of economic development professionals who are as concerned about the quality of economic activity generated (i.e., the quality of jobs created) as the old generation was concerned about the quantity of jobs resulting from development efforts. The newer emphasis on quality as much as quantity is another reason for the focus on nurturing local and regional economic opportunities in addition to industrial recruitment strategies. Developing local economic opportunities requires programs to build local human and social capacities. The International Economic Development Council (IEDC), in its 2010 report *Creating Quality Jobs, Transforming the Economic Development Landscape*, urges inclusion of quality into the economic development equation, insisting that high quality jobs equate to higher quality workforce and community welfare. They provide the following advice: "The goal for economic developers is to provide opportunities across a spectrum of skill levels and industries to build advancement into a community's economic structure (IEDC, 2010, p. 6). Further, they state that an economic development approach encouraging support for both creating quality jobs and improving jobs already in the community "is more likely to provide broadly distributed benefits to individuals, society and the economy" (p. 9).

"Broadly distributed benefits?" The overlap between economic and community development is becoming even more apparent. It is this wider interpretation and inclusion of additional factors and considerations that holds the promise of moving economic development toward a more beneficial practice aimed at fostering improved quality of life. Blair explained several decades ago that economic development, while focusing on production, consumption, and other resource allocation issues "should not lose sight of the fact that local economic development is part of a larger process of community development" (1995, p. 15). Some definitions have gone so far as to include environmental and social dimensions, bringing them close to what is considered to be "sustainable development." Others describe community economic development as a holistic approach connecting capacity-building processes and outcomes of community development with those of economic development to achieve desired economic, social, and environmental goals (Haughton, 1999; Phillips & Pittman, 2009). Conceptions of community economic development continue to evolve. For example, an explanation of community economic development from the recent past provides a more typical or expected emphasis on approaches to the practice and shows how conceptions are shifting:

> We maintain that community economic development occurs when people in a community analyze the economic conditions of that community, determine its economic needs and unfulfilled opportunities, decide what can be done to improve economic conditions in that community, and then move to achieve agreed upon economic goals and objectives. (Shaffer, Deller, & Marcouiller, 2006, p. 61)

A newer definition incorporates both concepts of sustainable development and social equity, reflecting a broader or more holistic approach:

> Community economic development, and its values and practices, are indeed important strategies to help forge a stronger base for addressing key challenges going forward such as (1) development that protects the environment while opening opportunities for the poor to build wealth and opportunity, and (2) assisting in the larger project of strengthening the economic competiveness of cities and regions. (Anglin, 2011, p. xx)

This leads us to a definition of community economic development, which we agree is a merging of aspects of the fields of community development and economic development, implying practice aimed at community betterment and economic improvement at the local level, preferably encompassing sustainable development approaches.

THEORY AND PRACTICE OVERVIEWS: COMMUNITY ECONOMIC DEVELOPMENT

We will now utilize the contributions of the authors of the chapters in this volume to summarize the salient theories of community economic development practice. A particularly appropriate place to begin the summary is with Shaffer's classic overview of sustainable development. Ron Shaffer was the founding director of the University of Wisconsin's Center for Community Economic Development and a director of the National Rural Economic Development Institute—his continuing influence on the theory and practice of community economic development is profound. Shaffer's focus on sustainability was innovative and slightly controversial in 1995 when this article was published. As he described, *sustainable community economic development is about changing perceptions and choices regarding community resources, markets, rules, and decision-making capacity.* He was among the first to focus on the importance of capacity, and building that capacity for community improvement. He proposed four main elements in designing sustainable economic development programs—decision making, resources, markets, and rules. Dykeman (1990) provides a definition of sustainable community economic development included in this chapter—it has much relevance for practice twenty years later. Shaffer has provided an excellent discussion on the theory behind sustainable development and community economic development, including pointing out the role of Schumpeter's creative destruction. The chart of paradigm shifts illustrates how the practice and precepts of community economic development have moved from traditional viewpoints to a more inclusive one incorporating sustainability.

In Chapter 3, Bradshaw and Winn expand Shaffer's view of sustainable development by adding ecological factors into the sustainability equation. Ted Bradshaw was the former editor of *Community Development*; his legacy of community development work continues to inspire developers and community leaders. Bradshaw and Winn introduce the concept of the third wave economic development. By this they mean those economic development strategies aimed at reducing incentives and shifting emphasis from firm-based programs to broader regional programs, especially leadership, information, and brokering—[as] the essential tools by which states can establish their industrial policies ... These policies are based on extensive strategic planning, public-private partnerships, foundations of technology, human resources and capital, and the development of strategic industrial clusters. (Bradshaw & Blakely, 1999, p. 229)

The authors advance the recommendation that sustainable development must meet the needs of businesses, helping them grow into viable long-term generators of wealth and economic vitality while minimizing or reversing long-term damage to the environment from economic activity. They point out that economic development and ecological sustainability are not incompatible and illustrate this position with examples of gleaners, do-gooders, and balers. A do-gooder is defined as someone who serves as a "watchdog of public welfare who evokes collective guilt over the extent of consumption that goes with affluence," while "balers, people making housing out of stacked and plastered bales of straw, are examples of the viability of sustainable technology in industries in which ecological alternatives are viewed with both suspicion and hostility." Gleaners are those who gather recyclable materials throughout both the urban and the rural environments. Their agenda for realizing sustainable development concludes this chapter.

Chapter 4 presents another framework for envisioning the interrelationship between community development and economic development. Building on work by Phillips and Pittman (2009), Pittman et al. point out the need to bring in social capital theory. The framework centers on the idea that community development increases the capacity of a community to act, which in turn builds social capital, defined as the extent to which members of a community can work together effectively to develop and sustain strong relationships, solve problems and make group decisions, and collaborate effectively to plan, set goals, and achieve accomplishments (Phillips & Pittman, 2009). Social capital is positively associated with community educational levels, better access to high quality medical care, and cultural amenities, often referred to as quality of life features. It is also noted for its ability to mobilize resources for economic development. Both of these relate to community economic development outcomes—quality and quantity of jobs and wealth creation. The economic development outcomes are positively associated with community capacity-building, completing the reciprocal cycle of community and economic development. Pittman et al. provide empirical evidence supporting this logic by analyzing data from surveys of community and economic development professionals in Louisiana.

Crowe, in Chapter 5, compares how different kinds of community capitals, natural, built, social, and human, contribute to implementing economic development strategies. Using key informant interviews in seven rural towns in Washington and Oregon, Crowe concluded that human capital was not important to either industrial recruitment or self-development outcomes. She utilized the Flora et al., 1992 definition of self-development as "activities fostering local businesses and other entrepreneurial activities along with relying on local resources to aid in development from within the community," with examples including "revitalizing downtown businesses, promoting local tourism, and retaining or expanding locally owned businesses." Towns that had implemented the most industrial recruitment strategies were high on at least two of the three capitals—social capital, natural capital, or built capital. Communities with high or moderate levels of both natural capital and social capital implemented a moderate number of self-development projects. This further supports the theory of social capital as applied to community economic development practice.

In contrast to traditional style industrial recruitment, Chapter 6 by Besser and Hanson and Chapter 7 by Halebsky examine how new kinds of industrial recruitment strategies affect community economic outcomes. Besser and Hanson provide a different slant on industrial recruitment by considering the outcomes of rural towns' successful efforts to attract new prisons. Rural towns with new state prisons built between 1990 and 2000 were worse off in 2000 compared to their situation in 1990 than matched small towns without new state prisons. New prison towns had higher poverty rates, higher unemployment rates, fewer total jobs, lower household wages, fewer housing units, and lower median value of housing in 2000 when 1990 population and economic indicators are controlled. Clearly the economic development strategy of attracting a new prison did not provide economic benefits for small towns, at least in the short term.

Halebsky addresses the impact of chain retail stores on community economies with a case study. Rural communities may not actively recruit chain stores and in many cases they actively discourage them. But past studies provide little evidence about the economic impact on the community of chain stores (non-local owners) vs. locally owned stores. The author contends that although the retail sector often receives little respect from economic developers and scholars due to its suspected low multiplier effect, it is valuable to local economies because it provides jobs, wealth, and income for owners, goods and services for locals, and tax revenue, and is a purchaser of local services and goods. To ascertain the "multiplier effect" of locally owned retail firms, Halebsky develops an indicator which he calls retails' "unique contribution." This indicator measures the extent to which profit is retained in the community and goods and services (especially financial and producer services) are purchased locally. In this case, the unique contribution of local ownership amounts to 14 percent of retail revenue or $42 million annually. Both chapters demonstrate the weakness of industrial recruitment strategies and further illustrate the need to move toward a more inclusive and broader conceptualization of economic development.

SUGGESTIONS FOR IMPROVING COMMUNITY ECONOMIC DEVELOPMENT

Several chapters suggest ways in which community economic development can be improved. In Chapter 8, Muske and Woods focus specifically on techniques for improving self-development strategies. Their research examined the microbusiness sector (for profit enterprises with fewer than 10 employees) to determine the elements important for business success. The authors argued that this sector is important for community economic vitality because these businesses provide jobs, income for owners, and sales tax revenue. The business owners in this study reported that their main needs are for help with financing, marketing, financial reporting, general record-keeping, and government regulations.

Sullivan's Chapter 9 and Bessant's Chapter 10 present a more comprehensive approach suggesting that broader resident participation and additional resources are imperative for generating effective community economic development. Sullivan argues that broad resident involvement is essential to effective community economic development efforts. He uses prior research to document the value of having citizen participation. Because economic development agencies handle public money and often have direct access to city powers such as condemnation power, it is imperative that their activities be transparent and reflect citizens' interests and welfare. Sullivan then concludes that city officials and business leaders are heavily involved in economic development agency functions, but private citizens are not. One of the reasons is that many economic development organizations do not have any private citizens on their boards and do not publically advertise their meetings or have open meetings.

In the final chapter, Bessant examines how Manitoba communities balance the goals of community development and economic development as manifested in the structure and goals of the local agency charged with these functions. Theoretically, community development corporations are local self-help entities organized to promote location-specific economic and social betterment. They are intended to be broadly inclusive and reflect local objectives and needs. Bessant found that most of the local organizations focus their efforts largely on business and economic development even though they have a broader community development mandate. In effect, they have become community economic development organizations instead of community development organizations. Although Bessant concludes that the development organizations include representatives from a broad array of community sectors, they admit that city officials, chamber officers, and business leaders constitute the majority of board members. This supports Sullivan's findings about low private citizen participation in community economic development. Shortages of leadership, finances, knowledge, and expertise were identified as limiting the capacity of small town community development organizations. He recommends more closely aligning the goals of community betterment and economic improvement in these organizations and finding ways to enhance leadership and other resources.

DIRECTIONS FOR FUTURE RESEARCH

The contributions in this book suggest several substantive areas that would benefit from future research, and as a group, the chapters reveal places where methodological triangulation would strengthen and advance our understanding of this subject. We list these suggestions below. We believe that pursuing these suggestions will assist the field of community economic development to continue to be a valuable resource for communities as they face ever-changing challenges to their economic vitality and quality of life.

1. Theoretical and empirical explorations specifically on the role of amenity development in rural community economic and quality of life outcomes.
2. Updated research comparing economic and quality of life outcomes of sustainable development approaches, industrial recruitment, and self-development.
3. Comparisons of communities with high resident participation in community economic development to those with less involvement. What are the consequences for economic and quality of life outcomes?
4. More case studies and large sample examinations to provide best practices examples.
5. Continued exploration of quality of life dimensions for addressing these aspects of community economic development processes and outcomes, using both quantitative and qualitative study approaches.

REFERENCES

American Economic Development Council (AEDC). (1984). *Economic Development Today: A Report to the Profession*, Schiller Park, IL: AEDC.
Anglin, R. (2011). Promoting sustainable local and community economic development. London: CRC Press.
Beauregard, R. (1993). Constituting economic development: A theoretical perspective. In R. Bingham and R. Mier (Eds.), *Theories of local economic development: Perspectives from across the disciplines* (pp. 267–283). Newbury Park, CA: Sage.
Blair, R. (1995). Local economic development, analysis and practice. London: Sage.

Bradshaw, T., & Blakely, E. J. (1999). What are "third-wave" state economic development efforts? From incentives to industrial policy. *Economic Development Quarterly*, 13(3), 229–244.

Cauchon, D. (2011). "Ohio is spending $1.4 billion to attract jobs. Will it work?" *USA Today*, April 25, 2011, http://usatoday30.usatoday.com/money/economy/2011-04-26-job-creation-shovel-ready.htm

Community Development Society (2012). Retrieved September 23, 2012 from http://www.comm-dev.org

Dykeman, F. W. (1990). Developing an understanding of entrepreneurial and sustainable rural communities, in F. W. Dykeman (ed.) *Entrepreneurial and Sustainable Communities.* Sackville, NB: Rural Studies and Small Town Research and Studies Programme, Department of Geography, Mount Allison University.

Eller, D. (2012). Orascom says it will build fertilizer in southeast Iowa. *Des Moines Register*, September 5.

Emery, M., & Flora, C. (2006). Spiraling up: Mapping community transformation with community capitals framework. *Community Development*, 37(1), 19–35.

Flora. J., Green. G., Gale, A.E., F.. Schmidt, F.E., & Flora, C. (1992). Self development: A viable rural development option? *Policy Studies Journal* 20:276-88.

Green, G. P., & Haines, A. (2007). *Assets building and community development*. Thousand Oaks, CA: Sage.

Haughton, G. (1999). *Community Economic Development,* London: The Stationery Office.

International Association for Community Development. (2012). Retrieved September 23, 2012 from http://www.iacdglobal.org/about/strategic-plan

International Economic Development Council. (2010). *Creating quality jobs, transforming the economic development landscape*. Washington, DC: IEDC.

Phillips, R., & Pittman, R. (2009). *Introduction to community development*. Abingdon: Routledge.

Rangarajan, R., Long, S., Ziemer, N., & Lewis, N. (2012). An evaluative economic development typology for sustainable rural economic development. *Community Development*, 43(3), 320–332.

Shaffer, R., Deller, S., & Marcouiller, D. (2006). Rethinking community economic development. *Economic Development Quarterly*, 20(1), 59–74.

Shaffer, R., Deller, S., & Marcouiller, D. (2004). *Community economics, linking theory and practice.* London: Blackwell.

ACHIEVING SUSTAINABLE ECONOMIC DEVELOPMENT IN COMMUNITIES

By Ron Shaffer

ABSTRACT

The options available for communities to work toward sustainable community economic development are explored through four fundamental elements of community economic development theory. Sustainable community economic development is about changing perceptions and choices regarding community resources, markets, rules, and decision-making capacity. The idea of new knowledge and reframing issues is offered as a method to create new options. The dimensions of time, space, marginalized social-economic groups, and dynamic economies broaden the concept of sustainable development beyond the more traditional physical-biological definition.

INTRODUCTION

Community developers are increasingly struggling with fundamental questions about whether their efforts will have continuing impact and not unintentionally foreclose future options for community residents. The idea of sustainability is advanced to capture this struggle. While the concept of sustainability is influenced substantially by one's values, this paper uses four fundamental elements of community economic development theory to explore the options available for communities to work toward sustainable community economic development.

Sustainable community economic development is about changing perceptions and choices regarding community resources, markets, rules, and decision-making capacity. The idea of integrating new knowledge and reframing issues is a method to create new options. By understanding these forces, the community improves its capacity to manipulate them to the community's advantage. The dimensions of time, space, marginalized social-economic groups, and dynamic economies broaden the concept of sustainable development beyond the more traditional physical-biological definition. The balance of the paper explores the substantial shift in our conceptualization of development, and the necessary

Ron Shaffer is Professor of Agricultural Economics and Community Development Economist, University of Wisconsin–Madison/Extension. An earlier version of this paper was shared at the International Conference on Issues Affecting Rural Communities, Townsville, QLD Australia, July 14, 1994.

conditions for sustainable community economic development. The paper does not reach conclusions, but attempts to summarize the thinking of one person trying to give personal meaning to an important question facing communities and those who work with them.

THE PARADIGM SHIFT

In many respects sustainable development represents a shift in paradigms about how development occurs and which aspects of development are crucial. Table 1 offers two contrasting paradigms about how our socio-economic-biological system works. No small part of the current sustainability debate is about which paradigm most accurately reflects the conditions of today and desires for tomorrow. The distinctions in Table 1 are exaggerated to expose what I believe to be the different perspectives and move us toward some general ideas regarding sustainable development.

The elements in Table 1 represent parts of two alternative views of how we frame the question of community economic development and indicate both how it will occur and the likely outcomes. These differences are not new. The first more visible appearance probably occurred in the 60s, when communities, neighborhoods, community activists, and public officials started to deal with the initiatives of the Kennedy–Johnson Administrations.

The old paradigm can be summarized in terms of more of the same, technological fixes, everyone will naturally benefit, and little connection among the elements of the community and elsewhere. The new paradigm suggests that there will be substantial transformations in how we do business; social interactions and networks are substantial parts of the fixes; conscious efforts are required to insure those we seek to help are actually helped; and the connections among all of us are stronger and often more indirect than we realize.

While these ideas have ebbed and flowed in the academic literature, policy debates, and community meetings, the emergence of the interest in sustainable development has given some legitimacy and renewed attention to how community economic development occurs and what outcomes we expect. Several themes come together in helping me make some sense of what this means in my professional career and how I might work with communities exploring their choices. The ideas contained in the concept of sustainable development help me look at how a community's economy is organized, what are key components, and how it changes over time.

Sustainable Development

In defining sustainable development, most analysts start with the World Commission on Environment and Development (Brundtland Report) definition of sustainable development as "that which ensures the needs of the present are met, without compromising the ability of future generations to meet their own

Table 1. Paradigms Describing Community Economic Development

Old	New
Growth is preeminent (more of the same)	Development is preeminent (long-term transformation)
Benefits of growth will naturally trickle down and out to others	Equity considerations require conscious policy efforts
Individuals are wise and all-knowing	Individuals can comprehend only part of what is happening and needed
Technological change is either always good or will solve most problems	Technological change is only one of many possible solutions, and may not even be one of the better choices
Tomorrow will look like today	Tomorrow may look like today, but certainly no guarantee
Externalities of space, time, and class typically of minor concern and likely to take care of themselves	Externalities of space, time, social groups must be explicitly considered
Dynamic economies are growing	Dynamic economies are creating new choices, reframing of issues, changing perceptions of markets and resources, changing values
Socio-economic-biological elements are largely independent or can be treated that way	Socio-economic-biological elements are so interdependent that failure to consider linkages creates problems

needs" (1987, p. 9). The balance of the Brundtland Report emphasizes management and control over development, plus a holistic approach to problem solving. This is a perspective most community developers feel reflects their values. An overlooked aspect of the report is recognition that "development is not a fixed state of harmony,[1] but rather a process of change in which the use of resources, direction of investments, orientation of technological development, and institutional change are made consistent with future as well as present needs" (World Commission, 1987, p. 9).

Part of the dilemma facing many of us is that the definition remains fluid. One expansion of the Brundtland definition includes

> ... a system that secures effective participation in decision making, provides for solutions that arise from disharmonious development, and is flexible and has the capacity for self-correction. ... a production system that respects the obligation to preserve the ecological base for the future while continuing to search for new solutions (Sustainable Rural Communities Committee, 1991, p. 6).

---

[1] Schumpeter (1983) defines development as *creative destruction*.

The addition of disenfranchised groups in decision making is an important advancement. While their involvement in the actual decision making may not be a reality, the inclusion of their interests and perspectives in the choices considered is paramount. This dimension is particularly crucial to community developers.

The importance of time becomes significant when considering that many families and communities are having increased difficulty earning an acceptable standard of living and are experiencing an increasing sense of marginalization. This sense certainly places a premium on decisions favoring this generation and attempting to capture the "good life."[2]

For community developers, this idea of time and sustainable development should not imply maintaining or returning to some nostalgic recollection of how things once were. A form of nostalgic misdirection is that every community and its historic role should be protected from outside forces and has a right to survive. Rather, greater emphasis needs to be put on the future and what may be possible with respect to maintaining options or choices for the future.

To close this section, Dykeman's (1990, p. 6–7) definition of sustainable community economic development is particularly helpful.

> . . . those communities that manage and control their destiny based on a realistic and well thought through vision. Such a community based management and control approach requires that a process be instituted within the community that effectively uses knowledge and knowledge systems to direct change and determine appropriate courses of action consistent with ecological principles. The process must be comprehensive and address social, economic, physical, and environmental concerns in an integrated fashion while maintaining central concern for present and future welfare of individuals and the community.

SUSTAINABLE COMMUNITY ECONOMIC DEVELOPMENT

Figure 1 displays the essence of my conception of how community economic development occurs.[3] The nodes in Figure 1 represent four significant elements that influence the economic change of a community (Shaffer, 1989). The diagram could be better displayed as a hologram, in motion with different images at different angles.

Two elements of Figure 1 that transcend the sustainability discussion are the need to be comprehensive in the strategies of change (Pulver, 1979) and the need

---

[2] For some marginalized groups the "good life" is rising above subsistence (Rural Sociological Society, 1993).

[3] Wilkinson (1991) and others argue that developing the social system called a community is far more important than just the economic dimensions of that community. The present discussion is limited to sustaining the economic dimensions of the community rather than the general concern of sustaining the community, but they are inseparable ideas.

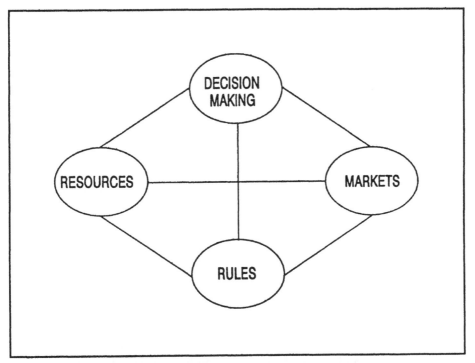

Figure 1. Crucial elements of community economic development.

to incorporate the various components of the community's economy in problem definition and the creation of options (Shaffer, 1989).

The resource node reminds us of the need to incorporate capital (financial, buildings, public infrastructure, housing), labor (workers, skills, educational outcomes), and technology (management systems, waste disposal or production, skill requirements) as important aspects of the community. Some policies communities create within this node include industrial parks, revolving loan funds, vocational training, management training, and low/moderate housing. The resource node can be thought of as the supply aspect of community's economy. It is the ability of the community to produce the desired goods and services.

The market node represents the demand side of community's economy. It is the nonlocal and local markets in which the community operates. These nonlocal markets could be international, in the next state, or in the next county. This is the export base idea of community economic development that probably best represents the old logic in Figure 1. It also represents the sense of how community economies change for an alarming portion of community and economic developers. The efforts to attract businesses to the community are the most obvious community policies emerging from this node. It is important, however, not to ignore the local market form. The local market generally affects community residents most directly. It relates to what goods and services are available locally, customer relations, store hours, parking, and ADA access. Shopper surveys, mainstreet renovation, and parking facilities are examples of local market focus community activities.

The aspects of the community's economy contained within the rules node are the more visible legal and the less visible cultural/values structures. Examples of visible legal structures include zoning, housing safety, taxing, forms of business organization, inheritance transfers, contracts, and utility regulation. The less visible cultural/value aspects of rules are the standards of conduct that are encouraged or accepted. A recent example of this element is the communitarianism ideas present in such work as Etzioni (1993). The recent work by Putnam (1993) and the Floras (1993) on social capital is another form of the less visible cultural/value dimensions.

The decision making node involves leadership, which most community developers would feel is their *entrée*. While leadership captures some parts of this node, it really is much more comprehensive than typically found in the leadership literature. This node clearly includes distinguishing between symptoms and problems, implementation of action efforts, and how internal and external forms of knowledge are integrated.

Sustainable community economic development is about changing perceptions and choices regarding community resources, markets, rules, and decision-making capacity. While not obvious in Figure 1, sustainable development requires the use of accumulated knowledge (both scientific and experiential) to reframe questions that change the set of perceived options available. *Sustainable* must not be redefined into meaninglessness, but the choices we make regarding the four nodes of Figure 1 and their definition go a long way in making sustainable development attainable.

A dynamic economy adds the important aspect to sustainable development—recognition of the changing circumstances in which the community functions. These changes can be depletion or revaluation of a resource (e.g., groundwater, mineral deposits, scenic vistas), technological changes (e.g., genetic engineering, fiber optics), market shifts (e.g., aging population, single parent families, working couples, shifts in defense spending), changes in political-economic institutions (e.g., eligibility for federal programs, discharge standards, NAFTA/GATT) or economic structure (e.g., transnational corporations, relative decline of manufacturing employment). These changing economic circumstances alter the choice set for community response. Sustainable communities recognize these changes and create responses that allow the community to maintain and improve its economic position now and through time.

Four characteristics are associated with communities which appear to be economically sustainable (Shaffer, 1991). They are, in no order of importance: a slight level of dissatisfaction; a positive attitude toward experimentation; a high level of intra-community discussion; and a history of implementation. In a few words, communities that demonstrate the qualities of sustainability believe they, and they alone,[4] make and/or control their own destiny. This recognizes that while individual communities are given different economic circumstances (resources, economic structure, access to markets, growth of local markets), the sustainable community will capture the economic possibilities available.

Sustainable community economic development means using new knowledge to create new choices and options through time regarding the nodes in Figure 1. Now resources take on new meanings including assimilative capacity, marginalized groups, nonrenewable resources, lower energy use technology, and different skill sets for people. Likewise, markets start including buying locally whenever possible, recycling, consuming green products, and green lifestyles. Decision-making capacity now adds sensitivity about the biosphere, sensitivity about inter-generational implications, sensitivity about marginalized groups, and sensitivity about spatial flows. The rules of the economic game now include discharge permits and markets, compensation to people adversely affected, development impact hearings, and taxes on transboundary environmental use.

The themes that emerge from the expanded definition of sustainable community economic development lead to policies that explore how to increase community self-reliance, increase niche marketing (i.e., less volume, more value), increase ecological awareness (e.g., diversification of production from mono-culture, recycling wastes or reducing waste stream), change labor and management relations, and increase demands on knowledge and creativity.

Necessary Conditions For Sustainable Development

Economists contend that a major theme in sustainable community economic development is the externality of decisions and actions. Externalities can be both positive and negative, but are generally not accounted for in the market prices used to allocate resources across groups, space, and time.

In sustainable community economic development, time and future generations are explicitly brought into consideration for decisions and actions. If decisions and actions adversely affect future generations then current prices need to reflect that. To assert that time is important begs the question: relative to what? To argue that some resources should be preserved for the future does not answer the economic questions of what alternatives are foregone—now or in the future. Who is being impacted by the choice of preserving a resource? The end result of this blanket acceptance of future over present value could lead to the sacrificing of current legitimate interests for undefined future legitimate needs. Either condition leads to equally inappropriate decisions.

Another externality is that the benefits and costs of a decision or action are distributed spatially to separate groups, minimizing the possibility that market

---

[4] The term *alone* is used to place responsibility on ourselves, not on others or external institutions. It does *not* mean isolation in action or response.

prices will create self-correcting signals. So, rather than getting corrective feedback, the system becomes self-reinforcing. The interaction between urban and rural economies is an example of spatial flows. Changes in urban markets (e.g., natural or artificial fibers, use of rain forest wood) and rules (e.g., water quality standards, prevailing wage standards) often play out in rural economies in a perverse manner. The transboundary flows of sulphur dioxide, ozone-depleting chemicals, or poorly educated migrants are other examples of externalities over space and time.

An aspect of sustainable community economic development that appears to have generated little direct discussion is the Schumpeterian (1983) idea that development is "creative destruction" with the associated economic dynamics that creates winners and losers. The sense of gains/losses may only be relative, but often is absolute (i.e., displaced worker, family, community).[5] The inability of some adversely affected groups to contribute to decisions leads to reinforcing patterns of shifting burdens to those groups. Economists deal with this in statements about needed adjustments (migration, training, identifying new business opportunities) in a dynamic economy. It is insufficient to expect the market to handle many of the noneconomic aspects of these adjustments given asset fixity, family, gender, education, personal traits, age and race (Hite & Powell, 1993).

Some suggest that people consciously make short-run non-sustainable decisions and even imply that the economic system discourages longer term sustainable development choices. The reality is that we often do not know what the full range of options and their implications are and often do not face the choices at the same time. A minimum precondition for sustainable development is an active effort to acquire and improve access to knowledge regarding the range of choices available and their implications. This will require a substantial personal and societal investment to create a culture that explores alternatives.

SUMMARY

In summary of my thinking to this point, sustainable development explicitly recognizes increasing limits (biological/physical), given past and current economic/cultural/social norms and knowledge. It is not absolute; relative to shifting constraints, it embodies different forms of capital (i.e., renewable and nonrenewable), and has the capacity to accommodate change. Sustainable development incorporates linkages between economic and ecological issues and is sensitive to distribution across generations (time), space, socio-economic groups, and economic sectors.

---

[5] An example of gains/losses and creative destruction is contained in the recent ending of the cold war. Most would agree that it represents a structural transformation and opens a host of new choices, but some communities, tied to the defense industry, obviously see themselves as losing.

Recognizing that changing norms, knowledge, technology, and markets lead to shifting needs for capital, labor, and space, I contend that sustainable community economic development is less a natural/physical/biological and more an institutional phenomenon. Sustainable development is less an issue of technical feasibility, and more an issue of what policies, behaviors, and institutions are required to achieve it in practice. Have we framed the questions appropriately? For example, energy is associated with economic growth,[6] so it has been assumed that we must increase energy use to have economic growth. If we adopt energy conserving technology or if we adopt new product configurations (lower hydrocarbon content), we can conserve energy usage and still have growth and development.

The preceding example exemplifies the importance of re-framing questions from either/or to multiple options. The paradigm shifts (see Table 1) that must occur include reframing the growth/non-growth dichotomy; market/state directed dichotomy, and the assumption that since marginalized groups will not improve their relative position, absolute growth is the only choice available. There is a need to explore new procedures with new partners. For example, collaboration rather than competition becomes the guiding principle (Bryson & Crosby, 1992). Some of the new processes that sustainable communities will need to master include negotiation and conflict management skills. A crucial component is accumulating and incorporating new knowledge into the choices considered and made (Buxbaum & Ho, 1993).

Sustainable development, in its most admirable form, consciously reminds us that the system we are dealing with is complex (e.g., time, marginalized groups, and externalities) and that the stock of resources (e.g., physical, social, human capital) used to produce the outputs desired is both nonrenewable and renewable. It is not a "no growth" concept, but one in which different forms of growth are encouraged. It recognizes that a dynamic economy is not a euphemism for growth, but refers to changing choices, reframing issues, changing perceptions of markets and resources, and changing values. Nostalgia is replaced with the reality of changing needs and functions. Insistence on maintaining some historic view (e.g., production processes or community role) will only delay making needed choices. Economic choices are guided by both market and nonmarket (including intergenerational) values. There is concern about how change is creating increased disenfranchisement based on gender, skills, ethnicity, space, or economic status. The pursuit of sustainability implies an effort to increase access to decision making and to provide a fuller array of knowledge for decision making.

---

[6] Energy is also associated with development, to the extent electricity transforms how we conduct our lives.

SELECTED REFERENCES

Bryson, John M. & Barbara C. Crosby. 1992. *Leadership for the Common Good*. San Francisco: Jossey–Bass Publishers.

Buxbaum, Stephen, & Robert Ho. 1993. *Innovation and Collaboration: Challenges for State Rural Development Councils*. Aspen, CO: Aspen Institute.

Dykeman, Floyd W. 1990. Developing an understanding of entrepreneurial and sustainable rural communities, in F. W. Dykeman (ed.) *Entrepreneurial and Sustainable Communities*. Sackville, NB: Rural Studies and Small Town Research and Studies Programme, Department of Geography, Mount Allison University.

Etzioni, Amitai. 1993. *The Spirit of Community: Rights, Responsibilities, and the Communitarian Agenda*. New York: Crown Publishers.

Flora, Cornelia B., & Jan L. Flora. 1993. Entrepreneurial social infrastructure: A necessary ingredient. *The Annals of the American Academy of Political and Social Science* 529 (September): 48–58.

Hite, James, & Roy Powell. 1993. Economics of the hinterland. Unpublished manuscript. Clemson University and New England University.

Pulver, Glen. 1979. A theoretical framework for the analysis of community economic development policy options. In Gene Summers & Arne Selvik (eds.), *Nonmetropolitan Industrial Growth and Community Change*. Lexington, MA: Lexington Books.

Putnam, Robert D.. 1993. The prosperous community: Social capital and public life. *The American Prospect* 13: 35–42.

Rural Sociological Society. 1993. *Persistent Poverty in Rural America: Rural Sociological Society Task Force on Persistent Rural Poverty*. Boulder, CO: Westview Press.

Schumpeter, J.A. 1983. *The Theory of Economic Development*. New Brunswick, NJ: Transaction Books.

Shaffer, Ron. 1991. Building economically viable communities: A role for community developers. *Journal of the Community Development Society* 21(2): 74–87. .

Shaffer, Ron. 1989. *Community Economics: Economic Structure and Change in Smaller Communities*. Ames, IA: Iowa State University Press.

Sustainable Rural Communities Committee. 1991. *Sustainable Rural Communities*. Guelph, ONT: University of Guelph.

Wilkinson, Ken P. 1991. *The Community in Rural America*. Westport, CT: Greenwood Press.

World Commission on Environment and Development. 1987. *Our Common Future*. Oxford: Oxford University Press. (Generally referred to as the Brundtland Commission).

GLEANERS, DO-GOODERS, AND BALERS: OPTIONS FOR LINKING SUSTAINABILITY AND ECONOMIC DEVELOPMENT

By Ted K. Bradshaw and Karri Winn

ABSTRACT

Sustainability and economic development are typically treated as conflicting goals in the literature and in practice. In this paper gleaners, do-gooders, and balers are used metaphorically to suggest that certain people outside the mainstream economy are in fact contributing to employment and generating wealth while acting in a sustainable manner, thus providing an example of how sustainable principles can complement economic development in all types of businesses. Third wave economic development strategies are shown to be compatible with gleaners who turn waste into a resource, do-gooders who find profit in being virtuous about conserving resources, and straw-bale house builders who find ways to cut through the cost barrier to develop sustainable technologies that are both better and cheaper. Local economic development officials can support these technologies through the use of third wave tools of leadership, information, and brokering, thereby helping to promote local economies that satisfy the short-term goals of businesses, support interdependent networks of growing firms, and minimize environmental damage.

INTRODUCTION

Sustainability is one of the most ubiquitous words in contemporary development discourse (President's Council on Sustainable Development, 1996b), but also one of the least understood (Dixon & Fallon, 1989, Gale & Cordray, 1994). During the 1990s countless articles and books were written on the benefits (Auty & Brown, 1997; Brown, 1996; Panayotou, 1993), the potential (Hawkin, 1993; Kinsley, 1994; Meadows, 1996; Morris, 1993), or the challenges (Daly & Cobb, 1991; McDonough & Braumgart, 1998) of planning for and achieving sustainability in all parts of the world. Sustainability is a well-accepted value as far as environmental protection is concerned, but its implementation has been slow because of perceived conflicts with other community goals, especially economic development.

Ted K. Bradshaw and Karri Winn, Department of Human and Community Development, University of California, Davis. An earlier version of this paper was presented at the 1998 meetings of the Community Development Society, Kansas City. Support from the Sustainable Communities Consortium and the Experiment Station at University of California, Davis, is appreciated.

Conflicts between these goals lead to policy and planning problems that affect competing uses of resources, priorities for development, and tensions over property or land use. For example, Campbell (1996, p. 298) notes that environmental protection, equity, and economic growth are three conflicting goals that must be accommodated in sustainable development. Farrell and Hart (1998) suggest that getting to sustainability requires finding a balance among competing economic, social, and ecological goals, though it is not clear that a balance will please everyone. Arrow et al. (1995) conclude that even in the most affluent places economic growth generates environmental problems (sometimes exported to poor countries) that demand strong environmental policy and institutions. The conclusion of most analyses of sustainability is that to a greater or lesser degree environmental protection and economic development are in conflict.

We propose that economic activity is in fact compatible with environmental protection. In contrast to those who mainly see conflict between economic growth and the environment, we see an option out of the dilemma through the metaphorical lessons learned from gleaners, do-gooders, and balers. Consider these unconventional examples:

- In many urban neighborhoods, technically unemployed people make their 5 a.m. rounds with borrowed grocery carts *gleaning* cans and bottles from trash and recycling bins. Their daily load of recyclables provides the collector a cash income totally outside the structure of modern employment, beyond the reach of federal tax agents or data collectors from the Employment Development Department. In the process they help society reuse valuable resources and reduce urban waste streams.
- Energy consumption, once thought a motor for economic growth and well-being, is now being replaced with conservation as the most cost-effective way to run utilities or businesses. The early conservationists were *do-gooders* who preached virtue as a motive, but in the process they proved that sustainable practices were not only more profitable but created better communities. Conservation is among the most profitable investments a company can make, but it is difficult to measure because it does not show up as new products, jobs, or income.
- Straw bales are cheap and plentiful, but stacked, reinforced, and coated with plaster they make super insulating walls for low-cost houses. Straw bale housing enthusiasts, sometimes calling themselves *balers* (Rice, 1997), help lead grass-roots efforts to adopt new technologies, materials, and community institutions to meet housing and other economic needs. Straw bale houses are only one of a number of alternative housing construction technologies that provide super energy-efficient, low-cost, and durable housing. Often constructed by groups of friends rather

than contractors, these houses are just one of many sustainable technological solutions that illustrate how major industries can be transformed by environmentally friendly technologies.

These examples of sustainability do not fit within the parameters of most traditional economic development programs, but they are immediately cost-effective, contribute to long-term community well-being, and are frugal in their use of non-renewable resources. They are an obviously fringe sub-set of examples that demonstrate the viability of sustainable economies, help create jobs and small businesses, and provide examples of how economic developers can encourage sectors of the economy that were previously unattractive and disregarded. For too long economic development has focused on attracting businesses within the "basic sector" (e.g., export industries thought to create new jobs and produce tax revenues). In contrast, "third wave" approaches to economic development (Bradshaw & Blakely, 1999; Ross & Friedman, 1990) provide communities with more resilience through a holistic approach to helping communities compete in the new economy. The third wave approach can be easily utilized by economic developers to help communities invest in sustainability and benefit from an economy in which environment plays a positive role (Hawkin, 1993).

The approach taken in this paper is drawn from the sociological tradition of Everett C. Hughes (1971), who explored the deep structure of social systems in the unexpected and out of the ordinary. By looking at low-prestige occupations he discovered deeper insights into the work behavior of professions. For example, Hughes (1971, p. 316) suggests that, "The psychiatrist and the prostitute must both take care not to become too personally involved with clients who come to them with rather intimate problems," and that the "dirty work" of cleaning up other people's messes is obvious among janitors, but also a problem for nurses and other professional groups. In our case, by looking at how people far from the center of industry are forging sustainable economic opportunities, we can discern the potential of bringing these activities to scale under the guidance of effective public policy.

We do not suggest that gleaners, do-gooders, and balers are new inventions of the 1990s to meet the challenge of sustainability (indeed gleaners predate industrialization); rather, our purpose is to derive from them lessons in bridging the gulf between sustainability and economic development. In all of the writing on sustainability, there is scant discourse on understanding the everyday lives and choices of people whose actions contribute to goals of sustainability in the broadest sense, e.g., enabling healthy people, communities, and ecosystems. In this context, we suggest that individual values represented by gleaners, do-gooders, and balers are given agency through new third wave economic development efforts. Sustainability is ultimately achieved by people being creative and making personal choices that benefit businesses, community, and environment.

SUSTAINABILITY AND THIRD WAVE
ECONOMIC DEVELOPMENT

Sustainability is surprisingly difficult to define, though at its core a commonality of definitions can be distilled from the United Nations Bruntland Commission Report (1987, p. 47), in which sustainability is defined as the ability to "meet the needs of the present without compromising the ability of future generations to meet their own needs." Embedded in this definition is an ethical choice that people living today should not reduce options for those who will live after them. Other definitions more explicitly acknowledge limiting human impact on the environment. For example, Farrell and Hart (1998, p. 7) define sustainability as "improving the quality of human life while living within the carrying capacity of supporting ecosystems."

Sustainable economic development needs to address multiple aspects of the relation between business and the environment. Hawkin (1993, p. 12) identifies these relations to enable of three issues that business must face to enable sustainability: what it wastes, what it takes, and what it makes. Gleaners, do-gooders, and balers address these three issues respectively. In terms of economic development efforts to achieve sustainability, waste management, creative conservation of inputs, and using technology to redefine what is made reflect a *comprehensive agenda for successfully competing in the new economy*.

An economic development strategy for sustainability must meet the imperatives of business success, however. Unlike strategies that attempt to achieve sustainability by persuading people to change their consumption patterns or through regulatory strategies and pricing mechanisms that aim to reduce unsustainable options,[1] local economic development practitioners achieve sustainability by being sensitive to the needs of local businesses. Thus, an economic development strategy must satisfy three criteria: 1) Sustainability initiatives must satisfy the short-term needs of the businesses that implement them, by being affordable, cost effective, and low risk; 2) sustainability initiatives must be able to grow into long-term viable industrial sectors that do not require ongoing assistance; and 3) sustainable economic development initiatives must minimize and reverse long-term damage to the natural resource system by protecting and expanding options for future generations. These three criteria go hand in hand to provide communities with the tools for sustainable development as illustrated by the metaphors of gleaners, do-gooders, and balers.

Emergence of Third Wave Economic Development Strategies

Economic development practices in the "smokestack chasing" tradition deservedly received a bad reputation for their single-minded focus on business locations and jobs, disregarding quality of jobs or environmental impacts. Yet, newer economic development approaches that have evolved through several transformations now enable a perspective on sustainable local economies. These changes are part of the transition within economic development from first and second wave strategies based on firm-level incentives to the holistic approach of the third wave.

The notion of "third wave" economic development was introduced by Ross and Friedman (1990) and Herbers (1990). In their model, the first wave included offering out-of-the-area firms incentives such as tax abatements, land deals, low interest loans, and other subsidies to encourage relocation. In the second wave, economic developers and communities questioned why benefits should go only to recruits. New community-based programs were introduced in the second wave, such as retention and expansion assistance, small business creation, loan programs available to all businesses, and technical assistance to help firms already in the area be more profitable and successful while maintaining tax revenues.

Third wave techniques are still emerging and supplement rather than replace earlier techniques. The focus of the third wave is on a holistic approach to supporting businesses in a region through information, leadership, and brokering to solve problems and improve the area's business climate (Bradshaw & Blakely, 1999). Third wave developers nurture collaborative programs designed to build industrial clusters—integrated networks of industries in a region that gain a competitive edge because of their proximity to each other (Bradshaw, King, & Wahlstrom, 1999; Porter, 1998). Industrial clusters are third wave building blocks for successful economic development that integrate key production firms with other businesses that are suppliers, distributors, marketers, financiers, trainers, researchers, inventors, lawyers, technicians, or information distributors. The third wave looks for regional advantages for clusters of firms, and then supports these advantages through coordination and planning to take advantage of the changes inherent in the new economy.

GLEANERS: WASTE IS A RESOURCE FOR SUSTAINABILITY

Urban gleaners who use carts and wagons to collect trash and recyclable materials are part of a long tradition of poor people who survive on discards. In rural areas, collections of items scavenged from old cars, farm machinery, buildings, and businesses are often traded and bartered in an informal economy. The fact that gleaners are unauthorized and outside the mainstream economy is not remarkable on its own except that the current gleaner culture exists in (and because of) such an overall affluent society. The lessons of the gleaners are that waste is an asset and has economic potential.

It is not known just how many poor live by selling discards recovered from trash, but gleaning cans and bottles from trash in urban areas provides short-term income for many people who lack other options. According to a recent article (Selna, 1998) about "canners" in the San Francisco Bay Area, hundreds of persons sift through trash and recycling bins to collect cans and bottles that are sold to distributors. One scrap company that buys recyclable materials from the poor who collect their bottles in grocery carts reported regularly receiving bottles and cans from about 350 canners who collectively earn about $1.5 million a year. While only a fragment of the state's total recycling business, gleaning is not only a source of income for some of the poorest of the urban poor, but it is an asset to the community and a service to the community by removing some bottles and cans from streets, parks, and trash cans. San Francisco reports about 20 tons/week of cans and bottles brought in by cart-people, while Oakland has about the same. Other cities in the region also see large volumes of discarded trash brought in by the poor. Earning between $5 and $30 per cartload, this source of income is outside the welfare system (Fagan, 1999).

Gleaners are a model for sustainable economic development because they show how waste recovery and marketing can be an economically viable resource for creating jobs and improving the environment at the same time. Gleaners do the "dirty work" of implementing recycling for very low pay outside the mainstream economy.

Short-Term Gains from Waste Management

The short-term advantage of gleaning for sustainable economic development extends beyond the urban poor. Just as the gleaner finds value in other people's discards, numerous experiences and examples now demonstrate that it is highly economical for firms to minimize their waste production, reuse discarded materials, and support recycling and waste reduction (Hawkin, 1993; President's Council on Sustainable Development, 1997). Increasingly, leaders in mainstream industry are recognizing that recycling is economically viable, but these efforts are largely hidden from economic reporting and are often unrecognized by executives and community leaders. The benefits of waste reduction and resale are attractive for firms in the short term, and third wave economic developers can assist in promoting the benefits of a waste reduction economy.

Community-based organizations are also key allies in making waste reduction economically attractive. For example, recycling businesses in poor communities can be organized to create valuable jobs and economic growth. Many nonprofit organizations have found that they can employ urban poor and generate income from recycling, often buying from independent collectors. Non-profits can be entrepreneurial. Bethel New Life in Chicago, for example, provides poor neighborhoods with recycling services and employs people who have few job opportunities.

Economic developers can utilize third wave techniques to promote waste recycling and create jobs. One of the best examples of community-scale gleaning is a Berkeley firm, Urban Ore.[2] Founded in 1979 by Dan Knapp, a professor of sociology who wanted to put what he was teaching about environmental issues into practice, the company started by separating resellable materials from the city dump. Recovered building materials, appliances, and office equipment, as well as household items generated a brisk business. Their location, adjacent to the waste transfer station, became an alternative supplier for both the bargain and treasure hunter.

Waste Management as a "New" Industrial Strategy

Waste management strategies also have long-term benefits. Urban Ore has grown more complex, moving from gleaning reusable goods at the Berkeley City Dump transfer station, to a diversified set of suppliers. However, the salvage aspect of the company's operation is now only 25 percent of the business because most items are obtained from local businesses and building contractors before they are discarded.

Third wave economic development strategies are obvious in the way Urban Ore conducts its business, which increasingly is recognized as helping to establish an emerging cluster of waste recycling industries. The leadership of Knapp and cooperation from the city are partly responsible for Urban Ore's ability to attract five other recovery businesses that are located near the city of Berkeley (two other non-profit organizations, and three for-profit organizations). Of these, Urban Ore is the largest employer with 25 full-time staff positions. Knapp's intent is to help create "incubator" sites where small businesses specializing in solid waste recovery and recycling can operate together to increase each other's efficiency. Knapp estimates that the United States could support some 20,000 small businesses such as his in the waste recycling and recovery industry. Information supporting the industry will help achieve this goal.

Eco-industrial parks are another model of how economic developers can selectively nurture groups of firms into an industrial area based on their symbiotic sharing of wastes, transformed into resources. Co-generation of electricity from industrial processes and sharing of heat among networks of firms save considerable energy and money in industrial parks. The waste outputs of one firm (such as waste materials, byproducts, or even toxic chemicals) can become inputs to another firm. Even whole cities get involved in this regional sustainability network. Chattanooga, Tennessee,[3] for example, has developed an old polluted brown-field industrial area into a "zero emissions" zone with firms using each other's waste (President's Council on Sustainable Development, Fall 1997, pp. 59-64). In another area, the city is developing a cluster of environmental industries that attract and support firms in environmental research, recycling, and waste remediation/reuse. In each of these projects, leadership and brokering link firms together, and community centers showcase the firms' waste-free interdependence, host visitors and researchers, and provide training. As a result, Chattanooga has transformed its economic base from being ranked the nation's "worst polluted city" to being a model for a turnaround and the headquarters for sustainable communities. The Chattanooga Institute, an educational program and a think-tank, was formed to continue research and conduct training for visitors who may be interested in replicating some aspects of a waste-reducing community.

DO-GOODERS: SUSTAINABILITY AND THE PUBLIC GOOD

Reduced consumption, pollution prevention, and control of toxic substances are often thought to require sacrifice—we are told to "do good" and cut back. The "do gooder" is the watchdog of public welfare who evokes collective guilt over the extent of consumption that goes with affluence. The moral imperative to reduce the use of scarce resources is presumed necessary because of the widespread belief that it will erode economic growth or even stability and that the environment will be unable to support future generations. Recently, moral outrage over the disproportionate use by U.S. consumers of world resources has fueled the anti-consumerism movement (Hempel, n.d.; Roseland, 1998).

Energy conservation is a good example of how the pursuit of an ideal can lead to unexpected local benefits for participants. During the energy crisis of the mid-1980s people were told to turn down their thermostats, reduce the amount of air-conditioning or lighting in their houses and workplaces, or drive less: this would avoid more serious electrical brownouts or catastrophic fuel shortages. Energy use at that time was believed to be necessary for economic growth, and any cuts in energy use were assumed to result in a lower GNP (see the predictions of Lovins' critics in Lovins & Nash, 1979). More recently, the Global Climate Coalition (a lobbying organization for the energy and automotive industries) is reported to have an economic model concluding that a 10 percent reduction in 1990 emissions would cost the United States 3 percent of its gross national product (Gelbspan, 1998, p. 26).

However, in one sector after another doing good has not led to sacrifice but short- and long-term benefits. Amory Lovins (1977) and others have shown that energy conservation is a good investment not only for the global environment, but also for households and businesses. In contrast to those predicting serious economic costs, some economists actually believe that emissions could be cut 30 percent or more with no loss in GNP (Gelbspan, 1998). The money saved from conservation is an asset that is invested into the community, generating additional jobs and economic opportunity. It turns out that conservation, like recycling, is economically beneficial, and along the way doing good has allowed businesses to grow.

Plugging Leaks

The Green movement, advocating recycling and conservation, plays an important role as a spokesperson for the do-gooders. While they contribute to our awareness of waste, they also help us understand the need to conserve both at the individual and community levels. From an economic development perspective, awareness of more frugal consumption patterns can free resources for other desired activities. The short-term savings made possible by better insulation or compact florescent light bulbs, for example, have payback periods of a year or two, after which time the energy saving investment has been paid for and all savings are profit.

It is useful to review how far energy conservation has come since the energy crisis of the early 1970s. Average automobile mileage has doubled and truck mileage is up 50 percent (Feldman, 1996), household appliance efficiencies have improved, and industrial applications often use no more than half their original energy requirement. On the horizon, emerging technologies promise even greater conservation of resources. Flavin (1996, pp. 234-235) notes that new technologies promise huge gains: "From light bulbs to refrigerators, many of these [emerging] technologies are at least 75 percent more efficient than the current standard." He goes on to state that maximum electric generation fuel efficiencies increased 50 percent in the last decade alone, and automobile fuel economies in hybrid vehicles are approaching three to four times the current standard.

At the community level, information dissemination can promote significant economic development benefits from reducing energy use. Kinsley (1994) reports that a weatherization, lighting, and conservation program in Usage, Iowa, was so successful that each family on average saved $900 per year on fuel and electricity, money that previously leaked out of the community and that can now be spent locally to stimulate businesses or to improve the lives of the community members. This infusion of over $1.2 million into the local economy enhanced both the community's local sustainability and its economic well-being. Kinsley calls this type of effort "plugging the leaks."

Conservation and Long-Term Investments

The process of transferring sustainable business practices from do-gooders to mainstream has gone through four stages according to Hart (1999). In the first stage (1900-1960), pollution was accepted as the inevitable costs of development. Then, during the 1970s, end-of-pipe regulations tried to reduce the negative impact of pollution and involved forcing companies to invest in control and reduction technologies. In the third stage, from 1980-1990, the emphasis turned to pollution prevention and project stewardship, essentially recognizing that doing business in a "green" way was environmentally friendly and cost effective. Looking into the future, however, Hart suggests a fourth stage, in which companies of the future will profit by product management and, more importantly, by a complete transformation to clean technologies and visionary products that are inherently environmentally friendly. This transformation fits closely with third wave holistic strategies where solving a resource problem leads to an exponentially larger opportunity for advanced technology and products.

The barriers to investment in innovative sustainable technologies are considerable in spite of their attractiveness and call for greater third wave economic development participation. Consider the high returns for low risk associated with investments in energy conservation. Casten, for example, argues that commercial buildings in the U.S. could easily save 30 percent of the energy they use, for an annual savings of $25 billion. Investments in capturing these savings are estimated to have a 20 to 30 percent return on investment, with a near zero risk since most buildings are occupied and generate revenue to repay the investment. These returns compare to the rate venture capital hopes to achieve, but venture capital has enormous risk. In fact, conservation investments have the risk of government bonds but with much higher returns.

Communities in which economic development leadership supports environmentally sound decisions about conservation have achieved remarkable benefits in excess of do-gooders' admonitions. Community sustainability was such a central part of the work of the President's Council on Sustainable Development (1999) because of the realization that individual do-gooders and progressive firms could not make a difference in isolation. Third wave economic development strategies are aimed at the holistic approach of a sustainable community and providing the supportive capacity for individuals and firms to create networks where people and firms are not isolated but are partners in the new economy.

BALERS: TECHNOLOGY FOR SUSTAINABILITY

Balers, people making housing out of stacked and plastered bales of straw, are examples of the viability of sustainable technology in industries in which ecological alternatives are viewed with both suspicion and hostility. The housing industry is one of the most significant for local economies, yet it has made few environmentally significant improvements over the last half century (Office of Technology Assessment, 1992). Today, with issues of housing affordability rising to the top of national and local political agendas, the search for solutions needs to look toward new technologies that value environmental performance as much as cheap initial costs.

Straw bale housing is constructed with exterior walls made by stacking bales of any locally available hay on a foundation and then reinforcing them by driving rebar through the layers. The bales are then coated with plaster, sealing them from weather, making a super-insulated and long lasting wall that works effectively in hot and cold climates. The plastered bale walls are generally impervious to rot and insects, are resistant to fire, and stand up well in earthquakes. Rice straw is attractive not only because it is a cheap material that is in fact a waste and air quality problem since it would otherwise be burned, but its use conserves wood for other uses. Finally, the ease of construction and the widespread local availability of the materials make straw bale houses affordable to people who might otherwise have limited shelter options (Steen, Steen, & Bainbridge, 1994, chap. 2).

The sustainability of straw bale technology from a housing and environmental perspective is favorable, although limitations exist in high density cities. Some of the oldest standing straw bale houses constructed early in the twentieth century in Nebraska serve as a model for a recent construction boom and growing international interest in bale houses. Balers have a near evangelical fervor, reflected in this introductory passage from a popular book:

> Straw bale building has become as much a process of building communities as a highly efficient and sensible way of building affordable and environmentally sound buildings. People seem to change fundamentally when they gain the added security that comes from knowing they are capable of providing their own shelter. When a community of people possess that confidence and come together to help create one another's homes, it necessarily makes the world a better place to live (Steen, Steen, & Bainbridge, 1994, p. xvi).

The lesson from the balers is that sensible solutions to common environmental problems and viable ways of overcoming the economic barriers to affordable housing can involve simple technologies. Over time these individual-level projects can provide solutions to community needs and environmental problems, and can transform whole industries. Like the lesson of the gleaner, the baler provides a model of how sustainability can become a local community's advantage in the new economy.

The Potential of New Housing Technologies

The potential for developing a sustainable economy often involves new applications of technologies that are counter to market trends. In third wave economic development the goal is to build a support system for a growing technology that will generate regional advantage for an industrial cluster capable of generating firms. A growing network of housing specialists and enthusiasts of straw bale houses are beginning to understand that new housing technologies may be a growth industry, and they are producing the key third wave roles of providing information, exercising leadership, and brokering deals that link firms with each other.

Alternative housing technology is not limited to one technology. Dozens of new technological alternatives to standard housing construction are available that promise both affordability and environmental benefits. For example, the newest generation of Swedish housing is so energy efficient that these houses do not have heating systems in spite of the long cold Swedish winter (Bradshaw, 1995; Schipper, Myers, & Kelly, 1985). This is possible because the houses are constructed with excellent insulation and are so air tight that lights, body heat, hot water heaters, and other appliances can provide what heat is needed. Yet super efficient houses cost no more than other similar houses because the extra insulation is more than paid for by the savings from not installing an expensive heating and cooling system. Annual energy savings of these near-zero energy houses amount to thousands of kroner each year.[4]

The Swedish housing example demonstrates the benefits of sustainable technologies that "cut through the cost barrier."[5] Typically, technologies are evaluated on how an incremental cost produces corresponding benefits. However, some technologies achieve a quantum leap in benefits because they produce dramatically better results with actual lower costs. In many parts of the hot United States as well as other countries, the largest energy conservation potential is from reducing air conditioning in hot weather. Electric utilities have peak demand on hot summer afternoons, and shaving some of the air conditioning demand at peak times when electricity generation costs are highest benefits both the utilities and consumer (see Bevengton & Rosenfeld, 1990; Meier, Wright, & Rosenfeld, 1983). The potential for a near-zero energy house for peak summer afternoons could solve many of the energy problems that lead to summer brown-outs. Since the requirements of a house that stays cool in hot summer heat are more challenging than for a house that stays warm in the winter, the following discussion focuses primarily on near-zero cooling.

Government and utility programs have provided incentives for incremental improvement of housing energy efficiency, but have come far short of taking the sensible step of suggesting zero-energy for heating or cooling. Balers and advocates of several alternative housing technologies, however, already have demonstrated that affordable housing could be built that need no air conditioning during hot summer afternoons.[6] The key is heavily insulated houses with very tight construction, with air quality maintained by air-to-air heat exchangers if needed. Building technologies that optimize insulation need not cost more than traditional technologies. For optimal summer cooling, large amounts of interior thermal mass (concrete or rock) help store daytime heat to be vented during cool nights. In addition, most successful near-zero energy houses use coated multi-pane windows, overhangs and trees to shade the house, white roofs, and optimal orientation to limit exposure to the sun. Several of the most attractive near-zero energy techniques include bonding thick foam panels between sheets of strand board (stress skin), spraying concrete over foam cores, or filling foam molds with concrete. Rammed earth, adobe, and solid concrete houses often perform well during hot months but their lack of insulation makes them hard to heat during cold winter months. Several innovative concrete technologies insert foam in the mix or activate chemical reactions to make a lightweight concrete material that has reasonable insulation value. One of the most attractive technologies makes walls in a factory using reinforced concrete around thick foam panel cores and transports them to the building site. Even traditional housing with studs and insulation in-between can be used if the walls are super-insulated with foam insulation panels on the outside and 6-inch wide studs are spaced further apart (24 inches) so that more insulation can be placed inside the walls. A convincing demonstration of this strategy is Bigelow homes in the Chicago area (Andrews, 1994; Carlson, 1992) which builds regular-sized houses that are priced no more than other houses in their area but are guaranteed to have a winter heating bill of no more than $200 per year.[7]

Sustainability and economic growth also emerge from innovations that recycle materials to form new-generation building components. Recycled plastics alone or in combination with wood fibers can be formed into weather-proof decking materials. Old wood or scraps can be reused to make chipboard, a strong building material that avoids cutting new timber. Recycled materials can be used in pipes, wires, paving, and other housing construction. Old concrete is frequently pulverized to become aggregate for new cement mixes. The housing industry illustrates the many ways new technologies can serve an industry employing around 5 percent of the labor force. Given housing shortages in many areas and the fact that housing costs average one-quarter or more of the average family expenditures, it is no wonder that nonprofit housing organizations and private builders alike are looking to find sustainable alternatives.

THE PROBLEM OF TECHNOLOGY TRANSFER
FOR ECONOMIC DEVELOPMENT

Alternative technologies have been advocated since the "small is beautiful" era as a viable solution to problems of sustainable communities. Where implemented, they provide environmentally friendly economic development. In one industrial sector after another, technology transfer of sustainable alternative technologies is slowly moving from concept to partial implementation and acceptance, and in some cases is making significant impacts. For example, organic farming, once considered odd, is now a significant agricultural market. Ecologically sensitive tourism is catching on in developing countries as well as developed places. Sustainable forest management practices increase profits as well as long-term yield on forest lands. New hybrid automobile engines are achieving much higher efficiencies than combustion engines with less pollution. Even in dry cleaning, new technologies are replacing toxic chemical processes with "wet" water-based processes suitable for most garments. Finally, electronic controls in all parts of industry and households are increasingly able to improve efficiency and generate profits at the same time. However, adoption of these sustainability innovations lags in importance from a business as well as environmental perspective.

Implementing the new technologies may involve third wave techniques of information, leadership, and brokering. For example, Mills (1991) shows that energy efficiency in refrigerators could be greatly improved by better design and insulation, often at no additional cost. In a series of projects in Sweden, more efficient refrigerators were introduced by competitions among producers for better design. The program paid viable contenders some of the initial cost of their engineering and design studies, but the competition had as its primary reward the guaranteed purchase of hundreds of thousands of refrigerators to be put in the country's extensive network of public housing. Winning designs turned out to exceed target energy efficiency goals, but were also lower cost because they needed smaller compressors and motors. While the competition was not part of an economic development program, it had enormous consequences for the competitiveness of Swedish appliance manufacturers and led to exports around the world.

The search for new technologies that do not compromise performance and that simultaneously cut through the cost barriers is the top priority for third wave economic development aiming to promote sustainability. Fortunately, as balers show, these technologies are emerging in virtually all sectors of the economy, and can be captured locally by developers using third wave approaches.

A SUSTAINABLE AGENDA

The potential for a sustainable economic development agenda is illustrated by the gleaners, do-gooders, and balers. Each works partially outside the traditional wisdom of modern industrial society. Correspondingly, each finds solutions to the tension between economic development and environmental protection. Waste reduction is not a problem but a profit center. Conservation involves smart investment, not sacrifice. New technologies teach us how to cut through the cost barrier. In each of these arenas economic developers have found ways to bring to scale and create community supporting clusters of interdependent industries that can provide long-term economic growth with lower environmental consequences.

Government needs to be a partner in the creation of a sustainable future. Deposits on beer and soft drink cans and bottles have helped create a more lucrative market for gleaners, but interestingly, along the way containers without deposits are also collected and recycled. Recycling zones (offering similar benefits to enterprise zones) have been established to entice firms that utilize recycled materials in making new products (such as making porch decking out of recycled plastic bags). State and local requirements on reducing the amount of trash put into landfills created an urgency for recycling that may not have been present otherwise. Mileage requirements forced major auto makers to place more emphasis on less polluting and more efficient cars, and increasingly tight regulations on toxic wastes created programs that provided incentives for the introduction of new less toxic technologies (see, for example, Roseland, 1998).

Third wave economic development strategies are a vehicle by which local communities can intervene to create sustainability. While governments can create situations in which sustainable economies can emerge, it depends on local leaders to actually generate sustainable communities. Although the key concepts of sustainability illustrated by gleaners, do-gooders, and balers remain outside the traditional measures of economic success, they provide direct links to emerging clusters of industry which will become the backbone of many local economies. Third wave economic developers are key players in this process. Rather than offering incentives to attract outside businesses as was characteristic of the "smokestack chasing" approach, sustainable economic development efforts require a holistic perspective on the community and the businesses that can support it. Third wave economic developers know the advantages of creating clusters of industries in which the waste from one firm supplies another, of improving profitability by conserving scarce resources, and of nurturing technologies that cut through the cost barrier.

The emerging role of economic development in creating community well-being thus transcends simply generating more jobs and dollars in the local economy. The economic development agenda in a sustainable world is to build economic networks that promote an equitable set of opportunities for all to share in the wealth of the present while supporting a wide range of options for the future. However, as the gleaners, do-gooders, and balers have shown, these benefits often are not measured by traditional measures of economic activity such as jobs, more expenditures, or tax revenues. Third wave economic development efforts can provide leadership, information, and brokering to achieve the potentials of an economy that values more efficient and less wasteful use of the resource stream, the promotion of environmentally sound and innovative technologies, and the pursuit of the public good.

NOTES

1. For example, new taxes or regulations tend not to work at the local level because businesses move to avoid them. State and federal reforms that fairly price environmental externalities and that regulate behaviors can not be so easily avoided, but are often opposed because they are politically unpopular and costs are passed on to consumers.

2. Based on interviews, August 1998.

3. Many other cities have gained attention for their success in sustainability, but space does not permit including them as other examples.

4. Interview with Bjorne Karlsson, Linkoping University, Linkoping, Sweden (1993).

5. Amory Lovins, Presentation at the Energy and Resources Group, University of California, Berkeley, November 1998.

6. Admittedly, housing construction technologies would be more challenging in parts of the United States with high summer humidity since the electrical air conditioning also removes excess moisture.

7. Most recently the guarantee is for no more than $300.

REFERENCES

Andrews, S. 1994. Perry Bigelow: Energy efficiency maestro. *Home Energy* (March): 11.

Arrow, K., B. Bolin, R. Constanza, P. Dasgupta, C. Folke, C. S. Holling, B. O. Jansson, S. Levin, K. G. Maler, C. Perrings, & D. Pimentel. 1995. Economic growth, carrying capacity, and the environment. *Science* 268: 520-521.

Auty, R. M., & K. Brown. 1997. *Approaches to Sustainable Development*. Washington, DC: Pinter.

Bevengton, R., & A. H. Rosenfeld. 1990. Energy for buildings and homes. *Scientific American* 263: 77-86.

Bradshaw, T. K. 1995. *The Potential of Near-Zero Housing in California*. Berkeley: University of California, California Institute for Energy Efficiency. Mimeo.

Bradshaw, T. K., & E. J. Blakely. 1999. What are third wave state economic development efforts? From incentives to industrial policy. *Economic Development Quarterly* 13(3): 229-244.

Bradshaw, T. K., J. King, & S. Wahlstrom. 1999. Catching on to clusters. *Planning* 65(6): 18-21.

Brown, L. 1996. We can build a sustainable economy. *Futurist* 30(4): 8-12.

Bruntland Commission. 1987. *Our Common Future*. Oxford University Press.

Campbell, S. 1996. Green cities, growing cities, just cities: Urban planning and the contradictions of sustainable development. *Journal of the American Planning Association* 62(3): 296-311.

Carlson, D. O. 1992. Suburban Chicago's Begelow Homes guarantees annual heating bill of $200: Maintains attention to detail does it. *Automated Builder* (August): 10-12.

Casten, T. 1998. *Turning Off the Heat: Why America Must Double Energy Efficiency to Save Money and Reduce Global Warming*. Amherst, NY: Prometheus Books.

Daly, H. E., & J. J. Cobb. 1991. *For the Common Good*. Boston: Beacon.

Dixon, J. A., & L. A. Fallon. 1989. The concept of sustainability: Origins, extensions, and usefulness for policy. *Society and Natural Resources* 2: 73-84.

Fagan, K. 1999. Heavy load: Cart-pushers recycle tons of bottles and cans. *San Francisco Chronicle*: A19.

Farrell, A., & M. Hart. 1998. What does sustainability really mean? *Environment* 40(9): 5-31.

Feldman, D. L. 1996. Revisiting the energy crisis. Pp. 1-19 in D. L. Feldman (ed.), *The Energy Crisis*. Baltimore: The Johns Hopkins University Press.

Flavin, C. 1996. Sustainable energy for tomorrow's world. Pp. 230-248 in D. L. Feldman (ed.), *The Energy Crisis: Unresolved Issues and Enduring Legacies*. Baltimore: The Johns Hopkins University Press.

Gale, R. P., & S. M. Cordray. 1994. Making sense of sustainability: Nine answers to "What should be sustained?" *Rural Sociology* 59(2): 311-332.

Gelbspan, R. 1998. A good climate for investment. *Atlantic Monthly* 281(6): 22-27.

Hart, S. 1999. Business decision making about the environment: The challenge of sustainability. Pp. 77-90 in K. Sexton, A. A. Marcus, K. W. Easter, & T. D. Burkhardt (eds.), *Better Environmental Decisions*. Washington, DC: Island Press.

Hawkin, P. 1993. *The Ecology of Commerce*. New York: Harper Collins.

Hempel, M. n.d. *Sustainable Communities: Guide for Grassroots Activists*. Claremont, CA: Population Coalition.

Herbers, J. 1990. A third wave of economic development. *Governing* 3(9): 43-50.

Hughes, E. C. 1971. Mistakes at work. Pp. 316-325 in *The Sociological Eye: Selected Papers on Work, Self, and the Study of Society*. Chicago: Adeline Press.

Kinsley, M. 1994. Sustainable development. *Public Management* 76(10): 6-9.

Lovins, A. 1977. *Soft Energy Paths*. New York: Harper and Row Publishers.

Lovins, A., & H. Nash. 1979. *The Energy Controversy: Soft Path Questions and Answers*. San Francisco: Friends of the Earth.

McDonough, W., & M. Braumgart. 1998. The next industrial revolution. *Atlantic Monthly* 282(4): 82-92.

Meadows, D. 1996. Envisioning a sustainable world. In *Getting Down to Earth*, International Society of Ecological Economics. Washington, DC: Island Press.

Meier, A., J. Wright, & A. H. Rosenfeld. 1983. *Supplying Energy Through Greater Efficiency*. Berkeley: University of California Press.

Mills, E. 1991. *Evolving Energy Systems: Technology Options and Policy Mechanisms*. Lund, Sweden: University of Lund, Department of Environmental and Energy Systems Studies.

Morris, D. 1993. *Ecology Nurtures Community*. Minneapolis: Institute for Local Self Reliance.

Office of Technology Assessment, U. S. C. 1992. *Building Energy Efficiency*. Washington, DC: Government Printing Office. OTA-E-518.

Panayotou, T. 1993. *Green Markets: The Economics of Sustainable Development*. San Francisco: Institute for Contemporary Press.

Porter, M. E. 1998. Clusters and the new economics of competition. *Harvard Business Review*: 77-90.

President's Council on Sustainable Development. 1996a. *Eco-Efficiency Task Force Report.* Washington, DC: The White House.

_____. 1996b. *Sustainable America: A New Consensus.* Washington, DC.

_____. 1997. *Sustainable Communities Task Force Report.* Washington, DC: The White House.

_____. 1999. *Towards a Sustainable America.* Washington, DC: The White House.

Rice, N. 1997. Balers, builders, and believers. *The Last Straw* 20: 32.

Roseland, M. 1998. *Toward Sustainable Communities: Resources for Citizens and Their Governments.* Gabriola Island, British Columbia, Canada: New Society Publishers.

Ross, D., & R. E. Friedman. 1990. The emerging third wave: New economic development strategies. *Economic Development Quarterly*: 3-10.

Schipper, L., S. Myers, & H. Kelly. 1985. *Coming in From the Cold: Energy-Wise Housing in Sweden.* Washington, DC: Seven Locks Press.

Selna, R. 1998. Can do folks. *San Francisco Examiner*, September 27, D, pp. 1-4.

Steen, A. S., B. Steen, & D. Bainbridge. 1994. *The Straw Bale House.* White River Junction, VT: Chelsea Green Publishing.

The Community and Economic Development Chain: Validating the Links Between Processes and Outcomes

Robert Pittman

Janus Economics, Atlanta, GA, USA

Evan Pittman

Brattle Group, Boston, MA, USA

Rhonda Phillips

School of Community Resources and Development,
Arizona State University, Phoenix, AZ, USA

Joe Cangelosi

College of Business, University of Central Arkansas, Conway, AR, USA

The community development and economic development literatures have evolved largely independently with little recognition of the critical relationship between the two disciplines. This omission is not so obvious when researchers focus on individual components of each discipline in isolation, but upon examination of how community and economic development systems work in theory and practice overall, this shortcoming becomes apparent. A proposed framework illustrates the links between community and economic development capacities, factors, and functions and shows the importance of community development to economic development outcomes. In particular, it focuses on the link between social capital and the outcome of community development and an economic development ready community. The framework provides an overarching paradigm that helps tie together some of the research in the two fields. Using data from a statewide survey, correlation coefficients are calculated, showing the connections between capacity factors, development factors, and development functions. Strong statistical results provide evidence to support the community and economic development framework and validate the use of subjective data.

This article sets forth a framework of community and economic development as interrelated processes and outcomes and tests that framework with statewide survey data from Louisiana.

The authors would like to thank Dr. Nancy Bliwise, Senior Lecturer, Department of Psychology, Emory University, Atlanta, GA, for her assistance with the statistical analysis.

Because of difficulties in measuring the often subjective community and economic development processes and capacities, these factors are often underrepresented in empirical analyses. Even using "hard" objective measures of community and economic development factors can be problematic in research studies because the factors can be measured in many different ways, often at the discretion of the researcher. As an alternative analytical approach, this study utilizes subjective survey data to measure community and economic development factors and functions which do not lend themselves to quantitative measurement. This article shows that, by not recognizing the important links between community development and economic development, many previous studies have produced results of limited dimensionality. Future research in community and economic development, both theoretical and empirical, will be more robust if this overarching framework is acknowledged and further explored.

A FRAMEWORK FOR COMMUNITY ECONOMIC DEVELOPMENT

Community development is defined in many ways in the literature, with some definitions emphasizing the processes of community development and others emphasizing the outcomes. From these different approaches, a simple but broad definition of community development can be derived:

> A *process*: developing or increasing the ability to act collectively; and an *outcome*: taking collective action, and the result of that action for improvement in a community in any or all realms: physical, environmental, cultural, social, political, economic, etc. (Phillips & Pittman, 2009, p. 6).

There is a large body of literature that, while recognizing the importance of the skills and abilities of individuals, also identifies *social capacity* (or *capital*) as a factor that facilitates community development and *capacity building* as an exercise in creating or increasing the stock of social capital. This relationship can be further described as follows: "the *process* of community development is social capital/capacity building which leads to social capital which in turn leads to the *outcome* of community development" (Phillips & Pittman, 2009, p. 5; italics original).

Economic development can be viewed as a process and outcome as well. This has been well established in the literature for many years. An early definition from the American Economic Development Council illustrates this view:

> [Economic development is] the process of creating wealth through the mobilization of human, financial, capital, physical, and natural resources to generate marketable goods and services. The economic developer's role is to influence the process for the benefit of the community through expanding job opportunities and the tax base. (American Economic Development Council [AEDC], 1984, p. 18)

Definitions of community and economic development are clearly parallel: community development produces assets for improving the quality of life and business climate, and economic development mobilizes these assets to realize benefits for the community. Community development, therefore, can be viewed as creating a "development ready" community: a good place to live, work, and play with a good labor force, quality of life, infrastructure, education system, government, and so on that attracts and retains businesses and facilitates successful economic development. The process of economic development was defined earlier; the outcome is more and better jobs, increased incomes and wealth, and an increase in the standard of living. This can be represented schematically, as in Figure 1.

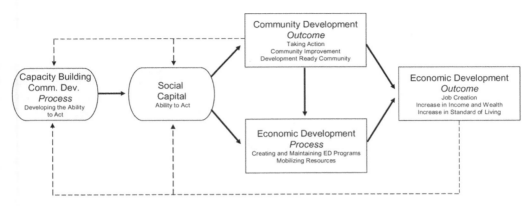

FIGURE 1 Community and economic development chain. (*Source*: Phillips & Pittman, 2009)

The community development part of the chain is as described previously: capacity building (the process of community development) leads to social capital (capacity), which In reply to: turn leads to the outcome of community development—taking action and improving the community in any or all realms: physical, environmental, cultural, social, political, and so on. In addition, the lower branch of the chain shows that communities with social capital or capacity (the ability to act) are inherently more capable of creating good economic development processes. When these communities take action (community development outcome), they can create and maintain effective economic development programs that mobilize the community's resources and lead to positive economic development outcomes. As mentioned above, they also improve their physical and social nature and become more development ready, which also facilitates success in economic development outcomes (new business attraction, existing business retention and expansion, small business development, etc.). Figure 1 also depicts a feedback loop, showing the cumulative and reiterative nature of the model. Success in the outcomes of community and economic development creates more resources the community can use to strengthen its capacity building process and social capital.

Shaffer, Deller, and Marcouiller (2006) describe the relationship and synergy between community development and economic development in a similar way:

We maintain that community economic development occurs when people in a community analyze the economic conditions of that community, determine its economic needs and unfulfilled opportunities, decide what can be done to improve economic conditions in that community, and then move to achieve agreed-upon economic goals and objectives. (p. 61)

They also point out that the link between community development and economic development is sometimes not understood or appreciated:

Economic development theory and policy have tended to focus narrowly on the traditional factors of production and how they are best allocated in a spatial world. We argue that community economic development must be broader than simply worrying about land, labor and capital. This broader dimension includes public capital, technology and innovation, society and culture, institutions, and the decision-making capacity of the community. (p. 64)

The authors make it clear that community development and economic development are inextricably linked and if scholars and practitioners of economic development do not address community development, they are missing an important part of the overall equation.

One of the main reasons why the link between community and economic development is not recognized is the difficulty of measuring all the aspects involved. For example, traditional factors of production are easier to measure than more subjective capacity factors or community capabilities. How are aspects of a community's social capital, such as "effective planning," or "ability to work together and avoid factionalism," measured? For that matter, development factors such as work ethic, quality of labor, and recreational opportunities are also subjective and difficult to measure, yet are important in economic development and business location decisions (Pittman, 2006). Even those factors, such as K-12 education, for which objective metrics are available can be measured in different ways, none of which are definitive. Do you measure the "quality" and "availability" of education by graduation rates, test scores, teacher/pupil ratios, or any of dozens of other metrics?

Measurement difficulties have hampered inquiry into the role of subjective factors in community and economic development. Measurement difficulties also introduce potential measurement errors in studies using "hard" measures of objective factors that are often selected at the discretion of the researcher. For example, Wong (2002) used cross-section regression analysis to explain changes in employment as a function of objective and readily-measurable factors such as wage rates, housing prices, proximity to large cities, and a host of other variables. She acknowledged the potential role of "institutional capacity" or the "coherence of local policies and the cooperation among local actors to provide support and assistance to economic development activities" but did not attempt to measure this and therefore did not include it in her statistical analysis.

There are many studies like Wong's that attempt to explain economic development success (outcome) as a function of various characteristics of communities and regions such as labor force, transportation, or distance to major highways (see, for example, Blair & Premus, 1993, or Carlton, 1979, 1983). Again, they do not include subjective capacity and other factors in their models, perhaps because of measurement difficulties or because they do not posit a role for these factors in business location. These studies focus on a small part of the community and economic development chain. In Figure 1 there is a relationship between "development ready" in the community development outcome box and job creation in the economic development outcome box.

As Figure 1 is designed to depict the holistic relationship between community and economic development processes and outcomes, it does not include exogenous factors that can affect economic development outcomes. These exogenous factors, many of which are the subject of studies such as Wong's, include physical location (i.e., location relative to major markets, highways, ports, etc.), natural resources, physical topography, and a whole host of variables not under the control of a community (Shaffer, Deller, & Marcouiller refer to these as traditional factors of production). However, many variables that affect business location decisions and economic development outcomes—such as a skilled labor force, good education system, quality of life, local infrastructure, and attitude towards development—are factors in the community and economic development chain that communities can influence to make themselves development ready (as depicted in Figure 1). It is this segment of the community development chain—the link between social capital, the outcome of community development, and a development ready community—that is the focus of this article. Future research by the authors will examine more of the chain, from social capital to community development outcome and economic process, then finally to economic development outcome.

METHODOLOGY

Data for this article comes from an on-line survey completed in 2006 by Louisiana Economic Development and the authors, as part of a project to assess community and economic development assets and needs throughout the state. Invitations were sent to approximately 1,440 community and economic development officials and community leaders, 389 of whom responded for a 27% response rate. The final data set included 277 usable responses with the level of analysis at the parish (county) and community levels. Regional data were not included as regional economic development programs are of a broader scope than is the focus of this research. The surveys were administered via online software. Data were gathered in groupings of factors: 8 capacity factors, 28 development factors, and 10 development functions (see listings to follow).

After the data were sorted, correlation coefficients were calculated for all the variables. This method was selected to examine the strength and direction of relationships between variables.

Capacity and Development Factors

Survey participants were given a list of 36 community and economic development (CED) factors and asked to rate each as an asset, liability, or neutral for their community or parish, depending on which they selected as their primary provider of economic development services. The results of these factor ratings at the community level are shown in Table 1, sorted in descending order by mean. When interpreting the mean, note that asset, neutral, and liability were coded as 3, 2, and 1, respectively. Factor ratings at the parish level differed somewhat but not materially and are not shown. Also note that for Tables 1 and 2 below, the rows do not necessarily sum to 100% because of "don't know" responses.

Some factors are subjective while others are objective in nature. The first eight factors are subjective and can be called *capacity factors*, or "society and culture, institutions and decision-making capacity" factors (Shaffer et al., 2006, p. 2). The remaining 28 factors cover a broad spectrum of issues that affect community and economic development: infrastructure (water and sewer, electricity, Internet service), transportation (air, water, highway), education (K-12, higher education), labor (availability, quality), and quality of life (cost of living, recreation, arts and culture) can all be referred to as *development factors*.

Development Functions

All respondents, regardless of their primary source of economic development services, were asked whether or not ten community and economic development (CED) functions were performed in their community and parish. These results for the community level are displayed in Table 2, sorted by mean in descending order. When interpreting the means, note that "does" and "doesn't" responses were coded as 3 and 1, respectively. Again, also note that the rows do not sum to 100% because of "don't know" responses.

TABLE 1
CED Factor Ratings (Community Level)

Factor	Asset	Neutral	Liability	Mean
Capacity Factors				
Positive attitude towards development	65%	27%	7%	2.59
Participation by citizens in community activities	49%	39%	10%	2.41
Quality of local government	53%	29%	16%	2.38
Leadership in economic development	37%	45%	18%	2.19
Effective planning	35%	35%	27%	2.09
Effective implementation of our plans	29%	39%	28%	2.01
Unified vision for economic development	33%	35%	33%	2.00
Ability to work together and avoid factionalism	28%	36%	35%	1.93
Development Factors				
Proximity to interstate or major state highway	71%	8%	8%	2.71
Availability/quality of higher education	64%	22%	7%	2.61
Recreational opportunities	64%	13%	13%	2.56
Safety from natural disasters	59%	29%	8%	2.53
Availability of high-speed Internet service	57%	29%	11%	2.48
Historic preservation	51%	30%	10%	2.45
Cost of living	48%	37%	7%	2.44
Arts and cultural opportunities	51%	24%	16%	2.39
Water and sewer infrastructure	48%	35%	13%	2.36
Availability of financing	41%	31%	12%	2.34
Water transportation	43%	28%	16%	2.32
Downtown redevelopment/Main St. program	45%	27%	17%	2.32
Electricity cost and service	42%	42%	13%	2.30
Appearance of community	49%	28%	20%	2.30
Crime rate	41%	40%	16%	2.26
Availability of industrial sites and buildings	39%	33%	18%	2.23
Retail/shopping available	42%	34%	20%	2.23
Work ethic	39%	33%	23%	2.17
"Walkability" of community	39%	34%	23%	2.17
Local taxes	25%	55%	13%	2.13
Racial harmony	31%	43%	19%	2.13
K-12 education	35%	35%	25%	2.10
Availability of labor	35%	30%	29%	2.06
Quality of labor	29%	36%	28%	2.01
Availability of funding for economic development	27%	31%	28%	1.99
Local business incentives	19%	43%	29%	1.90
Availability of air passenger service	17%	37%	37%	1.78
Public transportation	6%	31%	55%	1.47

Some of the functions in Table 2 would be considered community development (e.g., neighborhood redevelopment) and others economic development (e.g., business retention and expansion assistance) in nature, but the variables in Table 2 are activities that communities or parishes do or do not perform as opposed to factors or traits that are rated as assets or liabilities in Table 1.

As with Table 1, there are measurement challenges for the community and economic development functions. For example, the researcher could personally verify that a community had a workforce development program of some sort, but how would programs across communities be

TABLE 2
CED Functions at Community Level

	Does do function	Doesn't do function	Mean
Historic preservation	69%	16%	2.62
Leadership development	63%	23%	2.46
Workforce development/training	56%	21%	2.45
Assessment of strengths and weaknesses for CED	51%	21%	2.43
Small business start-up assistance	53%	24%	2.38
House improvement/affordability assistance	40%	24%	2.26
Business retention and expansion assistance	41%	25%	2.25
Land-use planning	42%	29%	2.19
Downtown redevelopment	31%	26%	2.09
Neighborhood redevelopment	34%	36%	1.98

compared? One community's workforce program could be exemplary while another's could be rudimentary. Measuring the quality of workforce development programs is just as problematic as measuring some of the subjective and objective capacity and development factors in Table 1. In the end, it is proposed that asking informed community and economic developers and leaders whether or not these programs exist in their community is a useful measurement technique. Note that the survey did not ask respondents to specify the geographic coverage of the functions in Table 2.

ANALYSIS

To ascertain relationships between the capacity and development factors and functions, and to look for evidence supporting the community and economic development framework in Figure 1, correlations were calculated among all the variables. The phi coefficient was used to assess the degree of association among the variables. The phi coefficient, a special case of the Pearson correlation coefficient, is used for data of a dichotomous nature. It is preferred when at least one variable represents an underlying continuum and is equivalent to the Pearson correlation coefficient when both variables are dichotomous. (Chen & Popovich, 2002).

In reality, the factors being measured in the survey are continuous. Respondents' opinions toward the CED factors (e.g., positive attitude towards development) would be better measured on a Likert scale, from 1 (*strong liability*) to 10 (*strong asset*). Likewise, the CED functions (e.g., historic preservation) would be better measured using a Likert scale from 1 (*no activity in this area*) to 10 (*strong activity in this area*). However, to make the survey easier to take and increase sample size, expanded range Likert scales for more continuous measurement were not used. Thus, the survey represents a dichotomous approximation to an underlying continuous distribution.

Two separate runs were made: one using community level data and the other using the parish level data. Several clear patterns emerged from the correlation analysis in support of the community and economic development model (as shown in Tables 3 through 6). The results for community and parish were similar; however, only the community level results are reported ($N = 83$).

TABLE 3

Correlations Among Capacity Factors

	United vision for economic development	Effective planning	Effective implementation of plans	Ability to work together	Leadership in economic development	Quality of local government	Positive attitude towards development	Citizen participation in community activities
United vision for economic development		0.812	0.757	0.726	0.582	0.445	0.405	0.479
Effective planning	0.812		0.837	0.599	0.668	0.530	0.401	0.355
Effective implementation of plans	0.757	0.837		0.680	0.686	0.470	0.420	0.457
Ability to work together	0.726	0.599	0.680		0.535	0.543	0.499	0.585
Leadership in economic development	0.582	0.668	0.686	0.535		0.407	0.531	0.393
Quality of local government	0.445	0.530	0.470	0.543	0.407		0.536	0.448
Positive attitude towards development	0.405	0.401	0.420	0.499	0.531	0.536		0.597
Citizen participation in community activities	0.479	0.355	0.457	0.585	0.393	0.448	0.597	

Note. All coefficients significant at the 1% level.

TABLE 4
Correlations of Capacity Factors With Development Factors

Development factors	Capacity factors							
	United vision for economic development	Effective planning	Effective implementation of plans	Ability to work together	Leadership in economic development	Quality of local government	Positive attitude towards development	Citizen participation in community activities
Education								
K-12 education	0.2593*	0.2388*	0.3213**	0.2306*	0.0978	0.2849*	0.1022	0.2391*
Higher education	0.3929**	0.4128**	0.3350**	0.2416*	0.2883*	0.2598*	0.2456*	0.2226
Infrastructure								
Water/sewer infrastructure	0.3638**	0.2881*	0.2653*	0.2676*	0.1588	0.3998**	0.2746*	0.2937**
Availability of hi-speed Internet	0.3035**	0.3447**	0.3486**	0.2837*	0.2968**	0.2245*	0.3542**	0.2606*
Business climate/readiness								
Local taxes	0.3574**	0.3458**	0.3943**	0.2831*	0.3419**	0.3351**	0.2914*	0.2416*
Incentives	0.3796**	0.3871**	0.4949**	0.3991**	0.4702**	0.2956*	0.3290**	0.4040**
Availability of sites and buildings	0.1724	0.2393*	0.2609*	0.0346	0.3428**	−0.0092	0.1464	0.0517
Quality of life/appearance								
Downtown redevelopment	0.4375**	0.4658**	0.3713**	0.3194**	0.3389**	0.4493**	0.3450**	0.2462*
Arts and culture	0.2100	0.2613*	0.1638	0.1099	0.2790*	0.0119	0.2696*	0.1077
Historic preservation	0.3364**	0.4237**	0.4095**	0.2044	0.2814*	0.2474*	0.2307*	0.3772**
Appearance of community	0.3919**	0.4958**	0.5977**	0.4263**	0.5297**	0.3837**	0.4483**	0.4099**
Racial								
Racial harmony	0.3292**	0.3079**	0.2933*	0.2842*	0.3699**	0.3239**	0.3638**	0.0512

*significant at 5% level, **significant at 1% level.

TABLE 5
Correlation Among Development Factors

	Labor availability	Labor quality	Work ethic	K-12 education
Labor availability		0.5410**	0.4344**	0.2502*
Labor quality	0.5410**		0.6992**	0.4386**
Work ethic	0.4344**	0.6992**		0.4850**
K-12 education	0.2502*	0.4386**	0.4850**	

	Arts and culture	Historic preservation	Appearance of community	Retail available
Higher education	0.4117**	0.3259**	0.2914*	0.3291**

*significant at the 5% level, **significant at the 1% level.

Correlations Among Capacity Factors

Correlations among the eight capacity factors were first examined to discover patterns in how respondents rated them as assets or liabilities. Table 3 shows how strongly respondents' ratings of the community and economic development capacity factors (the first eight in Table 1) are correlated—all of the coefficients were highly significant at the 1% level. Again, these variables can be interpreted as social capital or capacity factors as depicted in Figure 1. For each factor such as visioning, planning, implementing, or running local government, where a respondent believes the community does a good job, the factor would be rated as an asset (or a liability, if vice versa). The results clearly show how the capacity or social capital factors reinforce each other: strong citizen participation is associated with visioning (and vice versa), working together is associated with good leadership (and vice versa), and so on. The fact that the capacity factors are highly correlated is consistent with the community development theory that social capital and capacity building systematically lead to strong capacity and more functional communities, as opposed to a random process where some communities are functional in some areas but not in others.

Correlations of Capacity Factors with Development Factors

Table 4 shows significant correlations found among the eight capacity factors and the other 28 CED factors that make for a development-ready community, as depicted in Figure 1. (Factors with mostly non-significant correlations are omitted from Tables 4, 5, 6, and 7 for clarity of exposition). This shows the link between social capital and community development outcomes. There are four distinct groupings of development factors that are highly correlated with the capacity factors: education, infrastructure, business climate/readiness, quality of life/appearance, and racial harmony.

In the case of K-12 education, it is likely that the causality stems from the capacity factors to quality K-12 education, although it could be argued that well-educated citizens are more likely to perform the capacity factors well. For higher education, the more convincing argument might be that the causality is reversed—better availability of higher education would imply a higher level of education among local citizens (including faculty members), which in turn might lead to

TABLE 6
Correlations of Capacity Factors With Development Functions

	Capacity Factors							
	United vision for economic development	Effective planning	Effective implementation of plans	Ability to work together	Leadership in economic development	Quality of local government	Positive attitude towards development	Citizen participation in community activities
Development functions								
Assessment of strengths and weaknesses	0.1889	0.2959*	0.2720*	0.2383	0.2672*	0.3270*	0.2232	0.2906*
Workforce development	0.2058	0.3047*	0.2941*	0.2619*	0.2173	0.0972	0.1669	0.2015
Downtown redevelopment	0.0781	0.1174	0.1308	0.0242	0.1284	0.2299	0.1140	0.0000
Historic preservation	0.2728*	0.3776**	0.4021**	0.3225**	0.2880*	0.1452	0.2607*	0.2251
Neighborhood redevelopment	0.3948**	0.5093**	0.4293**	0.3004	0.4929**	0.2588**	0.2049	0.1349
Leadership development	0.1943	0.2335	0.2655*	0.3347**	0.3811**	0.2861*	0.4133**	0.2540*
Small-business start-up assistance	0.1441	0.1701	0.2008	0.1462	0.1945	0.1707	0.1159	0.2650*
Business retention and expansion assistance	0.3694**	0.3025*	0.3843**	0.3917**	0.3827**	0.4044**	0.3945**	0.2508
Land-use planning	0.5433**	0.6992**	0.5219**	0.4242**	0.3720**	0.4849**	0.3723**	0.4068**
House improvement and affordability assistance	0.4976**	0.4111**	0.4657**	0.4160**	0.3500**	0.4403**	0.2035	0.4965**

*significant at 5% level, **significant at 1% level.

TABLE 7
Correlations of Development Functions With Development Factors

Development functions	Development factors			
	Labor quality	Work ethic		
Workforce development	0.3805**	0.2730*		
	Downtown redevelopment	Historic preservation	Community appearance	Retail available
Historic preservation	0.3909**	0.4334**	0.3353**	0.3129*

*significant at 5% level, **significant at 1% level.

better performance in the capacity factors. The causality for one other factor in Table 4, racial harmony, might arguably run both ways as well. Better race relations might lead to more success in the capacity factors, but on the other hand, success in the capacity factors might facilitate racial harmony. However, for the remaining development factors the causality is intuitively clear: success in the capacity factors leads to asset ratings for the development factors. Reverse causality is unlikely (for example, good government and local planning would facilitate good water and sewer infrastructure, not vice versa).

The business climate/readiness group reflects a community's attractiveness to business in terms of local taxes (interpreted in this case as reasonable for services provided), the availability of incentives, and available sites and buildings. The quality of life/appearance group reflects a community's attractiveness to business in terms of a redeveloped downtown, good arts and culture, historic preservation, and a good overall appearance. The importance of these type factors on business location and success in economic development is noted by researchers (Johnson & Rasker, 1995; Pittman, 2006).

Correlations Among Development Factors

As shown in Table 5, there were strong correlations among labor availability, labor quality, work ethic, and K-12 education. The correlation among the three labor factors is not surprising: labor quality and work ethic are related, and if both of these factors are rated as assets, the respondent might be more likely to report labor availability as an asset as well. The presence of a large number of unskilled, inexperienced workers might not be considered synonymous with labor availability. The correlation of K-12 education with the labor factors shows the expected relationship that good local education helps build a good local labor force. Table 5 also shows the correlation between higher education rated as an asset (indicating close proximity of higher education resources) and arts and culture, historic preservation, appearance, and retail.

Correlations of Capacity Factors with Development Functions

Table 6 shows correlations among the eight capacity factors and the 10 CED development functions from Table 2 and provides more evidence of the strong link between social capital-community and economic development outcomes as shown in Figure 1. Table 4 showed the link between social capital and development *factors* contributing to a development ready community. Table 6 provides more evidence that social capital leads to strong outcomes in community development (the upper branch of Figure 1); in this case, development programs or *functions* contribute to a development-ready community. Importantly, Table 6 also shows the relationship between social capital and economic development programs and *processes* (e.g., business retention and expansion assistance), as depicted in the lower branch of Figure 1 and discussed in the first section of this paper. Of the 10 CED development functions, only the presence of downtown development and small business development programs are not significantly correlated with the capacity factors. Assessment of strengths and weaknesses, historic preservation, neighborhood redevelopment, leadership development, business retention and expansion, land-use planning, and housing assistance are all significantly correlated with most of the eight capacity factors.

Again, like Table 4, the causality for some of the correlations between the capacity factors and CED functions could run both ways. The most obvious candidate would be the correlation between presence of a "leadership development" function and "leadership" as a highly rated capacity factor. Another would be the Strengths, Weaknesses, Opportunities, and Threats (SWOT) function and planning. The most likely causation would be planning leads to SWOT analysis, but engaging in SWOT analysis might induce a respondent to check "planning" and perhaps "working together" as assets. However, for most of the correlations it is intuitive that the causality would run from capacity factors to CED functions.

Correlations of Development Functions with Development Factors

Several interesting and expected correlations were found between some of the ten development functions and the 28 development factors as shown in Table 7.

The presence of a workforce development program is correlated with ratings of labor quality and work ethic as assets. The presence of an historical preservation program is correlated with ratings of redevelopment, historical preservation, appearance, and retail as assets. These correlations of development functions with related development factor asset ratings indicate that these programs do contribute to community and economic development outcomes.

CONCLUSION

The links between community development and economic development deserve further recognition as mutually beneficial activities. While the literature does not always acknowledge the relationship between the two areas, it is important to further explore and define the relationships. This article has presented a framework for community development and economic development as interrelated processes and outcomes and tested links within the framework. Evidence was found to support the link between social capital or capacity and the outcome of community development and economic development. This includes creating a development-ready community conducive to economic development success and the presence of economic development functions. Because of difficulty in measuring capacity, and also development factors, the study utilized subjective survey data from Louisiana as an alternative to "hard" objective data with its own set of limitations and measurement errors. Future research by the authors will utilize the survey data to further explore the links in the community and economic development chain.

The results of this research have significant implications for community and economic development policy and practice. Policy makers should recognize that community and economic development are inextricably linked. All too often, resources are committed to economic development without giving thought to the underlying base of community development processes and outcomes. This research has provided additional evidence that good community development outcomes (such as a development ready community, or a good place for people and businesses to locate) and processes (the ability to work together or strong social capital) are key enabling factors in economic development. When making policies and plans, communities, regions and states should consider community development and economic development as a unified system. Concerning applications, community development and economic development are often practiced independently of each other, leading to suboptimal results. To move communities forward and increase the standard of living for all residents, decision makers should allocate resources across the entire spectrum of community and economic development needs and programs.

REFERENCES

American Economic Development Council (AEDC). (1984). *Economic development today: A report to the profession.* Schiller Park, IL: Author.

Blair, J. P., & Premus, R. (1993). Location theory. In R. D. Bingham & R. Mier (Eds.), *Theories of local economic development* (pp. 3–26). Newbury Park, CA: Sage Publications.

Carlton, D. (1979). Why new firms locate where they do: An econometric model. In Wheaton, W. (Ed.), *Interregional movements and regional growth* (Coupe paper 2; pp. 15–16). Washington, DC: Urban Institute.

Carlton, D. (1983). The location and employment choices of new firms: An econometric model with discrete and continuous endogenous variables. *The Review of Economics and Statistics, 65*, 440–449.

Chen, P., & Popovich, P. (2002). *Correlation: Parametric and nonparametric measures*, Thousand Oaks, CA: Sage Publications.

Johnson, J. D., & Rasker, R. (1995). The role of economic and quality of life values in rural business location. *Journal of Rural Studies, 11*, 405–416.

Phillips, R., & Pittman, R. (2009). Introduction to community and economic development. In R. Phillips & R. Pittman (Ed.), *Introduction to Community Development* (pp. 3–19). New York: Routledge.

Pittman, R. H. (2006). Location, location, location: Winning site selection proposals. *Management Quarterly, 47*, 2–26.

Shaffer, R., Deller, S., & Marcouiller, D. (2006). Rethinking community economic development. *Economic Development Quarterly, 20*, 59–74.

Wong, C. (2002). Developing indicators to inform local economic development in England. *Urban Studies, 39*, 1833–1863.

Economic Development in the Nonmetropolitan West: The Influence of Built, Natural, and Social Capital

Jessica Crowe

An increasing amount of research has been dedicated to studying economic development at the community level. Although several scholars have examined the effect of one or more community capitals on economic development, few studies examine the full array of capital with respect to economic development. In particular, research has failed to examine community leaders' perceptions of how the different types of capital affect the implementation of businesses in the community. Using survey and interview data collected from seven communities in Oregon and Washington, I examine which forms of community capital: human, built, social, and natural community leaders perceive as having a substantive effect on local economic development as well as explain how such perceptions held by leaders relate to economic development implementation and promotion. Results suggest that community leaders perceive built, social, and natural capitals as having the most effect on economic development. Communities that had high levels of at least two of the capitals, natural, built, and social, had implemented the largest number of outside businesses or industries in the previous three years. On the other hand, the two communities with high natural capital, low built capital, and moderate social capital had implemented the most local businesses or industry in the previous three years. These findings illustrate the need for researchers, policy-makers, and community activists to heavily consider the complex ways that built, natural, and social capital work together to influence self-development and industrial recruitment.

Economic development is an important issue for rural communities, as many communities that were once dependent on natural resources and manufacturing have had to look elsewhere for jobs. This is because structural changes and technological advances in these sectors along with advances in shipping and "free trade" policies have led many of these jobs to move to less developed countries, thus posing a threat to the survival of rural communities as homes and places of work (Flora & Flora, 2008; Sharp, Agnitsch, Ryan, & Flora, 2002). The economic hardships that have hit many rural communities make conditions prime for increased tension over economic development. Perceptions of community capitals' effect on local economic development, regardless of actual impact, provide the foundation for which types of economic development are pursued—making community leaders' perceptions of particular importance. While some communities attempt to recruit outside business and industry to locate to their areas, other communities generate and encourage local businesses and other entrepreneurial activities from within the community.

Jessica Crowe, Department of Sociology, St. Mary's College of Maryland

In seeking to understand and adapt to such structural changes, analysts and policymakers have studied which community characteristics lead to effective economic development implementation (e.g. Crowe, 2008; Flora, Sharp, Flora, & Newlon. 1997; Sharp et al., 2002). Characteristics of communities that have been analyzed include social infrastructure, (Crowe, 2006; Flora et al., 1997; Sharp et al., 2002) human capital (Becker, 2002; Gordon, 2000; Schultz, 1961), information communication technologies (Pigg & Crank, 2005), natural endowments (Crowe, 2006, 2008; McGranahan, 1999), organizational structures of communities (Crowe, 2007), and physical infrastructure (Christopherson et al., 1999; Harrison, 1992).

While researchers see the need in examining the characteristics that lead to effective community-level economic development (e.g. Crowe, 2006; Flora et al., 1997; Putnam, 1993; Sharp et al., 2002), most sociological research has focused on the impact that one or two sources of community capital have on economic development. When studying economic development, it is important to analyze development activities with respect to the full array of capital from which a community can draw. In addition, it is important to consider the perceptions that community leaders have about each form of capital in relation to local economic development efforts. Serious questions remain regarding how community leaders view the effect of various community resources on local economies. Perceptions of how different community resources affect economic development are important regardless of the accuracy of such perceptions because such perceptions are the driving force for which development paths a community pursues and by what means. Which forms of community capital (human, built, social, and natural) do community leaders[1] perceive as having a substantive effect on local economic development? Furthermore, how do such perceptions held by leaders relate to economic development promotion and implementation?

This paper responds to these questions by exploring the views of community leaders on the effect of community capital on local economic development. I examine survey and semi-structured interview data of key leaders in seven communities throughout Oregon and Washington to evaluate which community capitals community leaders perceive as having the most effect on local economic development and how these perceptions influence which types of development to promote.

Economic Development Strategies in the United States

Community-level economic development involves direct or indirect actions that result in the creation of local jobs and a raise in the real incomes of residents (Shaffer & Summers, 1989; Summers, 1986). Historically, federal and state governments have been responsible for the role of economic development. In the past, federal and state governments boosted local economies by investing in physical infrastructure projects, such as the interstate highway program, and the construction of dams along the Columbia and Snake Rivers (Green, 2003). More recently, state governments have adopted a variety of new methods for stimulating economic development, ranging from enterprise zones and right-to-work laws to technology parks and public venture capital firms (Leicht & Jenkins, 1994). While state governments continue to actively promote economic development for their constituents, economic development is increasingly seen as a local responsibility. This is in large part a result of the loss of jobs and income rural communities witnessed during the 1980s recession. In the 1980s many local government officials took action to pursue new sources of revenue in order to retain residents and preserve the community atmosphere (Green, 2003).

Researchers have distinguished between two economic development strategies that communities employ: industrial recruitment and self-development (Eisinger,1999; Flora, Green, Gale, Schmidt, & Flora 1992; Sharp et al., 2002). Industrial recruitment involves efforts to attract outside firms and industries to locate to the community (Crowe, 2006, 2008; Sharp et al., 2002). These efforts include the provision of tax abatements, low-interest loans, and easy access to cheap land for infrastructure development. One attractive feature of industrial recruitment is its ability to generate a large number of jobs in a relatively short time period. In contrast to industrial recruitment, self-development activities foster local businesses and other entrepreneurial activities along with relying on local resources to aid in development from within the community (Flora et al., 1992). Examples of self-development activities include revitalizing downtown businesses, promoting local tourism, and retaining or expanding locally owned businesses.

Capital and Economic Development

Generally speaking, communities have seven types of capital from which they can use to enhance the local economy: cultural, human, social, financial, built, natural, and political. When one type of capital is emphasized over all others, the other resources become weakened (Flora & Flora, 2008). This can compromise the economy, environment, and social equity of a community. Thus, it is important to study community capitals in conjunction with each other. For the purposes of this study, I examine community leaders' perceptions of four types of capital: human, built, social, and natural in relation to the promotion and implementation of economic development.

Human Capital

Human capital includes characteristics of individuals that strengthen one's ability to earn a living and provide for one's community, family, and self-improvement. It consists of one's personal assets: health, formal education, skills, intelligence, leadership, and talents (Flora & Flora, 2008). The association between human capital and economic development originates from the early work of Schultz (1961). Schulz (1961) argues that economic growth is largely the result of investing in human capital. He suggests that investments in human knowledge and skill are the major determinants of economic growth. Education is necessary if communities lacking such capabilities ever expect to attract and benefit from economic development. Similarly, Becker (2002) states that education and training are the most essential forms of human capital. As for rural areas, Gordon (2000) suggests that education and training are crucial in an increasingly hi-tech global economy in determining which communities will economically flourish and which will fall behind.

When it comes to recruiting outside industry, Rainey, Robinson, Allen, and Christy (2003) argue that communities that are able to train and/or attract a technologically competent labor force will be more equipped to attract and retain globally competitive firms. According to Rainey et al. (2003), rural communities must develop or attract workers who can adapt to new technology quickly and who can make creative adjustments to the production process in order to develop sustainable economies. Flora and Flora (2008) similarly argue that the level of schooling of a community's residents is an increasingly important asset of a community. Industries that are currently growing are computer oriented and thus require more highly educated workers. Therefore, rural communities need to invest in human capital to not only be attractive to outside industry but to be able to provide for self-development.

Built Capital

Along with human capital, research cites built capital as a major contributor to economic development. Built capital, sometimes referred to as physical capital, is the permanent physical infrastructure used to support community activities. Historically, when development agents discussed built capital, they referred to water and sewer capacity and transportation infrastructure. However, built capital also includes electric and natural gas, waste-disposal facilities, telephone and fiber optic networks, schools, hospitals, fire-protection, police, and other public buildings.

Recent research reveals that communities with well-managed, high quality built capital are more likely to be successful in sustaining and attracting economic development. In order to attract outside industry, Harrison (1992) argues that communities need to attract such industry by providing high-quality physical infrastructure, such as roads, sewer treatment, waste disposal, water lines, and telecommunications. Similarly, Rainey et al. (2003) suggest that in an increasingly global economy, communities that have a deficient physical infrastructure will find themselves at a considerable disadvantage for attracting and/or maintaining industry.

Research also suggests that investment in built capital can also contribute to self-development. For instance, Christopherson et al. (1999) found that investment in a community's physical infrastructure can have a positive impact on local tourism and the economy as a whole. While elements of a community's built capital allow businesses and industry to be more productive, Flora and Flora (2008) argue that built capital alone cannot guarantee the economic well being of that community. They argue that social capital is necessary to construct a strategy that leads to long-term, successful economic development.

Social Capital

While there are many definitions of social capital, Putnam (1995:67) states that social capital refers to "features of social organization, such as networks, norms, and trust that facilitate coordination and cooperation for mutual benefit." While early studies linked social capital to individual outcomes such as educational attainment (Coleman, 1988) and wealth (Bourdieu, 1979, 1980), later studies, led by Putnam (1993), began to link social capital to larger units such as nations and communities. Under Putnam's conceptualization, communities and even nations could possess a "stock" of social capital. He argued that communities that build a "stock" of social capital would have higher levels of community development.

Flora and Flora (1993) have tested this notion with their concept of an entrepreneurial social infrastructure (ESI). Communities with high levels of ESI are tolerant of different perspectives and have networks that bridge across different groups in the community as well as to other communities and state agencies. Communities that are tolerant of differing perspectives are expected to have access to a broader array of choices and be more likely to come to an agreement that benefits all groups than do communities characterized by conflict and intolerance (Coleman, 1957; Sharp et al., 2002). Network diversity, is expected to facilitate the flow of information, resources, and support within a community by assisting in the exchange of information among groups as well as connecting organizations within the community to the state.

Several studies show a link between high levels of social infrastructure and economic development. Flora et al. (1997) show a positive association between the implementation of economic development projects and having an entrepreneurial social infrastructure. In particular, communities that have a relatively unbiased local media and horizontal and vertical linkages to other communities and governments have higher levels of economic development. With regards to the two forms of economic development, Sharp et al. (2002) argue that a community's social infrastructure is more positively associated with self-development than with industrial recruitment. This is because self-development relies greatly on local resources and diverse leadership, while industrial recruitment relies more on government policy and funding.

Natural Capital

Natural capital, also referred to as environmental capital, includes a community's base of natural resources: air, water, land, flora, and fauna (Green & Haines, 2002). These natural resources may have direct use values in the form of provisioning services (e.g., timber, crops), unpriced benefits obtained from the regulation of ecosystem processes (e.g., climate and erosion regulation), and/or nonmaterial benefits in the form of cultural services (e.g., aesthetic values, sense of identity, recreation) (Millennium Ecosystem Assessment, 2005). Ostrom (2000) similarly defines natural capital as the *available* complex array of biophysical resources that surround a particular community. This includes geographical and social properties such as accessibility, control over surrounding land and resources, and geographical space. Crowe (2008) operationally defines a community's level of natural capital as the extent to which it is accessible, has room for expansion, and can provide services through its ecosystem.

Of the different forms of capital that can impact economic development, natural capital is the least mentioned. Weinberg (2000) states that for rural development to succeed in a global economy, communities must invest in education (human capital) and physical infrastructure (built capital) and have adequate financing (financial capital). Rainey et al. (2003) argue that while human and built capital are necessary for rural economic development; financial capital should be replaced with social capital. This is because communities that have thriving social networks and institutions and high human capital will also have adequate financing. Flora and Flora (2008) suggest that natural capital can impact economic development, but in an indirect fashion. For instance, natural resources are transformed into financial capital through farming and timber production and the consumption of natural capital provides the foundation for built capital (e.g. public buildings, roads, pipelines).

Despite many researchers lack of acknowledgement of the direct role that natural capital plays with regards to economic development, studies show that natural capital can also directly impact economic development. McGranahan (1999) finds that counties with higher natural amenities, such as warm climate, varied topography, and water areas, have had significantly higher levels of employment since 1969 than counties that rate low in natural amenities. As for industrial recruitment, Crowe (2008) finds that communities with low natural circumscription (have ample room for expansion) and easy accessibility are more likely to implement outside industries while communities with high natural circumscription and that are hard to access are more likely to implement self-development activities.

The Present Study

Although several scholars have examined the effect of one or more community capitals on economic development (e.g. Becker, 2002; Christopherson et al., 1999; Crowe, 2006; Flora et al., 1997), few studies examine the full array of capital with respect to economic development. In particular, research has failed to examine community leaders' perceptions of how the different types of capital affect the implementation of businesses in the community. Acknowledgement of leaders' perceptions about local capital is important since such perceptions are the driving force for which development paths a community pursues, and by what means. Furthermore, because different types of economic development result in variation in the number and quality of additional jobs in the community, it is important to examine economic development in terms of the number and type of new businesses attained. By knowing community leaders' perceptions of the effect of local community capital on economic development and the reasoning behind those perceptions, researchers, policy makers, extension and program evaluators will have more information to amend economic development programs so that they can better accomplish their goals of preserving small communities as homes and places of work.

The present study seeks to enhance our knowledge about how local economic leaders view their community's supply of human, social, built, and natural capital with respect to local business implementation. I use survey and interview data collected from community leaders in seven Washington and Oregon communities to ask the following questions: (1) Which forms of community capital: human, built, social, and natural do community leaders perceive as having a substantive effect on local economic development? (2) How do such perceptions held by leaders relate to economic development implementation and promotion?

Methods

Study Locations

Seven rural communities in Oregon and Washington were selected as study locations based on the following criteria:

- The community is rural (i.e. Building density is relatively low and the community is surrounded by agricultural lands or by natural vegetation (forests).
- The community has a population between 1,000 and 9,000—making it large enough to have economic development, but similar in size so that comparisons between communities can be made.
- The community had previously participated in a survey of economic development that had been administered to community leaders in 100 communities throughout Washington and Oregon (see _____ 2008 for a more in-depth discussion). Communities were selected from the 100 original to represent a diverse range of recent economic development activity. Communities that had recently implemented several economic development strategies as well as communities who had little recent economic development activity were selected from each state.

Research Approach

The findings reported here derive from surveys and in-depth interviews conducted between fall of 2006 and summer of 2007. In the fall of 2006, survey data collected on the seven communities was part of a larger project that surveyed over 100 communities throughout Washington and Oregon on a variety of issues pertaining to economic development, built, and social infrastructure. For each community, surveys were mailed to five community leaders. Community leaders consisted of two representatives of city council (typically city managers and city council members), one representative of the chamber of commerce or economic development council, one representative of local schools (typically superintendents), and one representative of an active civic organization. City clerks and local websites helped identify participants. Surveys were mailed to participants using a modified Dillman (2002) method. Five contacts were made; however, the fifth contact was by e-mail rather than by special delivery. A modified version of the surveys used by Flora et al. (1997) and Sharp (2001) was used to determine levels of each town's economic development.

In-depth interviews were directed towards expanding on the number and characteristics of economic development activities that had been successfully and unsuccessfully implemented in the community and the perceptions that key leaders had on what type of development should be pursued and what factors facilitate and hinder economic development. Interview questions were designed to clarify, confirm, or deny results obtained from the survey data. Participants consisted of city managers, city planners, council members, port commissioners, economic development council members, and newspaper editors. An in-depth search of all community websites that touched on local economic development was implemented. Through this search, individuals were solicited based on their knowledge of economic development that had taken place in the community over the past three years, making sure to capture a variety of views toward local economic development efforts. While all leaders were knowledgeable about recent local economic development efforts that had taken place in the community, a variety of views about economic development were expressed. Some leaders were favorable and proactive toward economic development, several took a laissez faire attitude toward development, and still others were against development of any kind.

During the interview participants were asked to list all economic development activities that they had implemented in the past three years, all economic development that they had tried to implement but were unsuccessful, and all economic development activities that had expired over the past three years. They were also asked specifics about each economic development activity, such as how many people were employed. A timeline of three years was used because it is a long enough period to allow for economic development activities to be counted, yet it is recent enough so that community leaders can more accurately recall all economic development activities. A time period of three years is consistent with previous research on economic development activities that samples community leaders (e.g. Crowe, 2006; Flora et al., 1997; Sharp, 2001). Leaders were also asked to list which types of development the community should pursue, if any, and what factors facilitate and hinder economic development. Specific questions were tailored toward understanding how the different types of community capitals affect current and potential economic development activities. All of the interviews were digitally recorded and extensive field notes were written as soon as possible after each interview. Recorded interviews were then transcribed verbatim and coded for relevant themes. Data coding happened in two steps. First the transcript materials were sorted into large themes (natural capital, economic development, etc.) and then that material was re-coded into more focused themes within the general themes (growth constraints, outside industries etc.).

Measures of Economic Development

Economic Development Implementation. The number of outside owned businesses that were successfully implemented or expanded in the previous three years serves as a measure for industrial recruitment. The number of locally owned businesses that were successfully implemented or expanded in the previous three years serves as a measure for self-development.

Economic Development Promotion. Informants were asked whether or not a particular type of economic development activity had been pursued in the community in the past three years. Items asked about promotion of self-development activities included efforts: to promote agricultural diversification; to revitalize the downtown or retail sector of the community; to retain or expand locally-owned businesses or industry; to apply for financial governmental assistance to expand local businesses; to attempt to find buyers for local businesses; to develop or promote a local historic or cultural site or event to promote tourism; and to encourage local realtors or contractors to develop housing. Items asked about promotion of industrial recruitment activities included efforts: to organize a committee to recruit new business or industry; to attract a large scale agricultural producer or outside owned value-added processing firm; to develop and maintain contact with leaders in industry outside the area; to apply for government financial assistance to attract industry or business; to seek investments from corporations outside the community to expand business or industry; to bring a state or federal office or facility to the community; and to seek outside investors to develop single or multi-family housing.

Measures of Community Capital

Natural Capital. A community's natural capital is measured by its accessibility, natural circumscription, and ecosystem type. Table 1 provides indicators for each variable._Data are collected from the Washington (2007) and Oregon (2007) Departments of Transportation and from detailed atlases.

Built Capital. A community's built capital is measured by the possession and quality of physical infrastructure such as roads, natural gas, sewer, and water, as well as public services such as a hospital and police department. Indicators for each variable are located in Table 1.

Table 1. Indicators of Community Capitals

Community Capital	Description	
Natural Capital		
Accessibility	Freight rail runs through community	Yes, No
	Number of 2-lane highways that pass through community	1, >1
	Miles from closest interstate	>25, <25 miles
Natural Circumscription	Number of directions available to grow	1-4
Ecosystem Type	Community's ecosystem typology	Urban, Cultivated, Coastal, Inland Water, Forest
Built Capital		
Sewer	Sewer system in community	Yes, No
Water	Type of water system	Well water, City water
Roads	How often roads are congested	Always, Sometimes, Never
Hospital	Quality of healthcare offered in community	Excellent, Good, Fair, Poor, Terrible, None offered
Police	Local police department	Yes, No
Social Capital		
Legitimacy of Alternatives	Quality of local media's performance in providing a forum to air different views on community issues	Excellent, Good, Fair, Poor, Terrible
Network Diversity		
• Community Organizations activity	How active are community organizations in community improvement or economic development activities	Very active, Moderately active, not very active
• Among different groups in community	How often different groups of people in the community cooperated for community betterment (past five years)	Often, Sometimes, Rarely, Never
• With other communities	The number of types of issues that community joined with other communities to address (past three years) (environmental, economic development, tourism, government lobbying, leadership training, special events)	1-6
• With state and national organizations	The number of state and national economic organizations the community belongs to	>0
Human Capital	Percent of residents age 25-44 with at least some college education.	Percent

Social Capital. Two concepts: legitimacy of alternatives and network diversity are used to measure a community's social capital. A community's willingness to legitimize alternatives includes the quality of its forums that allow different views to be expressed in an open environment. Network diversity includes the activity of community organizations in economic development, the extent that different groups in the community work together on community improvement projects, and a community's linkages to other communities and state and national organizations. Table 1 provides indicators for each variable.

Human Capital. A community's human capital is measured by the percentage of individuals between the ages of 25 and 65 with at least some college. Data is taken from the U.S. Census.

Results

Perceptions of Community Capital[2] and Economic Development

Community leaders mostly attribute the success or failure of implementing economic development to their built and natural capitals. Leaders in two of three communities with high natural capital, Evanston and Taylor Heights, viewed deficiencies in built capital, particularly water and sewer, as the reason why they did not successfully implement outside businesses or industry in their communities. Evanston did not implement any outside industries in the past three years. Community leaders attribute the lack of outside industry or businesses coming to the town on the lack of sewer in the community. As one community leader put it:

> The biggest limiting factor to development here is the lack of sewer systems. Businesses haven't been able to come into town. If you look at Jonesburg, which is just north of us, there are lots and lots of development going on and they have sewer.

Community leaders in Taylor Heights perceive the lack of water and adequate roads as the main reasons the community was not able to obtain more outside industry and business. According to one community leader:

> We have a huge Wal-mart distribution center in the next town over. They actually approached Taylor Heights wanting to build here, but we just didn't have the infrastructure (water and access roads). There's one thing that you could say that not being prepared with our (built) infrastructure, we weren't able to serve something like that. We lost out on that.

Community leaders in Rose Creek, a hard to access community with high natural circumscription, attribute the community's success at implementing both types of economic development (eight industrial recruitment projects and six self-development projects in previous three years) to enhances in their built capital. Community leaders view a new natural gas line as contributing to economic development particularly outside industry:

> Bringing in Northwest natural gas, I feel was a very good move on our area. That has proved to be very successful. It's provided for other developments. Businesses are looking at our North Spit area for manufacturing. We never had natural gas out there before. Now we do and so we are getting responses. There are people looking at the North Spit for developing out there.

Rose Creek was also successful in expanding locally owned businesses or industry. Community leaders partially credit this to the built infrastructure, particularly putting in a rail line that connects the city proper to the North Spit:

We just put in eight miles of railroad that is just right on that spur. The railroad bridge (that connects the town to the North Spit) keeps the wood products going that is crucial for the new mill that's been built on the North Spit.

As with built capital, natural capital, particularly level of accessibility and opportunity for expansion, played a major role in the implementation of outside industry to a community. Sunset Valley and Shady Grove are both hard to access—only by one two-lane highway, and have little to no room for expansion as they are locked in by steep hills on one side, water on two sides and government-owned land on the other side. Sunset Valley did not implement a single outside industry, while Shady Grove successfully implemented one outside industry to the community. Lilac City, like Shady Grove and Sunset Valley, is also hard to access—only by one two-lane highway. However, it has more room for expansion, as only two sides are limited by water. Lilac City implemented one outside industry and one outside developer to build residential housing. In all three communities, community leaders perceived natural factors to be a barrier to development. As one community leader in Shady Grove put it:

Shady Grove and Sunset Valley too have a history of blue collar, manufacturing, work in saw mills, work in processing plants, and would like to see that come back. But I don't know if that's going to come back and there's a national trend that manufacturing is in decline, let alone manufacturing when there's no rail, and there's no natural gas, and there's no highway system. So we're kind of struggling. We would like to see small type manufacturing come and we'll work to try to continue to promote that. But it's difficult.

Another community leader in the same community perceived the lack of expansion as the main limiting factor to development:

The city itself has no property to dabble with because the state purchased us out at the south end by putting that big project in the south (salmon rehabilitation)…and the north end, actually the city limits ends and it becomes (another community), and we have the river to the west. So we have just the hills to the east. We are locked in.

On the other hand, Reeve, a community that is accessible by rail, highway, and is close to an interstate and has ample room for expansion, had successfully recruited seven outside industries or businesses and will implement three more in the near future. While not yet implemented, the community had successfully recruited a state penitentiary and state mental hospital as well as a bio fuel company to locate to the community in the near future. In all cases, community leaders perceived accessibility and room for expansion as major factors in being able to attract them:

The prison folks required 250 acres or something like that…and so Reeve was one of those sites. When the need for the hospital came up, one of the citing priorities was to find available land that was already in state ownership. So that's how we get two.

As for the bio-fuel company:

In the past three months, we've been working with the county on trying to get a bio-fuel company to locate here. We've set up a meeting with them and are looking for some land for them. They want rail access. They want to be close to the source, close to the farms, but be close to rail and close enough to the interstate as well. It's just finding the land that would work for them.

While community leaders mainly attributed the success or failure of economic development to built and natural capital, a few communities perceived social conditions to either hinder or facilitate economic development. For instance, leaders in both Shady Grove and Sunset Valley perceived their relationship with the Department of Ecology (DOE) as hindering both industrial recruitment and self-development. Their relationship with the state agency was caustic, as leaders in both communities viewed DOE agents as governmental officials who were out to deliberately thwart economic development in the communities without any sound reasoning. As one community leader in Shady Grove described the situation:

> On a whole for economic development, we want to work with them (DOE) in an effective manner. Not just for them to come down and regulate. We're looking for a partnership that has mutual respect and communication. We find that we're always up against a brick wall. We start a process and they come down and say "you can't do this." They don't work with you for the best method of resolving it. They are extreme stumbling blocks for economic development.

However, the lack of effective communication came from both the DOE and the two communities:

> We used to have signs out in the valley that said "communist environmentalist." So for a long time, they (DOE) would not set foot down in our county. They were afraid they would be shot.

While vertical linkages between the two communities and the government were poor, until recently, any links between Sunset Valley and Shady Grove were also poor. The two communities viewed each other as rivalries and, although only three miles apart from each other, did not want to cooperate on any projects. Each community had their own school district, civic groups, and until the past year, their own chamber of commerce. In over 100 years of existence, the two communities had just begun to start to work together on a major project-- the implementation of a combined wastewater treatment plant that would serve both communities.

While Shady Grove and Sunset Valley had poor vertical and horizontal linkages that leaders perceived to contribute to a slow process of economic development, leaders in Rose Creek perceive the strong links between the town and the nearby tribal reservation to have heavily contributed to the effective implementation of outside businesses to the community. When the local tribe purchased 50 acres in the community to develop, they included the community of Rose Creek from the beginning to help shape the type of economic development that the land would serve. As a liaison for the tribe described the process:

> We wanted five acres to grow our parking lot (for the casino) and they (owners of land) said, "why don't you by all 50?" So we bought all 50. We did a series of meetings with the community. We thought that whatever we do for development, we want the community to be involved. This is very rare for a tribe to do this. Tribes are usually very protective of their sovereignty and rightfully so, but we wanted the community involved. So we held a series of community meetings. We asked them, "What do you want on this site?" We had every kind of idea. Through a process, we evaluated every idea that was presented, did feasibility studies and came up with an idea of developing a mixed-use retail and entertainment center for the piece of property. We had a second meeting to give a progress report and at our third community meeting we made the announcement that we had made a partnership agreement with the Home Depot to anchor the development.

Table 2. Promoted and Implemented Economic Development for Each Community

Community	Promoted Industrial Recruitment	Promoted Self-development	Number of IR Implemented	Number of SD Implemented
Evanston	none	Promoted agricultural diversification; marketing or <u>locally owned</u>, value-added processing Attempted to find buyers for a local business Developed and/or promoted a local historic or cultural site or event to promote tourism	0	10
Taylor Heights	Organized/rejuvenated a committee to recruit new business or industry Sought to attract a large scale agricultural producer or <u>outside-owned</u>, value-added processing firm Organized to bring a state or federal office or facility to the community Applied for financial assistance from county, state or federal government to <u>attract industry or business</u> Sought investments from investors outside the community to expand business or industry	Promoted agricultural diversification; marketing or <u>locally owned</u>, value-added processing Worked to revitalize the downtown or retail sector Taken action to retain or expand <u>locally-owned</u> businesses or industry Attempted to find buyers for a local business Developed and/or promoted a local historic or cultural site or event to promote tourism	3	16
Sunset Valley	Applied for financial assistance from county, state or federal government to <u>attract industry or business</u> Sought outside investors to develop housing	Worked to revitalize the downtown or retail sector Attempted to find buyers for a local business Developed and/or promoted a local historic or cultural site or event to promote tourism	0	4
Shady Grove	Organized/rejuvenated a committee to recruit new business or industry Applied for financial assistance from county, state or federal government to <u>attract industry or business</u> Sought investments from investors outside the community to expand business or industry Sought outside investors to develop housing	Promoted agricultural diversification; marketing or <u>locally owned</u>, value-added processing Worked to revitalize the downtown or retail sector Taken action to retain or expand <u>locally owned</u> businesses or industry Attempted to find buyers for a local business Developed and/or promoted a local historic or cultural site or event to promote tourism	1	3

Table 2. Cont'd

Community	Promoted Industrial Recruitment	Promoted Self-development	Number of IR Implemented	Number of SD Implemented
Lilac City	Sought outside investors to develop housing	Promoted agricultural diversification; marketing or locally owned, value-added processing Worked to revitalize the downtown or retail sector Taken action to retain or expand locally owned businesses or industry Attempted to find buyers for a local business Developed and/or promoted a local historic or cultural site or event to promote tourism Created a local housing development organization or encouraged local realtors or contractors to develop housing	2	5
Reeve	Systematically developed and maintained contact with leaders in industry outside the area Organized to bring a state or federal office or facility to the community	Promoted agricultural diversification; marketing or locally owned, value-added processing Worked to revitalize the downtown or retail sector Taken action to retain or expand locally owned businesses or industry Developed and/or promoted a local historic or cultural site or event to promote tourism	7	5
Rose Creek	Organized/rejuvenated a committee to recruit new business or industry Organized to bring a state or federal office or facility to the community Applied for financial assistance from county, state or federal government to attract industry or business Sought investments from investors outside the community to expand business or industry Systematically developed and maintained contact with leaders in industry outside the area Sought outside investors to develop housing	Promoted agricultural diversification; marketing or locally owned, value-added processing Worked to revitalize the downtown or retail sector Taken action to retain or expand locally owned businesses or industry Attempted to find buyers for a local business Applied for financial assistance from county, state or federal government to expand local businesses Developed and/or promoted a local historic or cultural site or event to promote tourism Created a local housing development organization or encouraged local realtors or contractors to develop housing	8	6

Both community and tribal leaders attribute this success to the social networking that took place between the tribe and the community and the open forum that provided for a variety of ideas to be expressed in an atmosphere where each were considered to be legitimate.

Community leaders did not attribute success or failure of implementing economic development to human capital. None of the interviewed leaders mentioned skills training, leadership development, or level of education as factors that either contributed to or deterred economic development in their communities.

Economic Development Implementation and Community Capitals

Several themes emerge as to how a community's array of capitals relate to economic development. Table 2 shows the number of implemented development activities while Table 3 provides values of each community capital measure for each community. With respect to industrial recruitment, communities that had implemented the most outside industries in the previous three years ranked high for at least two of the three capitals: natural, social, and built. While Rose Creek had low natural capital, the community had extremely high levels of built and social capitals. Reeve had very high natural and social capital and moderately high built capital. The other five communities that had implemented few or no industrial recruitment activities in the previous three years had high levels of one or none of the three community capitals: natural, social, and built and either low or moderate levels of the other capitals. This is evidenced by both the leaders' perceptions of capitals as well as the survey and secondary data that objectively measure the capitals (see Table 3). Taylor Heights and Evanston both had high natural capital. However, both communities had low built capital and moderate social capital. Shady Grove and Sunset Valley had low natural and social capitals and moderate built capital, while Lilac City had low natural capital and moderate built and social capitals.

It appears that a community's human capital is unrelated to the number of outside businesses and industries recruited. The two communities with the highest proportion of working age adults with some college education (Lilac City and Evanston) had low levels of industrial recruitment in the previous three years (two and zero respectively). However, the two communities with the lowest proportion of working age adults with some college education (Sunset Valley and Taylor Heights) also had low levels of industrial recruitment in the previous three years (zero and three respectively).

With respect to self-development, a different pattern emerges. Communities that had high natural capital but low built capital had implemented the most self-development projects in the previous three years. Evanston and Taylor Heights with their high natural capital and low built capital implemented 10 and 16 self-development projects in the previous three years. The two communities with low natural and social capitals, Sunset Valley and Shady Grove, implemented the least number of self-development projects in the previous three years, four and three respectively. Communities with either high or moderate levels of both social and built capitals, Lilac City, Reeve, and Rose Creek, implemented a moderate number of self-development projects in the previous three years, five, five, and six respectively.

Once again, it appears that a community's human capital is unrelated to the number of local businesses and industries implemented. The community with the highest number of local businesses implemented in the previous three years, Taylor Heights, has the second to lowest proportion of working age adults with some college education (43.6%). However, the community with the second highest number of local businesses implemented in the previous three years, Evanston, has the second to highest proportion of working age adults with some college education (67.9%). In addition, the communities with the highest and lowest proportion of working age adults with some college education (Lilac City and Sunset Valley) had similar levels of self-development in the previous three years.

Table 3. Summary of Community Capitals for Each Community

	Evanston	Taylor Heights	Sunset Valley	Shady Grove	Lilac City	Reeve	Rose Creek
Natural Capital							
Natural Circumscription	3	3	0	1	1	4	0
Accessibility							
• Rail	no	yes	no	no	no	yes	yes
• Highway	1	2	1	2	1	2	1
• Interstate	9 miles	0 miles	56 miles	52 miles	80 miles	15 miles	82 miles
Ecosystem Type	Inland Water	Cultivated	Coastal	Coastal	Coastal	Cultivated	Coastal
Built Capital							
Roads	sometimes	sometimes	never	never	sometimes	sometimes	sometimes
Sewer	no	yes	yes	yes	yes	yes	yes
Water	well	city	city	city	city	city	city
Natural Gas	no	no	no	no	no	no	yes
Hospital	fair	good	good	fair	fair	good	good
Police	yes	yes	yes	yes	yes	yes	yes
Social Capital							
Legitimacy of Alternatives							
• Forum	fair	poor	poor	fair	poor	good	good
Network Diversity							
• Community Organization Activity	Not very active	Moderately active	Moderately active	Moderately active	Moderately active	Not very active	Very active
• Among different groups in community	sometimes	sometimes	sometimes	sometimes	sometimes	sometimes	sometimes
• With other communities	4	4	6	5	6	3	6
• With state and national organizations	3	3	3	3	4	2	6

Economic Development Promotion and Community Capitals

Overall, communities were more likely to develop methods to secure self-development projects than to secure outside businesses and industry. On the whole, the seven communities were successful at self-development. However, the two communities with the lowest levels of natural, social, and built capitals, Shady Grove and Sunset Valley, were the only two communities that were not successful at every method at securing self-development. Despite trying to revitalize the downtown or retail sector, attempting to find buyers for local businesses, and taking action to attain locally-owned businesses, both communities had failed at all methods; both communities' downtowns were littered with vacant buildings. While the two communities had experienced new businesses, an equal number had closed in the same period.

As for industrial recruitment, Rose Creek, Taylor Heights, and Shady Grove actively promoted outside industries and businesses, while Evanston, Lilac City, Shady Grove, Reeve did not actively pursue such development. Of the three communities to actively pursue outside industry, Rose Creek was the most successful. Despite having low natural capital, Rose Creek has high built and social capitals that leaders claim have aided in the successful recruitment of outside businesses to the community. Despite such efforts, Taylor Heights and Shady Grove were not as successful at recruiting outside businesses. Taylor Heights did apply for financial assistance from the state, but was unsuccessful. This has perpetuated the problem, according to one community leader:

> We've tried to pursue a public works trust fund loan for a new water reservoir to expand our infrastructure. We've been unsuccessful in that. That has a huge impact on our economic development because right now we are in a position where we have to have that in order to grow.

Despite having such success with self-development, Taylor Heights would like even more development by recruiting outside industries and businesses. Leaders believe that until they improve their built infrastructure, especially water and roads, their efforts will be in vain. However, because of Taylor Heights' high natural capital, once they are able to improve their built capital, their efforts for industrial recruitment may be more successful.

Unfortunately, Shady Grove will have an even tougher battle to secure outside industry to the community. All of the community's efforts to implement outside businesses have been unsuccessful. One major reason is the community's low natural capital. In the past three years, no outside industry or business came in. In fact, one outside industry and one outside developer wanted to come to Shady Grove but decided against it. In both instances, natural factors were to blame:

> The carpet company wanted to come in, but we didn't have any room. There was also an outside developer who has developed a bunch of ocean front condos and restaurants and golf courses in Westport, actually bought a water front restaurant in Shady Grove and had those plans to develop here. But my impression is that he got over extended and his funders would not fund him because they did not see the location as profitable. So he's actually selling that and decided not to enter into Shady Grove.

Thus, to be successful at both self-development and industrial recruitment, Shady Grove must develop its social and built capitals.

As for the four communities that did not actively pursue outside industries and businesses, two had high natural capital (Evanston and Reeve) and two had low natural capital (Lilac City and Sunset Valley). Because Evanston did not have sewer, the community's leaders did not attempt to recruit outside industry. Instead of actively seeking outside industry and business, they have been focusing on obtaining sewer:

> Sewer is our biggest issue. It has been for years now. It's been hard to think about anything beyond sewer. Economic development just has not been at the top of the list until now. It's now up there because we are getting sewers. For the last few years, all of our energy has been based on getting our sewer treatment plant.

Now that the work is mostly behind them, city hall and city council are now looking at economic development. Because of the community's high natural capital and moderate social capital, once they improve their built capital the community's economic future looks promising.

Reeve is an example of industrial recruitment success, despite its low efforts at pursuing outside industries and businesses to the community. Reeve takes a laissez faire attitude toward recruitment. As one community leader puts it:

> I sometimes think that economic development happens in spite of what everybody does to promote it. And that it sometimes comes from directions that you don't expect, like Camping World locating a store here.

Reeve's high natural and social capital, along with its moderate built capital play major roles in the community's success at attaining outside businesses, industries, and state facilities. The community had success with both methods of recruitment—organizing to bring in a state or federal facility to the community and systematically developing and maintained contact with leaders in industry outside the area—resulting in two large state facilities and five industries and businesses to locate to the community.

The last two communities, Lilac City and Sunset Valley neither actively pursued nor had much success at implementing industrial recruitment activities. Both had low natural capital and moderate built capital and either low or moderate social capital. Like Shady Grove, Sunset Valley must develop its social and built capitals to have success at both self-development and industrial recruitment. However, unlike Shady Grove, Lilac City has had more success at implementing self-development projects. This may be due to more time and resources spent on pursuing self-development as well as its moderate built and social capitals.

Discussion

Economic development is increasingly seen as a local responsibility. While economic development is important for the survival of small communities as places of home and work, taxes from new businesses and industry are important sources of revenue for the community. Perceptions of community capitals' effect on local economic development provide the foundation for which types of economic development are pursued—making community leaders' perceptions of particular importance. This research provides a starting point for thinking about how community leaders perceive the effect of community capitals on local economic development. In the cases of the communities studied, community leaders perceive built and natural capitals as having the most effect on economic development. However, for natural capital, community leaders perceived natural circumscription and accessibility to be the most important factors, while not perceiving their natural amenities as having an effect on economic development. This is an important distinction because instead of using their natural amenities to capture the "creative class" (McGranahan & Wojan, 2007) and thereby increasing economic development in professions that require these creative workers, such as science, arts, design, entertainment, and business ownership, Shady Grove and Sunset Valley spent their efforts in recruiting heavy industries to their communities. In addition to built and natural capitals, several communities also perceived social capital as having a major effect on successful economic development. However, none of the community leaders perceived human capital to have an impact, either positive or negative, on the successful implementation of economic development activities.

As for successful implementation of economic development, communities that had high levels of at least two of the capitals, natural, built, and social, had implemented the largest number of outside businesses or industries in the previous three years. This gives hope to communities with low natural capital. While it is hard to change natural capital, a community can work to strengthen its social and built capitals and have some success at industrial recruitment, as illustrated by Rose Creek. This may also explain why some communities' pursuit of outside industry and businesses were not successful. For example, despite heavily promoting industrial recruitment, Shady Grove was only successful at implementing one outside-owned business to the community in the previous three years. The results suggest that Shady Grove's low natural and social capitals may partially explain why their pursuit of outside industries and businesses were mostly unsuccessful.

For self-development, the two communities with high natural capital, low built capital, and moderate social capital had implemented the most local businesses or industry in the previous three years. Both of these communities perceived their low built capital as the hardest challenge to development and thus this recognition may have pushed them toward self-development that is smaller in scale and not dependent on improvements in built infrastructure. Clearly, Evanston would not even focus on recruiting outside industries and businesses until the community had acquired sewer. Both Evanston's and Taylor Height's efforts in promoting self-development despite their low built infrastructure were successful. Evidence suggests that this may be due to their high natural capital and moderate social capital. Furthermore, while Sunset Valley and Shady Grove had moderate levels of built capital, they implemented significantly fewer self-development projects than Evanston and Taylor Heights. Again, this may be due to their natural and social capitals as both communities had low levels of each capital. Alternatively, by focusing on their high natural amenities rather than their low accessibility and high natural circumscription, perhaps the two communities could be more successful at implementing self-development strategies that appeal to tourists.

There are some limitations of the study that future research should attempt to address. While the current study measures the promotion and implementation of self-development and industrial recruitment, it does not measure the outcomes each type of development has on the community. It would be instructive to know how implementing self-development projects compared to industrial recruitment projects affects various economic, environmental, and social conditions, such as income inequality and environmental degradation. In addition, while the findings illustrate how natural, built, and social capital influence community-level economic development, there is a need for more comparative studies to better evaluate the robustness of the findings. For instance, future studies may compare how the sources of capital influence local economic development in developed nations to that in less developed nations. Finally, more research is needed to conceptualize cultural capital and the role that it plays toward economic development. For instance, some communities in the study appear to have a more pro-active culture of getting things done by all means necessary, while other communities appear to have a laissez faire attitude or hand-out approach to development.

In conclusion, it is not surprising that issues surrounding economic development have begun to capture the attention of activists, researchers, and policy makers. With an increasingly global economy, researchers and communities alike continue to strive for development that is both economically and environmentally sustainable. While there is increasing recognition that different sources of capital influence community-level economic development, community leaders and researchers alike must recognize the intricate manner that each type of capital works in conjunction with one another to influence different kinds of economic development. This study shows that unless researchers, policy makers, and community leaders give sufficient attention to physical, natural, and social factors, communities may continue to spend time and resources pursuing certain types of economic development strategies to no avail, while failing to implement alternative economic development strategies that may be of extreme benefit to community citizens.

Notes

1 While community leaders can consist of civic, government, religious, and other types of leaders in the community, I focus on leaders who are knowledgeable about economic development. These leaders tend to hold positions in government or are in other positions where they have the ability to be heard by local citizens and outsiders and thus have the most influence with respect to local economic development. Thus their perceptions about economic development play a key role in deciding the economic future of a community.

2 Community leaders' perceptions of their communities' natural, social, and built capital are validated by survey and secondary data that empirically measure the three capitals for each community. However, since none of the leaders mentioned human capital as affecting local economic development, results mainly focus on the three other forms of capital.

References

Becker, G. S. (2002). Human capital. In *The Concise Encyclopedia of Economics*. Online; available: http://www.econlib.org/library/Enc/HumanCapital.html; accessed September 24, 2007.

Bourdieu, P. (1979). Les trois etats du capital culturel. *Actes de la Recherche en Sciences Sociales* 31:3-6.

Bourdieu, P. (1980). Le capital social: Notes provisoires. *Actes de la Recherche en Sciences Sociales* 31:2-3.

Christopherson, S., Alexander, T., Clavel, P., Lawhead, J., Reardon, K., Westmont, K., & et al., . (1999). *Reclaiming a regional resource: A progress report on the U.S. Department of Housing and Urban Development's Canal Corridor Initiative*. Ithaca, N.Y.: Department of City and Regional Planning, Cornell University.

Coleman, J. (1957). *Community conflict*. Glencoe, IL: Free Press.

(1988). Social capital in the creation of human capital. *American Journal of Sociology* 94: S95-120.

Crowe, J. (2006). Community economic development strategies in rural Washington: Toward a synthesis of natural and social capital. *Rural Sociology* 71:573-596.

(2007). In search of a happy medium: How the structure of interorganizational networks influence community economic development strategies. *Social Networks* 29:469-488.-

(2008). The role of natural capital on the pursuit and implementation of economic development. *Sociological Perspectives* 51:827-851.

Dillman, D. A. (2002). *Mail and Internet surveys: The tailored design method*. New York: Wiley and Sons.

Eisinger, P. (1999). State economic development in the 1990s: Politics and policy learning. Pp. 178-90 in *Approaches to Economic Development*, Blari, J. & Reese, L. (Eds.). Thousand Oaks, CA: Sage Publications.

Flora, C. & Flora, J. (1993). Entrepreneurial social infrastructure: A necessary ingredient. *The Annals of the American Academy of Political and Social Sciences* 529:48-58.

Flora, C. & Flora, J. (2008). *Rural communities: Legacy and change, 3rd edition*. Boulder, CO: Westview Press.

Flora, J., Sharp, J. Flora, C. & Newlon, B. (1997). Entrepreneurial social infrastructure and locally initiated economic development in the nonmetropolitan United States. *The Sociological Quarterly* 38:623-45.

Flora, J., Green, G., Gale, A.E., F., Schmidt, F.E., & Flora, C. (1992). Self development: A viable rural development option? *Policy Studies Journal* 20:276-88.

Gordon, R. J. (2000). Does the 'New Economy' measure up to the great inventions of the past? *Journal of Economic Perspectives* 14:49-74.

Green, G. (2003). What role can community play in local economic development? Pp. 343-352 In

Challenges for Rural America in the Twenty-First Century, Brown, B. & Swanson, L. (Eds.) University Park, PA: Pennsylvania State University Press.

Green, G., & Haines, A. (2002). *Asset Building and Community Development*. Thousand Oaks, CA: Sage Publications.

Harrison, B. (1992). Industrial districts: Old wine in new bottles? *Regional Studies* 26:469-83.

Leicht, K., & Jenkins, J.C. (1994). Three strategies of state economic development: Entrepreneurial, industrial recruitment, and deregulation policies in the American states. *Economic Development Quarterly* 8:256-269.

McGranahan, D. (1999). Natural amenities drive population change. Agricultural Economics Report No. 781, USDA, Washington DC, US Government Printing Office.

McGranahan, D. & Wojan, T. (2007). The creative class: A key to growth. *Amber Waves*. April 2005. United States Department of Agriculture Economic Research Service.

Millennium Ecosystem Assessment (2005). *Ecosystems and Human Well Being*. Washington D.C.: Island Press.

Ostrom, E. (2000). Social capital: A fad or a fundamental concept? Pp. 172-214 in *Social Capital: A Multifaceted Perspective*, Dasgupta, P & Serageldin, I. (Eds.) Washington, DC: World Bank.

Pigg, K. & Crank, L. (2005). Do information communication Technologies Promote Rural Economic Development?" *Community Development* 36:65-76.

Putnam, R. (1993). *Making democracy work: Civic traditions in modern Italy*. Princeton, NJ: Princeton University Press.

(1995). Bowling alone: America's declining social capital. *Journal of Democracy* 6:66-78.

Rainey, D. V.,Robinson, K.L.,Allen, I. & Christy, R.D. (2003). Essential forms of capital for sustainable community development. *American Journal of Agricultural Economics* 85:708-715.

Schultz, T. (1961). Investment in human capital. *American Economic Review* 51:1-17.

Shaffer, R. & Summers, G. (1989). Community economic development. Pp. 173-95 in *Community Development in Perspective*, Christenson, J. & Robinson, J. Jr. (Eds.) Ames, IA: Iowa State University.

Sharp, J. (2001). Locating the community field: A study of interoganizational network structure and capacity for community action. *Rural Sociology* 66:403-24.

Sharp, J., Agnitsch, K., Ryan, V. & Flora, J. (2002). Social infrastructure and community economic development strategies: The case of self-development and industrial recruitment in rural Iowa. *Journal of Rural Studies* 18:405-17.

Summers, G. (1986). Rural community development. *Annual Review of Sociology*. 12:347-71.

Weinberg, A. S. (2000). Sustainable economic development in rural America. *Annals of the American Academy of Political and Social Sciences* 570:173-85.

DEVELOPMENT OF LAST RESORT: THE IMPACT OF NEW STATE PRISONS ON SMALL TOWN ECONOMIES IN THE UNITED STATES

By Terry L. Besser and Margaret M. Hanson

ABSTRACT

Many rural communities desperate for economic development have turned to formerly resisted options, such as influencing the state to locate prisons in their area to revitalize their local economies. Without a vital economy, they fear a continuation of declining population and a diminished quality of life. This study uses 1990 and 2000 census data to examine the economic and demographic impact of new state prisons on small town economies compared to changes that occurred during the decade in all other small towns. The analysis shows that when 1990 economic and demographic factors and region are controlled, new state prison towns experienced less growth than non-prison towns except that prison towns had a greater increase in unemployment, poverty, and percent of minorities. The assumption that prisons represent a solution to distressed small town economies and a boost for community development should be reexamined by community leaders.

INTRODUCTION

The decade of the 1980s was devastating to rural towns in the United States. The plunge in agricultural revenue and the need to repay expensive loans taken out during the booming 1970s sent many farmers into bankruptcy (Davidson, 1990). Rural towns lost population, businesses, and tax revenue. State, federal, and non-profit agencies encouraged rural communities to diversify their economies by developing non-agriculture based industry. Many followed this advice and eagerly pursued manufacturers—viewed as the industry with the highest multiplier effect and hence the industry likely to have the greatest positive impact on the local economy. However, since the country as a whole was shifting at the same time from manufacturing to services as the dominant industrial sector, the manufacturing industries attracted to rural communities were seeking low wage, docile employees, and a "good business climate." More critically, the search for low wages and a good business climate has led many of these newly settled manufacturers to leave their rural facilities when moving to a site with even lower wages is feasible (Drabenscott, 2003). A fortunate few small towns attracted high-wage manufacturers like Saturn, Mercedes, or Toyota plants. The remainder sought alternative development options.

Terry L. Besser, Iowa State University, Department of Sociology M. Hanson, Iowa State University, Office of Social and Economic Trend Analysis

At the same time, another major change occurred in the United States—a dramatic increase in rates of incarceration. From 1980 until 1995, the number of inmates in prisons and jails grew by 5 to 6 percent per year. Then growth in the number of inmates slowed to 3.8 percent in state prisons but continued at about 5 percent growth in federal prisons (Hallinan, 2001). Since 1980, there has been a massive 326 percent increase in the rate of adult males incarcerated in state and federal correctional institutions (Sourcebook of Criminal Justice Statistics, 2001). In 2001, 896 of every 100,000 adult males were in state or federal prisons compared to 275 of every 100,000 in 1980. The number of U.S. residents incarcerated, including prisoners in jails and state and federal prisons, exceeded the 2 million mark in 2002 (Anderson, 2003). Fighting crime and incarcerating inmates is an expensive undertaking costing federal and state governments over $57 billion in total justice system expenditures in 1999, up from $11.6 billion in 1982 (figures not adjusted for inflation) (Sourcebook of Criminal Justice Statistics, 2001).

At first, many states handled the large influx of prisoners by packing them into already existing facilities. However, a federal court ruling in 1980 made it illegal to use prison inmates to guard other prisoners and ruled that inmate packing (among other practices) constituted cruel and unusual punishment (Hallinan, 2001). States were forced to build new prisons to comply with the court rulings. In addition, tough federal anti-drug and "Truth in Sentencing" legislation added substantially to the number of inmates incarcerated (Wood et al., 2002). Many states also passed legislation that required lengthy sentences, especially for drug offenders, taking away judicial sentencing discretion. The so-called "tough on crime" legislation, coupled with the overall increase in crime rates (in the 1960s, 1970s, and 1980s) and the court injunctions against overcrowding of prisons, caused a prison building boom in the 1980s and 1990s (Beale, 1995; Hallinan, 2001; Wood et al., 2002).

Prior to the 1980s, prisons were generally built in metropolitan areas (Grieco, 1978; Beale, 1995). The logic was that it was convenient and economical to locate prisons where most of the crime was committed. In any case, rural areas resisted siting prisons in their vicinity (Shichor, 1992). According to Beale, prior to the prison building boom of the 1980s, 62 percent of inmates were located in prisons and jails in metropolitan areas. Between 1980 and 1991, 47 percent of inmates in new prisons were located in metropolitan areas with 53 percent in non-metropolitan counties (1995, p. 25). As we will show below, an even greater percentage of inmates are housed in new prisons built in the 1990s in non-metropolitan areas.

The relocation of prisons from metropolitan to rural locations happened with the consent and indeed the enthusiastic support of rural community leaders. What had been viewed as a LULU (a locally undesirable land use) became a last resort for promoting economic development. Given the contemporary decline of rural community economies summarized previously, it is not hard to understand the change in sentiment. According to a Jasper County, Iowa, economic development official, the benefits of a new prison would be "many new jobs, population growth, an increased tax base and the development of additional businesses" (JEDCO, 1995). An article in the *Fort Dodge (Iowa) Messenger* estimated that the new prison in Fort Dodge would bring 300 correctional facility jobs, $11.5 million in direct payroll income, and $78 million per year in total economic benefit to the county (Hughes, 1998). Moreover, prisons are perceived to be non-polluting and provide recession-proof jobs (personal interview with an Iowa economic development official, 2002). These accounts summarize the local assumptions about the anticipated economic benefits from a local prison (Reynolds, 1995; 2001; Doyle, 2002).

There is a dearth of research on this topic prior to the late 1980s. This is partially explained by the fact that prisons would probably not produce a noticeable impact on metropolitan economies (Hooks et al., 2000), which is where most prisons were located. Three hundred new jobs would not be significant in Cincinnati or Kansas City. However, the addition of 300 jobs to Newton or Clarinda, Iowa, and other small towns is another matter. Over and above the likely greater impact of prisons on small town economies, it has become a more important area of inquiry because rural community leaders operate under the untested premise that prisons will benefit their community. Based on that assumption, they invest taxpayer money to "lure" a prison to their town. Fort Dodge, Iowa, raised $500,000 from private sources for a prison industries facility, donated 60 acres of land, and paid $150,000 from tax revenue for a back-up generator for the electric utility in their bid to attract a prison to their community (Shea, 1998).

Although an increase in economic activity (more jobs and businesses) is accepted by many as a worthy goal in and of itself, careful examination reveals that economic development is ultimately justified for its contribution to community betterment, i.e., an enhanced quality of life for residents. Significant sudden events that upset the community status quo, such as a prison or a large business opening or closing, reverberate throughout the community beyond the economic sector impacting community social relations and quality of life. Couch and Kroll-Smith (1994) suggest that communities confronted with "consensus crisis" events (Drabek, 1986), rally together to solve the common problems posed by the event. Residents develop a "spiritual kinship" and an enhanced sense of shared identity (Erikson, 1994). Our understanding of consensus crisis events comes from research about communities facing natural disasters. However, this work has theoretical applications to economic events as well. Alternately, "corrosive community" (Freudenburg & Jones, 1991) events split the community into angry warring factions. Albrecht, Amey, and Amir (1996) studied four communities selected as sites for nuclear waste disposal facilities. They found that value differences within the communities about economic development and environmental quality, and differences in perceptions of risks and benefits from the waste disposal sites led to heated acrimony that strained or ruined interpersonal relations extending beyond the siting debates, both in time and in subject matter. The impact on subsequent community quality of life is unexamined, but the authors imply a direct relationship between solidarity and quality of life.

A longitudinal study of energy boom towns reveals a slightly different pattern than that exhibited in either the consensus crisis event or the corrosive community conceptualization (Smith, Krannich, & Hunter, 2001). These researchers found that the initial gains in the economy associated with the plant openings were accompanied by declines in social well being. However, two decades later the economic gains remained and social well being rebounded to pre-boom levels. Thus, major economic events may lead to three different community outcomes: consensus and improved quality of life, corrosive relations with deep divisions in the community and possibly diminished quality of life, and an initial economic gain accompanied by a decline in social well being that rebounds after several decades. Albrecht et al. (1996) argue that the distinction between consensus and corrosive community outcomes depends on the presence of shared values about economic development and the perception by community residents of an equitable sharing of risks and benefits from the "event." If true, the non-economic impact of a new prison on a small town would depend on the perceptions of community residents about whether a prison is an appropriate venue for economic development, whether the economic gains to the town outweigh the costs, and whether the costs and benefits are shared equitably.

This study examines only the economic and demographic changes (gains or losses) associated with a new prison. We provide a review of the extant literature and utilize the 1990 and 2000 census data to compare small towns with and without new prisons on several economic and demographic measures. With this analysis, we hope to determine if new prisons provide the economic gains hoped for by community leaders, at least in the short term.

THE CONSEQUENCES OF PRISONS ON COMMUNITIES

Prisons provide jobs. Whether and how much the local community gains from those jobs is the issue. Reviews of the literature conducted by Smykla et al. (1984) and Carlson (1991) concluded that prisons have no negative affects on local economies. However, at the time of the studies included in the reviews, most prisons were located in metropolitan areas and one would expect that the consequences might be different for prisons in small towns (Hooks et al., 2000). Additionally, McShane, Williams III, and Wagoner (1992) point to serious methodological flaws with this body of research, the largest being the lack of controls for historical changes over time.

More recently, King et al. (2003) compared new prison small towns to matched non-prison small towns in New York. Matching comparable prison and non-prison towns can partially control for historical effects on the economic factors that should be approximately the same in matched towns. They discovered that the prison towns did not gain significantly in employment when compared to non-prison towns. Similar findings resulted from analyses of all U.S. counties (Hooks et al., 2000), new prison towns in Mississippi (Wood et al., 2002), and new prison towns in California (Huling, 2002). Citing yet to be released research by Ruth Gilmore, Huling (2002) reported that initially only about 20 percent of prison jobs in California small towns with new prisons went to local residents. This figure increases over time up to about 40 percent as commuting employees move to the community and local residents become eligible for employment. Possible explanations for the low employment are that local residents may not be qualified for correctional positions and/or are prevented by seniority and union rules from starting their career in corrections at the local facility (King et al., 2003). Private prisons are more likely to hire local residents; however, their turnover rate is three times higher than public prisons because of their lower wages and lower level of employee training associated with greater employee safety concerns (Huling, 2002).

If few local residents are hired by the prison, and prison employees commute to the prison from other towns, then the impact of the additional jobs provided by the prison on housing, local businesses, tax revenue, and property values will be less than if the employees reside in the local area. Studies conducted prior to the 1980s were mixed in their findings regarding the association of changes in property values and tax revenue with prison siting (Shichor, 1992). However, in a recent study in Iowa, new prison towns did not realize significant gains in tax revenue after the prison openings compared to the tax revenue changes over the same time period in matched non prison towns (DeLisi & Besser, 2003). Of course, public prisons pay no property or sales taxes and private prisons frequently are granted tax abatements. Therefore, there is no local tax revenue expected from those sources.

King et al. (2003), DeLisi and Besser (2003), and Wood et al. (2002) compared changes in housing and local business numbers from 1990 to 2000 in new prison and matched non-prison towns in New York, Iowa, and Mississippi respectively. The new prison towns fared no better than the matched towns in growth of housing or number of businesses. Apparently, prison employees do not purchase sufficient goods and services from the local area to spur the growth of local businesses whose employees and owners might boost the housing market. Also, it appears as if prisons are not purchasing their supplies from the local community (King et al., 2003). Clement (2002) argues that prisons themselves have few economic links with the local community. Local suppliers may not be able to meet the needs of the prison or purchasing decisions are centralized at the state level. Some prisons, especially in Southern states, attempt to be self sufficient, which provides few opportunities for local businesses to provide supplies and services to the prison (Hallinan, 2001).

Locating prisons in small towns, compared to metropolitan areas, brings unexpected consequences (Clement, 2002; Huling, 2002). Inmates may be counted as residents of the prison town for census and legal purposes. Since census demographic figures are the basis for various kinds of federal support to local areas, the addition of incarcerated "residents" boosts federal revenue to small communities. Clement (2002:3) cites Minnesota officials who estimate that each inmate provides an additional $200 to $300 per year in federal funding for prison towns. Census figures are also used to determine political boundaries. While inmates cannot vote, their presence nonetheless influences school boundaries and legislative districts. Communities compete to have inmates counted as residents (Clement, 2002). The real losers in this competition are the poor urban inner cities from which many inmates come. These areas lose federal revenue to small prison towns where their convicted residents are sent for incarceration. No wonder politicians in some states work to land prisons in their district and then craft policies and laws to keep the incarceration rates high (Wood et al., 2002; Hallinan, 2001).

The majority of inmates are minorities. By year end in 2001, only 36.1 percent of inmates in federal and state prisons were white non-Hispanics (Harrison & Beck, 2002). The overrepresentation of minorities in the prison population changes the racial composition of small prison towns for census purposes. Most small towns outside the South and West have a relatively low population of minorities. In 1990, the percent of minorities in towns with 10,000 or less in population was 6.5 percent in the Northeast, 4.4 percent in the Midwest, and 22.0 percent in the South and West (calculated from 1990 Census of the Population). Hence, a small town with a new prison will likely experience an exponential increase in minority population according to census figures while the actual diversification among town residents may be minimal.

Another related issue pertains to the potential danger posed by the prison. Many small town residents fear escapees and visits or in-migration of the friends and families of inmates (Doyle, 2002; Shichor, 1992). Studies conducted prior to the ruralization of prisons show that the arrival of "camp followers" to prison towns is not a major problem (Tully et al., 1982; Shichor, 1992) and prisons do not negatively impact local crime rates (Smykla et al., 1984; Daniel, 1991). However, the impact of these factors in rural communities is unknown. Since inmates are counted as local residents, crimes they commit while incarcerated will be included in local crime figures. Also, when a crime is committed by inmates, they are entitled to local public defender services. Huling (2002) points to the overload on the local criminal justice infrastructure that may result.

Finally, whatever other benefits and disadvantages result from prisons, one sure benefit according to proponents is that prison employment is stable and secure. Two factors challenge this assumption. Recent state budget problems have caused some states to furlough and not replace departing prison staff (DeLisi & Besser, 2003); some states are delaying the opening of new prisons (Clement, 2002; Wood et al., 2002); and the incarceration rate has leveled off (U.S. Department of Justice, 2003). All of these factors may lead to an overall decrease in employment in correctional facilities. Therefore, what were once recession-proof jobs are now subject to the same lay offs and "plant closings" that characterize private sector jobs.

As indicated in the research reviewed above, prisons appear to provide few benefits to small town economies. However, prior research is limited to studies of a single state, studies conducted prior to the ruralization of prisons, or national studies conducted before the findings of the 2000 census were released. This paper extends the research base by examining all new prison small towns on economic and demographic factors in 1990, before prison opening, and 2000, after the prison was in operation, compared to all other small towns for the same time period.

RESEARCH DESIGN

Information on state prisons built during the decade of the 1990s was assembled by perusing website information provided by the state department responsible for corrections in each of the 48 contiguous states, followed by e-mail contact, and if necessary by telephone calls. Information gathered directly from the states was verified with the Directory of Adult and Juvenile Correctional Departments (2001). For each new prison, we were provided with the date of opening, offender type (juvenile or adult, male or female, and security level), and design and actual inmate capacity of the prison. In this analysis, we used only non-work release adult facilities opened between 1990 and 2000 (not including those opened in 2000). Some states do not report both design and actual capacities of their prisons. We had more complete data for design capacity, and therefore that figure was used in this analysis. When design capacity was unavailable, we substituted actual capacity.

We chose to elaborate the impact of new prisons on towns and not counties. Without a doubt, the economic impact of a new prison is not confined to the boundaries of small towns, but instead extends out into the county and adjacent areas. Nevertheless, if there is a local impact from the prison, one would expect to see it in the prison's host town as well as in adjoining areas. It is important to know what if any consequences are experienced by the host town, not just the county or the multi-county area.

The town stated in the mailing address of the prison was considered the host town for the prison. We analyzed the population census data for each of the new prison home towns and all other towns in the 48 contiguous states for 1990 and 2000. Twenty-five new prison towns did not have FIPs codes. Thus, there were no census data for them. In those cases, we substituted the closest town that had a FIPs code and used that town's census data. Substituted towns ranged from 1.8 miles to 44 miles, with the median being 8.7 miles, from the prison town indicated in the address. There were 248 towns hosting 274 new state prisons built between 1990 and 2000. Included in that group are twenty-four towns with two new state prisons built in the 1990s, and one (Beeville, Texas) was the site of three new prisons.

Small towns are defined as incorporated places with 10,000 or less in population. It should be noted that in this analysis, the term "non-prison towns" refers to towns that were not the location of a new state prison built in the 1990s. These towns may have an older prison, a new federal prison, or a new private prison within their boundary. Even so, we believe it is safe to assume that the majority of the 19,253 non-prison small towns used here for comparison are not the location of a prison.

FINDINGS

Table 1 displays the distribution of new state prisons by community size, region, and year opened. Slightly more than 69 percent of the 274 new state prisons were opened in towns of 10,000 or less in population in 1990. The South built the greatest number of new state prisons with 151 (55.1 percent) and about two-thirds of the new state prisons were opened in the first half of the 1990s. The trend of moving inmates to new prisons in small towns continued into the 1990s. According to Beale (1995), prior to the 1980s, 62 percent of inmates were located in prisons in metropolitan areas. In the new prisons built from 1980 to 1991, the percentage of inmates located in metropolitan areas declined to 47 percent. The percentage of inmates in new state prisons in metropolitan areas built in the 1990s was slightly less than 10 percent. Additionally, 68.9 percent of the inmates of new state prisons are in prisons in small towns of 10,000 or less.

For the comparisons that follow, percent change from 1990 to 2000 statistics were calculated for all indicators for each town. Then the change statistics were

Table 1. Percent of New State Prisons by Size of Town, Region, and Year of Opening, 1990 to 2000

	N	%
Town Population in 1990		
< 10,000	190	69.3%
10,001-49,999	54	19.7%
50,000+	30	<u>10.9%</u>
		100%
By Region		
East	37	13.5%
West	34	12.4%
Midwest	52	19.0%
South	151	<u>55.1%</u>
		100%
By Year		
1990-94	183	66.8%
1995-00	91	<u>33.2%</u>
		100%

averaged for small new state prison towns and other small towns. There were 176 small towns with new state prisons built from 1990 to 2000. Since we utilize the full population of towns in this analysis, tests of statistical significance are not necessary. All observed differences reflect differences in the population. Whether the observed differences are substantively significant is a judgment issue.

Table 2 compares the average change in economic and demographic variables from 1990 to 2000 for small towns with a new state prison and all other small towns. It is noteworthy that changes in the unemployment rates are roughly equal in both kinds of towns and that public sector employment grew more in prison towns. In all other economic indicators, except changes in poverty rates, the new prison towns fared worse than the non-prison towns. Increases in total non-agricultural employment, retail sales, average household

Table 2. Comparison of Change in Economic and Demographic Indicators in New State Prison Small Towns and All Other Small Towns (From 1990 to 2000)

	New State Prison (N= 176)		All Other (N= 19,253)	
	Average % Change*	Standard deviation	Average % Change*	Standard deviation
Economic Variables				
Unemployment	2.64%	64.02	2.56%	112.39
Non-agriculture employment	12.28%	26.75	22.55%	71.07
Retail sales** (N=87 & 3051)	83.95%	92.49	127.83%	668.70
Average HH wage	49.20%	20.58	55.70%	133.09
Total housing units	10.95%	21.48	13.20%	58.90
Md. value of owner occupied housing	50.61%	28.91	61.53%	53.74
Poverty rate	-0.55%	39.79	15.72%	105.65
Public sector jobs	86.77%	175.90	53.28%	169.59
Demographic Variables				
Population	27.90%	67.74	12.49%	61.57
Population:				
Towns counting inmates (101)	45.44%			
Inmates subtracted	-0.08%			
Towns not counting inmates*** (75)	4.00%			
Population < 18 years	6.20%	25.32	15.17%	81.65
Percent minority	201.58%	913.39	143.44%	359.81

* The percent change was calculated for each town individually and then the average percent change for prison and non prison towns was calculated.

** The U.S. Census does not have retail sales information for all small towns. 1987-1997

*** When towns do not include inmates in their populations, they are counted as part of the institutionalized county population.

wages, total number of housing units, and median value of owner-occupied housing are substantially less in new prison versus non-prison towns. New state prison towns experienced a slight decrease in poverty rates between 1990 and 2000, while other small towns had, on average, higher poverty levels at the end of the decade.

On the whole, new prison towns experienced a substantial population gain over non-prison small towns from 1990 to 2000 (27.9 percent compared to 12.5 percent). However, 101 of the prison towns counted inmates as town residents. For the remainder, inmates were counted as county residents. When the prison towns are separated on the basis of whether or not inmates were counted in the 2000 population and the percent change is recalculated for the two groups, the towns counting inmates experienced population growth of 45.44 percent compared to a modest 4.00 percent gain for the other prison towns. Subtracting the inmates from the 2000 population figures for those towns that included them shows that those towns actually lost non-inmate population from 1990 to 2000 (-0.08 percent). The population figures also reveal the differential changes in minority and young population in prison and non-prison towns. New state prison towns experienced more than a 200 percent increase in minority population from 1990 to 2000 compared to lower growth in non-prison small towns (143.4 percent) and less than half the growth of non-prison towns in the percent of the population under 18 years of age.

To understand the impact of a new prison on small towns it is important to control for several factors that may also be affecting the outcomes shown in Table 2. It may be that the towns with the new prisons had the most depressed economies of all small towns before the siting of a prison. Indeed, the 1990 poverty rate of new state prison small towns is higher (21.08 percent) than other small towns (15.28 percent). Given new prison towns' disadvantaged position at the beginning of the 1990s relative to other small towns, one could argue that they are better off with the prison then they would have been otherwise. To address this issue, we conducted multiple regression analyses to determine the association of having a new state prison with each of the 2000 economic and demographic variables controlling for 1990 figures for population, poverty level, unemployment, median value of housing, population < 18 years, average household wage, and non-agricultural employment; and region of the country (South vs. non-South).

For this examination, prison was dummy coded with 1 = yes, 0 = no. Again, since we have the full population of small towns and not a sample, tests of statistical significance are not appropriate. Table 3 shows the unstandardized regression coefficients for new state prison regressed on each dependent variable (in separate regression equations) controlling for the variables mentioned above. When 1990 population and economic indicators and region are controlled, the patterns are similar to those shown in Table 2. At the end of the decade, new prison towns had on average a lower median value of housing ($3,010 less), an

Table 3. New State Prison Regressed on Economic and Demographic Variables for Small Towns (OLS Regression)

Unstandardized Regression Coefficients for Prison (1=yes, 0=no)		
	Coefficient	Standard Error
2000 Economic Dependent Variables		
Unemployment rate	.34	.33
Percent in poverty	1.96	.50
Median value of housing	-$3010.53	2571.87
Total number of homes	-82.80	47.93
Average HH wage	-$442.58	737.00
Non-agriculture employment	-86.62	47.89
Public sector jobs	53.45	4.96
2000 Demographic Dependent Variables		
Population	191.11	99.28
Percent of population 18 years or less	-28.92	29.49
Percent minorities	7.54	1.28

average 82.8 fewer housing units, lower average household wages (by $442.58), 86.62 fewer non-agricultural jobs, and 28.92 percent fewer youth than non-prison towns. Poverty levels, the unemployment rate, population, percent minorities, and public sector employment are all higher in new state prison towns compared to other towns. Except for public sector employment, all economic indicators show prison towns disadvantaged compared to non-prison towns in 2000 when controlling for key economic and demographic factors in 1990.

To provide greater insight into the extent of the differences between new prison towns and similar non-prison small towns, we calculated the means for key 1990 indicators (population, poverty level, average household wage, and non-agriculture employment) for the new prison towns. Then we selected all prison and non-prison towns that were equivalent to or more disadvantaged than the average for prison towns (the cutoff points are shown in Table 4). These parameters were met by 47 prison towns and 3,624 non-prison towns. The average percent changes shown in Table 4 compare new prison towns only to other small towns in an approximately equivalent position at the beginning of the 1990s.

Compared to other small towns roughly matched on 1990 economic indicators, the new state prison towns experienced substantially less growth in every economic indicator except total number of housing units and public sector jobs. At the end of the decade, prison towns had an increase in unemployment levels compared to a decline in non-prison towns. Prison towns experienced one fifth less reduction in poverty rates compared to matched small towns. Indicators of population change mirror the pattern from analyses of the full set of small towns in that there was more growth in population for the prison towns

Table 4. Comparison of Changes in Economic and Demographic Indicators for Economically Disadvantaged New State Prison Towns and Similaly Disadvantaged Non-Prison Towns*

	New Prison Towns (N= 47)		Non-Prison Towns (N= 3,624)	
	Average % Change	Standard deviation	Average % Change	Standard deviation
Percent Change 1990 to 2000 - Economic Variables				
Unemployment	15.63%	91.11	-4.46%	91.08
Poverty	-5.49%	28.11	-26.44%	30.85
Median value of housing	56.99%	26.81	58.90%	49.91
Total housing units	12.13%	17.34	6.40%	37.12
Average HH wage	54.80%	22.26	70.93%	81.96
Non-agriculture employment	8.80%	24.88	25.63%	69.29
Public sector jobs	69.90%	1.04	48.98%	1.54
Percent Change 1990 to 2000- Demographic Variables				
Population	49.22%	89.34	7.00%	42.55
Population:				
Towns counting inmates (34)	65.20%			
Inmates subtracted	-0.19%			
Towns not counting inmates (13)	7.44%			
Population <18 Years	3.19%	24.64	8.68%	71.23
Minorities	44.50%	77.67	90.03%	367.35

* 1990 Population ≤ 3560, 1990 Poverty ≥ 21%, 1990 Average HH Wage ≤ $26,000, and 1990 Non-agricultural Employment ≤ 1,335.

as a whole. However, when inmates were subtracted from the 2000 population for towns that counted them, there was a loss of population. The thirteen prison towns that did not count inmates realized a gain in population that exceeded slightly the amount of population growth in matched communities. Surprisingly, the percent change in minority population is less in new state prison towns than in the comparable small towns. This can be partially explained by the fact that among this sub-sample of towns, the new prison towns had a higher percentage of minority population in 1990 (40.63 percent) compared to the non-prison towns (25.0 percent) and therefore given the smaller denominator for the non-prison towns, a relatively small absolute change would result in a larger percentage change.

CONCLUSION

Small town leaders and state policy makers have perceived the heightened incarceration rates of the 1980s and 1990s in the United States as an economic development opportunity for rural areas, albeit a strategy of last resort. Findings in this paper reveal the continuing trend of prison movement from metropolitan areas to non-metropolitan locations. Only about 10 percent of inmates housed in state prisons built in the 1990s are located in metropolitan areas. Sixty-nine percent are in small towns with 10,000 or less in population. The untested assumptions of proponents of locating prisons in small towns are that prisons will bring stable government jobs. Prison employees will buy local houses, purchase local products and services, and increase local tax revenue. These factors will in turn result in an increase in local businesses, an increase in non-prison jobs, and additional growth in housing and tax revenue reflecting the multiplier effect of new jobs in a community. It is expected that the enhanced economic activity will cause an increase in population, especially among young families, and eventually stronger ties within the community and an enhanced quality of life for residents.

The promise of economic gain is so tantalizing to rural community leaders desperate for economic and community development that many have been willing to build infrastructure (roads, utilities, hospitals, and even prison facilities themselves) for public and private prisons and offer tax abatements to private prisons in order to attract them to their area. However, if there were differences within the community prior to prison construction about the merits of prisons as an economic development strategy, if residents come to believe that the costs of the prison outweigh the risks, or if they perceive that the costs and benefits are not shared equitably, then the prison can have negative consequences for the community beyond its economic impact. The corrosive community framework would predict that the contingencies just mentioned would lead to a diminution of the ability of community residents to work together for collective ends and a decline in residents' social well being.

Early studies conducted prior to the heightened building spree in the 1980s and 1990s and before the movement of prisons to small towns, discovered that prisons did not negatively affect communities (Smykla, 1984; Shichor, 1992). However, the metropolitan location of most prisons at the time of the studies and the methodological problems with this literature (McShane, Williams III, & Wagoner, 1992) make it difficult to have confidence in their applicability to the current situation of prisons in small towns. More recent research on single states (New York, Mississippi, California, and Iowa) concludes also that new prisons do not have a negative effect. But given the changed expectations of economic gain from prisons, not showing a negative effect is insufficient to support local assumptions and investments. This research expands understanding of the economic impact of prisons on small towns by using 1990 and 2000 Population Census data to compare changes in new state prison small towns to changes in non-prison small towns.

Findings in this paper revealed that small towns that acquired a new state prison in the 1990s experienced higher poverty levels, higher unemployment rates, fewer total jobs, lower household wages, fewer housing units, and lower median value of housing units in 2000, when 1990 population and economic indicators, and region are controlled, than towns without a new state prison. With these controls in place, new state prison towns realized an increase in public sector employment, population, and minority population.

Possible explanations for the lack of economic benefits from a new prison are that it takes a long time for the benefits to be realized and the phenomenon is too recent to see the net gain in the 2000 census figures. Another explanation is that prisons do not have extensive backward linkages to the community and therefore a minimal multiplier effect on the local economy. Small town businesses may not be able to meet the needs of prisons for supplies and services, purchasing decisions may be made centrally at the state level, or state prisons may be relatively self-sufficient needing little that the local town can offer. A final possibility is that prisons stigmatize communities. Thus, whatever gain is experienced from the multiplier effect of correctional jobs is negated by the loss of businesses and people who leave or chose not to locate in a "prison town." This is an especially critical factor for small towns where there may be no other major community image (think of the image of Silicon Valley, Seattle, Aspen) to act as counter weights to the prison image. Whether these or other explanations apply, these findings suggest that the establishment of new prisons is a dubious strategy for economic and community development for small towns. This is especially the case in many communities where residents were divided about the advisability of attracting a prison in the first place. In the presence of differences of views about attracting the prison, the investment of public money for the prison that then does not improve the local economy, may according to Albrecht et al. (1996) result in deep community schisms and diminished quality of life.

REFERENCES

Albrecht, S., R. G. Amey, & S. Amir. 1996. The siting of radioactive waste facilities: What are the effects on communities. *Rural Sociology* 61(4): 649-73.

American Correctional Association. 2001. *Directory of Adult and Juvenile Correctional Departments, Institutions, Agencies, and Probation and Parole Authorities*. 62nd edition. Lanham, MD.

Anderson, C. 2003. "U.S. prison population tops 2 million." *Associated Press Online*. April 7.

Beale, C. L. 1995. Rural prisons: An update. *Rural Development Perspectives*. 11(2): 25-27.

Carlson, K. A. 1991. What happens and what counts: Resident assessments of prison impacts on their communities. *Humboldt Journal of Social Relations*. 17(1&2): 211-237.

Clement, D. 2002. Big house on the prairie. *Fedgazette*. Federal Reserve Bank of Minneapolis. Jan.: 1-7.

Couch, S. R. & S. Kroll-Smith. 1994. Environmental controversies, interfactional resources, and rural communities: Siting versus exposure disputes. *Rural Sociology* 59: 25-44.

Daniel, W. 1991. Prisons and crime rates in rural areas: The case of Lassen County. *Humboldt Journal of Social Relations* 17(1&2):129-170.

Davidson, O. G. 1990. *Broken Heartland: The Rise of America's Rural Ghetto*. Doubleday: NY.

DeLisi, M. & T. L. Besser. 2003. *The Economic Impact of Prison Growth in Iowa*. Mt. Vernon, IA: Iowa Policy Project.

Doyle, Z. 2002. Does crime pay? Pros and cons of rural prisons. *Economic Development Digest* July: 1-4.

Drabek, T. E. 1986. *Human System Responses to Disaster.* NY: Springer-Verlag.

Drabenstott, M. 2003. Rural America's new economic frontier. *State Government News.* June/July: 8-11.

Erikson, K. T. 1994. *A New Species of Trouble: The Human Experience of Modern Disasters.* NY: W.W. Norton and Co.

Freudenburg, W. R., & T.R. Jones. 1991. Attitudes and stress in the presence of technological risk: A test of the Supreme Court hypothesis. *Social Forces* 69(4): 1143-1168.

Grieco, Alan L. 1978. New prisons: Characteristics and community reception. Quarterly Journal of Corrections 2:55-60.

Hallinan, J. T. 2001. *Going Up the River: Travels in a Prison Nation.* NY: Random House.

Harrison, P. M. & A. J. Beck. 2002. *Prisoners in 2001.* Bureau of Justice Statistics Bulletin July. U.S. Department of Justice.

Hooks, G., C. Mosher, T. Rotolo, & L. Lobao. 2000. Escape from the prison-industrial complex: Prison expansion and local economic growth in U.S. counties." Paper presented at the Annual Meeting of the American Sociological Association, Aug. Washington, DC.

Hughes, B. 1998. Pork industry provides 824 jobs in Webster Co. *Fort Dodge Messenger.* May 24.

Huling, T. 2002. Building a prison economy in rural America. In M. Mauer & M. Chesney-Lind (eds.), *Invisible Punishment: The Collateral Consequences of Mass Imprisonment.* NY: The Free Press.

JEDCO. 1995. *Prison Site Proposal: Department of Corrections.* Newton, IA.

King, R. S., M. Mauer, & T. Huling. 2003. *Big Prisons, Small Towns: Prison Economics in rural America.* Washington DC: The Sentencing Project.

Kniazkov, M. 2003. U.S. prison population exceeds two million for the first time. *Agence France Presse.* April 7.

McShane, M., F. Williams III, & C. P. Wagoner. 1992. Prison impact studies: Some comments on methodological rigor. *Crime and Delinquency* 38(1): 105-120.

Reynolds, Sandra. 1995. *Begging for LULUs: Locating Prisons in Small Communities.* Masters Thesis. Iowa State University, Ames, IA.

Shea, B. 1998. Council makes good on word. *Fort Dodge Messenger.* May 19.

Shichor, D. 1992. Myths and realities in prison siting. *Crime and Delinquency* 38(1): 70-87.

Smith, M. D., R. S. Krannich, & L. M. Hunter. 2001. Growth, decline, stability and disruption: A longitudinal analysis of social well-being in four western rural communities. *Rural Sociology* 66(3): 425-450.

Smykla, John Ortiz, Carl Ferguson Jr., David Cheng, Carolyn Trent, Barbara French, and Annette Waters. 1984. Effects of prison facility on the regional economy. *Journal of Criminal Justice* 12:521-539.

Sourcebook of Criminal Justice Statistics. 2001. Justice system direct and intergovernmental expenditures. Table 1.1: 2.

Sourcebook of Criminal Justice Statistics. 2001. Number and rate of sentenced prisoners under jurisdiction of state and federal correctional authorities on December 31, 2002. Table 6.23: 494.

Tully, H. A., J. P.Winter, J.E. Wilson, & T. J. Scanlon. 1982. Correctional institution impact and host community resistance. *Canadian Journal of Criminology* 24: 133-139.

U.S. Census Bureau. 1990. *Census of the Population*. U.S. Census Bureau.

U.S. Census Bureau. 2000. *Census of the Population*. U.S. Census Bureau.

U.S. Department of Justice. 2003. Bureau of Justice Statistics. After dramatic increases in the 1980s and 1990s, the incarceration rate has recently leveled off. Www.ojp.usdoj.gov/bjs/

Wood, P. B., R. G. Dunaway, M. R. Lee, & D. Parisi. 2002. Does prison construction generate economic development? The Mississippi case. Paper presented at the Southern Rural Sociological Society Meeting.

CD CASE

Chain stores and local economies: a case study of a rural county in New York

Stephen Halebsky

Department of Sociology/Anthropology, State University of New York-Cortland, Moffett Center, Cortland, NY 13045, USA

Retailing in rural America has been transformed over the last several decades by the explosive growth of retail chains. Cortland County, a rural county in central New York State, is examined to assess the effect of chain stores *en masse* on a rural county. Data on individual establishments were generated by an original census of all the chain stores in the county. Additional data came from the Economic Census and other sources. Results show that chains account for about two-thirds of sales in the county. The percentage of the proceeds of the sales at chain stores that leaves the county, and thus is not available to be recirculated locally, is estimated to be approximately 14%. It is argued that the contribution of chain stores to the local economy is less than that of local independent merchants. Chains, furthermore, have problematic implications for social capital, political capital, and other aspects of community development.

Students of community development have long been interested in the relationship between rural communities and the urban (and suburban) society of which they are a part. A key concern has been to understand the degree to which such communities can maintain independence and self-sufficiency in economic, social and political matters. Vidich and Bensman (1958, p. 101), in their classic study of "Springdale," a small town in central New York, conclude that "A central fact of rural life ... is its dependence on the institutions and dynamics of urban and mass society." The independence and economic health of rural communities in the US has been a concern since at least the 1940s, when technological change initiated a transformation of American agriculture, resulting in the ascendance of corporate agribusiness and the decline of independent farms and farmers (Albrecht & Murdock, 1990; Davidson, 1990). The fortunes of other rural areas have been tied more closely to manufacturing. Beginning in the 1970s and continuing into the present, deindustrialization and the search for cheaper labor have made many rural communities painfully aware of the extent to which their economic well-being is tied to the decisions of large corporations headquartered elsewhere (Falk & Lobao, 2003; Flora & Flora, 2008). Many communities saw their fortunes fall as local production facilities closed or moved abroad, while others (i.e., those in the sunbelt) saw their fortunes rise as they became the hosts of new facilities.

The decline of manufacturing and other production-oriented industries has been accompanied by the growth of services and consumption-oriented industries. One manifestation of the increasing importance of consumption is the increasing importance of retailing, as evidenced by the proliferation of stores, the appearance of stores in more and more venues (airports, museums, schools, etc.), and the merging of shopping with entertainment (Gottdiener, 2001; Lowe & Wrigley, 1996). The wave of rationalization that has swept over American industry since the 1970s has affected retailing as well and can be seen in the use of new and more sophisticated techniques and technology, especially in data processing, communications and logistics (Bluestone, Hanna, Kuhn, & Moore, 1981; Foster, Haltiwanger, & Krizan, 2006). One result of this rationalization is the decline of independent local merchants and the rise of corporate retailers who operate extensive chains of stores. The "retail revolution" has advanced to the point that most areas of retailing are now dominated by corporate chains. In the subsector of retailing that includes general merchandise stores, large chains (retailers with at least one hundred stores) account for 95.9% of all sales (US Census, 2002, *Economic Census, Retail Trade, Establishment and Firm Size*).

Many major cities have increasingly shifted from centers of production to centers of consumption (Urry, 1995; Wrigley & Lowe, 1999; Zukin, 1998), a phenomenon that has affected rural towns and cities as well. Small towns that were once hubs of farm-based activity or that boasted a number of factories are now home to an array of stores, restaurants, hotels and other consumption-oriented enterprises, and many of the small independent merchants that were the mainstay of rural retailing have been replaced by corporate chains (Flora & Flora, 2008). Vias (2004) reports that between 1988 and 1999 employment in retailing in nonmetropolitan counties increased 27.9% and average store size, operationalized as the average number of employees per store, increased 17.1%, an indication that small independent stores are being replaced by large chain stores.

The present research is an empirical examination of what these trends look like on the ground in one rural county, Cortland County in central New York, which happens to be about 65 kilometers from Candor, the small town made famous by Vidich and Bensman under the pseudonym of Springdale. While numerous journalistic accounts as well as a number of academic studies have focused on the effect of Wal-Mart superstores on small towns, the present research analyzes the impact of chain stores *en masse* on a community, based on data from the US Census, commercial sources, and an original census of local chain stores. And while previous studies of chains have used aggregate data only, the present study is based on estimates of sales and other statistics for *every* chain store in the county.

One important question that has not been addressed in the literature is— how much money do chain stores take out of local communities? The present research provides an estimate of this amount, referred to as the *unique outflow* and conceptualized as the amount (or percentage) of the proceeds from chain store sales that uniquely leaves the county, unique in the sense that these dollars would have remained in the county had they been generated by sales at a locally-owned establishment instead of a chain. The unique outflow is not a one-time event but reoccurs every year.

Also, historical data on the composition of the retail sector and the size of establishments are used to gauge how retail restructuring has affected the county over the last several decades, and the location of chain stores are plotted on a map to illustrate their centrifugal effect on commercial activity.

It is argued that when local retailing becomes dominated by chain stores, as has occurred in Cortland and many other communities, there are important implications for the local economy and other aspects of community development including social capital, human capital, political capital, and the built environment.

Retailing and community economics

"Retail" and "retail trade" refer to establishments included in the North American Industry Classification System (NAICS) sectors 44 and 45. Retail trade is divided into the following subsectors: motor vehicle and parts dealers; furniture and home furnishings stores; electronics and appliance stores; building material and garden equipment/supplies dealers; food and beverage stores; health and personal care stores; gasoline stations; clothing and clothing accessories stores; sporting goods, hobby, book, and music stores; general merchandise stores; miscellaneous store retailers; and nonstore retailers. An "establishment" is a separate location where business is conducted, so that a typical independent local retailer would operate just one establishment, while a corporate chain

would operate many. The essence of a chain is that similar establishments exist at more than one location, where establishments are similar insofar as they sell similar products and use similar signage, advertising, logos, and operating procedures. Because of the extensive similarity of their establishments, chains are known also as "formula" businesses.

A local economy may be conceived as an open system that produces and consumes goods and services (Hustedde, Shaffer, & Pulver, 2005; Shaffer, Deller, & Marcouiller, 2004). A community produces goods and services using a combination of local and non-local sources of raw material, labor and capital. Some portion of what is produced within the borders of a community is consumed locally; the rest is "exported" to other communities. An establishment that sells its product or service outside the community is known as a "basic" or "export" establishment. It is generally advantageous for a community to have export establishments because they bring money into the community, which can then be used to generate additional jobs and income.[1] While a manufacturing facility such as an automobile factory is the archetypal export establishment, a local retailer that attracts many customers from outside the community functions similarly (Pittman & Culp, 1995). Although it is typically considered beneficial for a community to have such retailers, touted by their promoters as "destination retail," most retailers sell mainly to local customers.

A key function of the retailers operating in a community is to provide the goods and services that local residents want. Beyond this, however, retailers can contribute to the local economy by employing local residents; generating profit, rent, and interest for local business owners, landlords, and financial institutions, respectively; and paying taxes to local municipalities. Given this model of community economics, we can specify the business practices that maximize retailers' contribution to the local economy and thus ultimately to local welfare: buy raw materials and goods locally, hire local residents, obtain financing from local financial institutions, rent or lease real estate from local landlords and landowners, use local business services, and generate profit for local owners (see Figure 1). For these actions to have maximum benefit the money received by the various parties must be spent or invested locally as well (Blakely & Bradshaw, 2002).

Business services, also known as producer services, include accounting, finance, advertising, marketing, printing, legal counsel, research and development, training, transportation, logistics, communications and data processing. These services are necessary to support a retail establishment and must be performed locally or elsewhere. If performed locally, as would be the case typically with an independent store, they would be done by the retailer or by another local business (e.g., a local accountant); if performed elsewhere, as would be the case typically with a chain store, they would be done by the corporation that owns the chain at its headquarters or by another corporation probably located outside the local area. When business services are not done locally some portion of the proceeds from sales dollars leaves the community, which has a negative impact on the local economy compared with having those same services done locally.

From the perspective of local economic development, the usual concern in regard to retailing is how to increase total sales. Maximizing sales, however, does not equate automatically to the maximization of community welfare. Increased sales may do a community little good if receipts leave the area in the form of wages paid to non-local residents, profits earned by non-local owners, rent paid to non-local landlords, and interest paid to non-local financial institutions. Similarly, the community gains little when local retailers purchase raw materials and goods from non-local companies or pay non-local companies to provide business services. Thus, sales volume should be seen as an indication of the potential, not actual, contribution of retailing to the local economy (Dixon, 2005). This applies to the number and size of retail establishments as well: while more and bigger stores may represent more shopping options, they benefit a community economically only to the extent they are able to put more dollars in the hands of local residents and businesses.

As noted earlier, the unique outflow is the amount (or percentage) of the proceeds from chain store sales that uniquely leaves the county, unique in the sense that these dollars would have remained in the county had they been generated by sales at a locally-owned establishment. This notion is derived from the model of retail activity and community economy presented in Figure 1, which is based on an understanding of a local economy as an input-output system with extensive linkages (an output in one part of the system may become an input for another part) (Shaffer, Deller, & Marcouiller, 2004). While dollars may leave a community in many ways, there are two that are unique to chain stores: via the use of non-local business services and via the transfer of net income (profit) to corporate headquarters. The unique outflow is operationalized as the sum of these two categories.

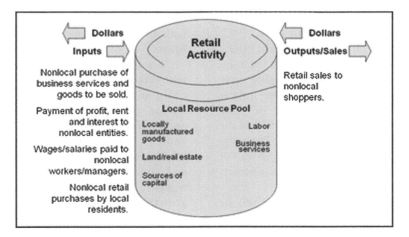

Figure 1.   Retail activity and the community economy.
Source: Adapted from Hustedde et al., 2005.

Literature review

Research on the impact of chain stores has been undertaken in a number of areas. Although much of this research focuses on Wal-Mart, most of the issues and problems pertain to other corporate chains as well. This research has generally been of two types: large-N comparative studies with counties as the typical unit of analysis and economic impact analyses concerned with the impact of one store (i.e., a Wal-Mart superstore) on one town.

One line of comparative research has investigated the impact of chain stores on local merchants. This research generally supports the view that the presence of a Wal-Mart superstore leads eventually to the demise of many smaller merchants. Stone (1995) and Stone, Artz and Myles (2002), in a series of studies of Iowa, Mississippi and other states, conclude that the opening of a Wal-Mart superstore is accompanied by an eventual decrease in the number of small merchants. Research by Muller and Humstone (1996), who also studied communities in Iowa, and Gruidl and Kline (1992), who examined

communities in Illinois, generally supports this conclusion. Peterson and McGee (2000) surveyed 428 businesses in five small towns in Nebraska and Kansas and found that the majority had experienced a decline in sales since the arrival of a Wal-Mart superstore. At a more global level, Jarmin, Klimek, and Miranda (2005) show that between 1976 and 2000 the mean number of retail establishments in rural counties in the US declined from 8.3 per one thousand residents to 6.4, while the mean number of employees per establishment increased from 38.2 to 52.7, indicating the replacement of many smaller stores by fewer but bigger stores.

Concern with the effects of chains on independent merchants overlaps with concern about their impact on Main Streets, downtowns and other central business districts where many independent merchants have traditionally been located. Corporate chains, especially those that operate superstores, often place their establishments near the periphery of rural towns and cities, thereby drawing consumers away from the central business district and undermining its vitality as a commercial center, civic center and public space (Beaumont, 1994, 1997; Kunstler, 1993; Moe & Wilkie, 1997; Worpole, 1992). There have been no systematic attempts to investigate these effects using a large sample. One indication, however, of the extent of these problems is the formation in 1977 of the National Trust for Historic Preservation's Main Street program, a direct response to the decline of Main Streets across the country.

In another study (Schaffer, 2006), he found that "income grew faster in those counties having a smaller average retail establishment size initially, or those having a larger proportion of small retail establishments" (p. 152). Zhang, and Ciccarella (2007), using data from all US counties, found that the opening of a Wal-Mart store reduced local retail employment by about 3%. This outcome is most likely attributable to Wal-Mart's superior operating efficiency and the fact that business services are performed at its headquarters in Bentonville, Arkansas. In a similar study Basker (2005) examined 1749 counties, three-fourths with a Wal-Mart that had opened between 1977 and 1998, and found that retail employment increased by about 100 in the year after the store opened and then declined by about 50 jobs over the next several years. She also found that employment in wholesaling decreased by about 20 jobs. Basker, however, is unable to conclude that this net increase is due to job loss in counties without Wal-Marts or whether it represents the replacement of full-time workers at other stores by part-time workers at Wal-Mart. Focusing on rural areas, Blanchard, Irwin, Tolbert, and Nucci (2003) examined all the nonmetropolitan counties in which a retailer with 100 or more employees opened between 1977 and 1996 ($N = 786$) and found a decline in both retail employment and number of retail establishments in the

South and the Midwest, the two regions with the highest concentration of Wal-Marts.

Another line of research has investigated the effect of firm size and chain stores on overall local prosperity, as measured by median income and poverty rate. Shaffer (2002) examined 700 US cities and found that "the average size of manufacturing and retail firms is negatively and robustly associated with subsequent growth rates of median household income" (p. 195). In another study (2006) he found that "income grew faster in those counties having a smaller average retail establishment size initially, or those having a larger proportion of small retail establishments" (p. 152). Goetz and Swaminathan (2006) found that the presence of a Wal-Mart was "unequivocally associated with smaller reductions in family-poverty rate in US counties during the 1990s relative to places that had no stores" (p. 223).

Retailers also affect the local economy through their fiscal effects. Proponents tout increased property and/or sales tax revenue associated with chain stores, while critics argue that such increases are either illusory, because they are offset by decreased revenue from other stores, or outweighed by the increased cost of providing necessary infrastructure (roads, signage, etc.) and services (police, sanitation, etc.) (Rockne & Milchen, 2003). Fiscal impact is also affected by the subsidies, tax abatements and other incentives that some cities use to attract retailers (Karjanen & Baxamusa, 2003; Mattera & Purinton, 2004). Comparative studies of fiscal effects using large samples remain to be done.

The other type of study, a local impact analysis, is typically undertaken *ex ante* by local officials faced with a proposed new chain store and attempts to measure its effect on the local economy. These studies are produced for local use, employ a variety of research methods, and rarely appear in peer-reviewed journals, making it difficult to generalize their results. A common strategy is to compare the impact of a proposed new chain store to the impact of existing independent merchants who expect to lose business, thereby highlighting the extent to which a locally-owned store is more beneficial because a larger percentage of the proceeds from its sales circulates and recirculates throughout the local economy.

Given that many scholarly examinations of the economic impact of large retail chains, with Wal-Mart as the exemplar, have concluded that their effects are negative, what explains their appeal? The answer is convenience, selection and, of course, prices. The most widely reported analysis of Wal-Mart's effect on prices is by Global Insight (2005), an economic forecasting firm, which found that between 1985 and 2004 Wal-Mart saved the average American $895 annually as a result of its effect on consumer prices. Bernstein and Bivens (2006) and Bernstein, Bivens, and Dube (2006) contest Global Insight's statistical analysis and argue that low prices on consumer goods do not make up for low wages because a larger percentage of consumer expenditures are devoted to other types of goods and services such as housing, medical care, transportation and education.

Relationship of the unique outflow to various analytical tools

There are a number of analytical tools that may be used to evaluate the contribution that various sectors make, or could make, to a local economy (Hustedde et al., 2005). The unique outflow is not intended to become another standard analytical tool but could serve as a complement to existing tools. One frequently used tool is the multiplier, a statistic that summarizes the effect of an increase in an export sector (or even just one export business) on the rest of the economy.[2] Multipliers are commonly computed for output (sales), employment, and income and take the general form: total change in local economy/ change in a particular export sector. If, for example, the income multiplier for a particular export sector is two, then every one dollar increase in wages and salaries in that sector will result in an additional one dollar increase in wages and salaries throughout the economy. The multiplier depends crucially on local linkages: the greater the local linkages—opportunities for money to be spent and respent locally—the larger the multiplier. Because the unique outflow represents money that is not available to be spent locally, it follows that the larger the unique outflow, the smaller the multiplier. Thus, the larger the unique outflow, the less impact that export businesses will have on the economy.

Other analytical tools include potential sales, trade area capture, and pull factor, all of which are statistics that measure the extent to which a municipality is garnering all possible sales from within its borders as well as from other municipalities. A related statistic is sales leakage, which measures the loss of sales that occurs when a local consumer or employer buys goods or services outside the municipality. While all these statistics focus on sales, actual and potential, the unique outflow focuses on what happens *after* sales take place; specifically, on how much of the proceeds of sales—regardless of where those sales dollars come from—remains in the local area.

Cortland County

Cortland County (population 48,369 [2007]) is located near the geographical center of the state of New York. The city of Cortland (population 18,382) is the only city in the county. Ithaca (population 29,974) is about 30 kilometers southwest of the city. The largest nearby cities are Syracuse (population 139,079), about 40 kilometers to the north of the city, and Binghamton (population 45,020), about 65 kilometers to the south. There are also three villages in the county: Homer (population 3270), Marathon (population 1025), and McGraw (population 961). The remainder of the county's populace is distributed sparsely or clustered in several dozen hamlets. The entire county is dotted with hundreds of farms, some large but most small. The small population, low density, lack of medium-size or large cities, and numerous farms combine to give the county a rural feel.

While obviously not representative of all rural counties, there are several characteristics of Cortland County that are typical of many rural counties and thus make it appropriate for a case study. Like many other rural counties it is struggling economically. Although it had substantial manufacturing employment during the first half of the twentieth century, it has suffered as factories have moved or gone out of business during the last several decades. A large Smith Corona (typewriters) plant closed in 1992, preceded by Brockway Motor Truck in 1977 and Wickwire (wire products) in 1971. Concurrently, the number of farms has declined slowly (US Census, 1977 and 2000, *County and City Data Book*). The condition of the local economy is reflected in the size of the population, which has remained virtually the same for the last 25 years (see Table 1). Moreover, median household income in the county is well below that for the state and the nation; the percentage of persons below the poverty line exceeds the percentage for the state and the nation; and the unemployment rate is greater than the rate for the state and the nation. Cortland County is typical also in regard to retailing. It has a full complement of chain stores, including Wal-Mart, most of which are located just outside the city. The city's downtown, like many others, is struggling to attract and retain businesses. And, like most rural counties, it does not have any retail establishments that qualify as destination retail, the marketing term applied to a store or group of stores that attracts a sizeable number of

Table 1. Population, household income, poverty, and unemployment: Cortland County, New York State, and the United States, 1980 and 2007.

	Cortland County	New York State	USA
Population, 2007	48,369	19,297,729	301,621,157
Population, 1980	48,820	17,558,072	226,545,805
Population change, 1980–2007 (%)	−0.9	9.9	33.1
Median household income, (2007) ($)	40,770	53,448	50,740
Poverty rate, (2007) (%)	14.8	13.8	13.0
Unemployment rate, (2007) (%)	5.2	4.5	4.6

Sources: Population, 2007: US Census. (2007). *Population estimates*; population, 1980: US Census (1996). *The population of states and counties of the United States: 1790 to 1990*; median household income and poverty rate: US Census. (2007). *small area income and poverty estimates*; unemployment rate: Bureau of Labor Statistics. (2007). *Local area unemployment statistics*.

out-of-town (or out-of-county) shoppers because of its uniqueness. There are no major tourist attractions in the county with the possible exception of Greek Peak, a ski resort.

Methodology

To study chain establishments in Cortland County it was first necessary to identify all such establishments, which I did by conducting a census of all the chain stores in the county. I investigated on foot and by car all streets with commercial establishments in or near the city of Cortland and the villages of Homer, McGraw and Marathon. Outside the city and the three villages, I drove through every settlement or hamlet marked on the most detailed map available. Chains were identified using common knowledge and the formulaic appearance that is typical of such enterprises. Reference sources *(S&P Register of Corporations, Directors and Executives*, 2007; *Lexis-Nexis Corporate Affiliations*, 2006; and *Million Dollar Directory*, 2006) and corporate websites were consulted to verify chain status. "Local" chains, in which all the locations or the headquarters are in Cortland County, were excluded. Each chain establishment was classified by NAICS 3-digit subsector.

County-level data were taken from County Business Patterns and the Economic Census. Two commercial directories, *Manning's Cortland Directory 1976–77* and *Dickman Directory Cortland County* 2006, were used to find out how many retailers were located on Main Street in the city of Cortland in 1977 and 2006.

Estimating the unique outflow

Three sources of data were used to estimate the unique outflow. Estimates of annual sales were obtained from InfoUSA, a commercial provider of information about individual business establishments. These estimates were provided in terms of a range of sales for each establishment, with the following response categories: less than $500,000, $500,000–$1 million, $1 million–$2.5 million, $2.5 million–$5 million, $5 million–$10 million, $10 million–$20 million, and $20 million–$50 million. The midpoint of each range was used (except as noted below). Estimates of non-local business services as a percentage of sales were derived from the Economic Census; estimates of net income as a percentage of sales came from the Fortune 500 (*Fortune*, 2008).[3]

To calculate the unique outflow it is necessary to use accounting categories. The income statement for a retailing business takes the following basic form (Tracy, 1994):

> sales
> *minus* cost of goods sold
> *minus* operating expenses
> *minus* depreciation expenses
> *minus* interest expenses
> *minus* income tax
> _____
> *equals* net income (profit)

Retailers buy goods from wholesalers or manufacturers and then sell them directly to consumers. The largest expense for any retailer is the cost of these goods (in accounting terms, "cost of goods sold"). Most of the goods sold at a typical establishment, whether a chain store or an independent merchant, comes from outside the community and thus a large percentage of the proceeds from sales at both chains and independent establishments leaves the community. It was assumed that there is no significant difference in the residential location (i.e., inside or outside the county) of chain and non-chain employees. It was also assumed that all types of retail establishments pay state and federal taxes equally. To simplify the analysis two relatively small income statement items, depreciation and interest, were ignored.

There remain two ways in which a portion of the proceeds from sales at chain stores leaves the local area: non-local business services and net income. Retail chains perform most business services in-house at their corporate headquarters or they contract for such services with other large corporations. Each individual Wal-Mart store, for example, does not conduct its own market research, develop its own employee training programs, have its own staff of information technology specialists, or maintain relations with the thousands of suppliers whose products it sells. Indeed, the centralization of

these functions, whether in-house or at another large corporation, is an important source of the economies of scale and scope that allow chains to outperform small independent merchants (Chandler, 1990). Net income is paid out as dividends to the owners or kept as retained earnings; in either case it leaves the community. Together, non-local business services and net income represent the unique outflow. Table 2 shows unique outflow estimates by retail subsector. Note that "sales" refers to chain store sales unless otherwise specified.

The unique outflow was derived as follows. First, estimate non-local business services as a percentage of sales for each subsector (column A). Operating expenses (also known as operating, selling, general and administrative

Table 2. Derivation of the unique outflow for Cortland County: chain establishments.

Retail subsector	A (%)	B (%)	C (%)	D ($1000s)	E (%)	F (%)	G ($1000s)
Motor vehicles/parts	6.5	7.4	13.9	20,500	6.7	0.9	2857
Furniture/home furnishings	19.0	3.9	22.9	3500	1.1	0.3	802
Electronics/appliances	12.6	3.1	15.7	1750	0.6	0.1	275
Building materials/supplies	12.7	3.7	16.4	30,500	10.0	1.6	4992
Food/beverage stores	10.6	1.7	12.3	90,242	29.6	3.6	11,133
Health/personal care	9.9	2.5	12.4	25,750	8.4	1.0	3184
Gas stations	6.4	8.8	15.2	46,250	15.1	2.3	7026
Clothing stores	14.4	5.5	19.9	4520	1.5	0.3	901
Sporting goods/hobbies	15.3	2.4	17.7	3500	1.1	0.2	618
General merchandise	8.2	3.2	11.4	67,319	22.0	2.5	7660
Misc. store retailers	17.3	4.2	21.5	4000	1.3	0.3	860
Nonstore retailers	23.7	4.2	27.9	7500	2.5	0.7	2091
Totals				305,331		13.8	42,399

A = non-local business services as percentage of sales.
B = net income as percentage of sales.
C = non-local business services as percentage of sales plus net income as percentage of sales (A + B).
D = Cortland sales by subsector.
E = subsector sales as percentage of total sales (D / 305,331).
F = non-local business services as percentage of sales plus net income as percentage of sales, weighted by subsector sales as percentage of total sales (C × E). **The sum (13.8) represents the unique outflow as a percentage**.
G = C × D **The sum (42,399,000) represents the unique outflow as an amount**.
Sources:
A: US Census. (2002). *Economic census, retail trade, sales and operating expenses by type and kind of business.*
B: *Fortune* magazine. (2008).
D: InfoUSA. (2007).

expenses) is a conglomerate category that includes all the various expenses of running a business. Non-local business services was operationalized as all the components of operating expenses except payroll, utilities, maintenance, rent, and (local) taxes. Examples of these components are "transportation, shipping and warehousing services" and "advertising and promotional materials" (US Census, 2002, *Retail Trade, Sales and Operating Expenses by Type and Kind of Business*). The Economic Census provides estimates of each of these components as a percentage of operating expenses, and an estimate of operating expenses as a percentage of sales, thus making it possible to estimate non-local business services as a percentage of sales.

Next, estimate net income as a percentage of sales for each subsector using the average percentage of the top three companies nationwide in each subsector (column B).

Add these two percentages to get the unique outflow as a percentage of sales for each subsector (column C).

To get the unique outflow (as a percentage) for the entire chain store sector it is necessary to adjust for the fact that different subsectors represent different portions of the sector. This requires sales estimates for each subsector (column D). Before making this adjustment two adjustments to the sales estimates were necessary. First, the initial estimate for the food/beverage subsector was $137,500,000, which is clearly too large as it exceeds the sales at all food/beverage stores (see Table 4). This overestimate is probably due to the use of the midpoint ($37.5 million) of the relevant sales range ($20 million–$50 million). One or more of the four large grocery chain stores that dominate this subsector must actually have had sales that are below the midpoint. As an alternative estimate,

90% ($90,242,000) of sales at all food/beverage stores was used. This is a conservative estimate because there are no large or even medium-sized independent grocery stores in the county, and while there are 20 independent stores, many of those are liquor stores or other small stores that NAICS includes in the food/beverage subsector. Second, the initial estimate for the general merchandise subsector was $68,500,000, a very slight overestimate because it exceeds the sales at all such stores ($67,319,000). As an alternative, the sales at all such stores was used because virtually all the stores in this subsector are chain stores and the two non-chains are small stores that garner a minuscule portion of total sales.[4]

To make the necessary adjustment divide the sales for each subsector by total sales and then multiply the quotient (column E) by the unique outflow for each subsector (column C). The products (column F) are then added to arrive at the unique outflow as a percentage (13.8%).

Finally, multiply column C by column D to get the unique outflow in dollars for each subsector (column G). Summing the figures in column G gives the unique outflow in dollars for all the chain stores ($42,399,000).

Results

Retailing represents an important part of the county's economy (see Table 3). Only manufacturing produces more revenue than retail, and only manufacturing, health care, and educational services provide more jobs. Moreover, the health care and educational services jobs are somewhat special insofar as they include a small regional hospital and a medium size campus of the State University of New York (SUNY), respectively. The retail sales pull factor for the county is 1.41, indicating that

Table 3. Economy of Cortland County, 2002.

Sector	Number of establishments	Revenue ($1,000)	Number of employees
Agriculture	569	39,708	N
Manufacturing	73	644,801	3819
Wholesale trade	33	112,062	283
Retail trade	212	456,035	2428
Information	15	N	158
Real estate	39	D	100-249
Professional & scientific services	80	D	500-999
Administrative & support services	35	20,512	756
Educational services	N	X	2634
Health care & social assistance	131	155,156	3362
Arts, entertainment & recreation	22	14,944	571
Accommodations & food services	135	53,045	1680
Other services	93	28,819	532

Note: Employment for educational services includes 1421 local public school employees on a full-time equivalency basis and 1213 SUNY Cortland employees (full-time and part-time). SUNY Cortland data are for 2007.

Sources: Agriculture; US Department of Agriculture, National Agricultural Statistics Service. (2002). *County summary highlights*; Educational services: US Census. (2002). *Census of governments, local government employment and payroll in individual county areas*; Human Resources Office, SUNY Cortland; All other sectors: US Census. (2002). *Economic census, geographic area series*.

D: Withheld to avoid disclosing data for individual companies.

N: Not available or not comparable.

X: Not applicable.

sales in the county exceed expected sales, based on population and per capita income, by 41%.[5] Cortland undoubtedly "pulls" sales from some of the seven bordering counties, although three of those counties have pull factors as high as Cortland's and only one has a pull factor less than one.[6] Cortland's pull factor may also reflect greater than expected spending (based on per capita income) by county residents. This may apply especially to the students at SUNY Cortland, whose spending may be out of proportion to their reported income. What the situation in Cortland indicates is that even a rural county with modest incomes and high unemployment—and without "destination retail" or other special attractions—can have substantial retail sales.

The majority of retail spending in Cortland County occurs at chain stores, which account for 67% of total retail sales (see Table 4). Chain stores take more than 50% of sales in every subsector except motor vehicles/parts, electronics/home furnishings, clothing stores, and nonstore retailers, evidence that the chain store phenomenon involves more than Wal-Mart. A significant number (83) of the 212 retail establishments in Cortland County are chain stores. Given that such stores are usually larger, often much larger, than local independent merchants in the same line of business, and one chain store can replace a number of smaller establishments, it is striking that chain stores account for such a large percentage of all retail establishments. While the data in the previous paragraph show that a rural community can have substantial retail sales, these data show that those sales primarily support an array of chain stores.

Using the procedure described above the unique outflow was estimated to be

Table 4. Number and sales of retail establishments: Cortland County, 2002/2007.

Subsector	Number		Sales ($1000s)		Chain sales/ all sales (%)
	chains	all	chains	all	
Motor vehicles/parts	10	39	20,500	104,040	20
Furniture/home furnishings	2	8	3500	5347	65
Electronics/appliances	1	9	1750	5572	31
Building materials/supplies	8	22	30,500	35,077	87
Food/beverage stores	9	29	90,242*	100,269	90
Health/personal care	9	11	25,750	36,541	70
Gas stations	22	23	46,250	50,117	92
Clothing stores	3	17	4520	12,977	35
Sporting goods/hobbies	2	8	3500	4088	86
General merchandise	11	13	67,319*	67,319	100
Misc. store retailers	4	21	4000	6388	63
Nonstore retailers	2	12	7500	28,300	27
totals	83	212	305,331	456,035	67

*See text.
Sources: US Census. (2002). *Economic census, retail trade.* Data on chains: InfoUSA. (2007).

about $42 million or about 14% of total chain store sales (or about 9% of total retail sales) in the county (see Table 2).[7] The importance of this statistic is discussed in the next section.

The census revealed that very few chain stores are located downtown. Most, in fact, are located just outside the city of Cortland in the township that surrounds the city (see Figure 2). It is not unusual for the majority of chain stores to be sited just outside the limits of the local "central city." There are a number of reasons for this (Halebsky, 2004): land is cheaper, zoning is less stringent, it is easier to assemble a large tract of land, and rural townships often lack a downtown of their own and are indifferent to the fate of those in nearby cities. Because they are so numerous, and because their buildings, parking lots, and signs are so large, the 83 chain stores physically dominate the landscape in this part of the county and present an aesthetic quite different from that of downtown Cortland.

Another finding is the scarcity of *any* retailers outside the city of Cortland, the villages of Homer, McGraw and Marathon, and the areas just outside their borders, even though nearly 60% of the county lives outside these municipalities. The reason for this lack of convenient retailing is unclear. Perhaps it is an effect of chain stores such as Wal-Mart: just as independent downtown retailers are squeezed when a significant percentage of consumers stops shopping downtown because they assume that a superstore on the outskirts of town "has everything" and is less expensive, people in the county's several dozen unincorporated settlements may stop patronizing local small retailers for the same reasons, leading to the eventual demise of whatever small retailers may have existed in the hinterlands. The result is that a large number of people, some of whom are congregated in settlements with the density of a small village, must drive a considerable distance to buy basic commodities, a situation that resembles somewhat the phenomenon of "food deserts" (Kayani, 2002).

Historical data reveal a number of changes since 1977, including a decline in the total number of stores (see Table 5).

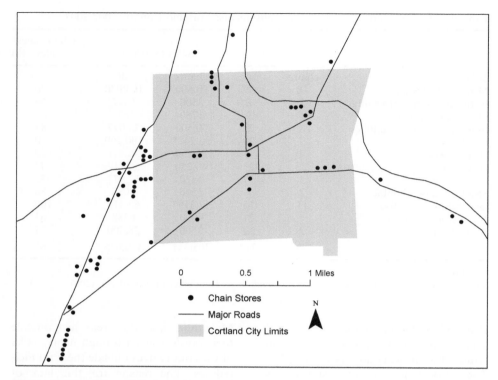

Figure 2. Location of chain stores.
Source: Map created by Dr. Wendy Miller, SUNY Cortland.

Table 5. Number of retail trade establishments: Cortland County, 1977 and 2002.

Subsector	1977*	2002	1977–2002
Motor vehicles/parts	38	36	−2
Furniture/home furnishings	11	8	−3
Electronics/appliances	9	9	–
Building materials/supplies	13	18	+5
Food/beverage stores	33	24	−9
Health/personal care	12	12	–
Gas stations	22	22	–
Clothing stores	30	14	−16
Sporting goods/hobbies/etc.	8	8	–
General merchandise	10	13	+3
Misc. store retailers	15	22	+7
Nonstore retailers	16	16	–
Totals	217	202	−15

Sources: US Census. (1977). *County business patterns, New York*, Table 2; US Census. (2002). *County business patterns, New York*, Table 6.
*Before 1997 business enterprises were classified using the Standard Industrial Classification (SIC). Data have been adjusted to allow comparison with current NAICS categories. In 1977 electronics/appliances were included with furniture/home furnishings, health/personal care stores with miscellaneous store retailers, gas stations with motor vehicles, sporting goods/hobbies/etc. with miscellaneous store retailers, and nonstore retailers with miscellaneous store retailers.

Table 6.   Retail establishments by employment-size class: Cortland County, 1977 and 2002.

Year	Number of employees per establishment						Totals
	1–4	5–9	10–19	20–49	50–99	100–249	
1977	124	42	30	19	2	2	219
2002	97	56	36	16	5	3	213

Sources: US Census. (1977). *County business patterns, New York*, Table 2; US Census. (2002). *County business patterns, New York*, Table 6.
Note: "Eating and drinking places" have been removed from the 1977 data to ensure comparability with the 2002 data.

This decline mirrors a nationwide decline in the number of stores (US Census, *Economic Census, Retail Trade, Establishment and Firm Size*, various years). At the subsector level there were marked declines in the number of clothing stores (from 30 to 14) and number of food/beverage stores (from 33 to 24).[8] While causality cannot be established, these declines correlate with the presence of the large general merchandise stores and large grocery stores, respectively, which tend to be chain stores.

Concurrently, there was a change in the distribution of stores by size (as measured by number of employees per establishment), with a decline in the number of small stores (those with one to four employees) and an increase in the number of large stores (those with 50 or more employees) (see Table 6). This also mirrors trends at the national level (US Census, *Economic Census, Retail Trade, Establishment and Firm Size*, various years). Again, causality cannot be established, but this pattern is congruent with the presence of the large grocery stores and general merchandise stores just mentioned.

With the displacement of independent merchants by chain stores and the predilection of chains to locate on the outskirts of town, what impact has the spread of chain stores had on downtown Cortland? Commercial directories, which list businesses by street address, were used to enumerate retailers located on Main Street, the heart of the city's central business district, in 1977 and 2006. The number of retailers with Main Street addresses declined from 38 in 1977 to 25 in 2006, a decline of 34%. In 1977 there were three general merchandise stores (all chain stores) on Main Street: Montgomery Ward, JC Penney, and JJ Newberry; today there are none. By locating on the outskirts of town the newer and larger chain stores have drawn shoppers away from Main Street. While still viable, Cortland's Main Street struggles to attract and retain businesses.

Discussion and conclusion

Data from a variety of sources were used to investigate the impact of retailing and chain stores in Cortland County, a rural county that, like so many others, is grappling with a stagnant local economy. This investigation has a number of implications for community development, beginning with the importance of retailing. As the data clearly indicate, retailing is a significant source of revenue and jobs. Even in communities that are economically stagnant and lack destination retail or other major attractions—as, in truth, most communities do—the retail sector remains substantial. This suggests that economic development officials should try to maximize the

COMMUNITY ECONOMIC DEVELOPMENT

benefit from those retailers that are present in their communities.

The unique outflow

Retailing has changed as a result of the retail revolution and the displacement of small independent merchants by corporate chains. While previous research has focused on Wal-Mart, the present research provides evidence that the chain phenomenon involves chain stores *en masse* and all subsectors of retailing. In Cortland, as in many other communities, Wal-Mart dominates sales of general merchandise, but that subsector represents only about 15% of retail sales; other chains dominate most other subsectors (Table 4). Does this dominance represent the maximum possible contribution of retailing to local economic development? As noted earlier, the contribution of retailers is maximized when they buy raw materials and goods locally, hire local residents, obtain financing from local financial institutions, rent or lease real estate from local landlords and landowners, use local business services, and generate profit for local owners. By these criteria chain stores fail to make the maximum contribution.

The main purpose of the unique outflow, estimated to be about 14%, is to quantify this limitation. As such it should be useful to citizens and officials who want to gauge the present and future benefits of retail development in their communities. While the unique outflow has been developed in the context of a case study of Cortland County, when expressed as a percentage it is dependent on the particulars of retailing in Cortland only insofar as it reflects the mix of chain stores in the county. In other words, it should be roughly the same in other communities with approximately the same mix of chain stores.

Is 14% high or low? There is no objective standard by which to judge. One way to evaluate its magnitude, however, is to compare it to a hypothetical economic development project. In Cortland the relevant question would be, what kind of project would contribute at least 14% of chain sales, or about $42 million, *annually*, to the local economy? A project of this size would clearly be a very large and significant project for the county. A similar question could be posed for other municipalities. Viewed this way, the unique outflow represents a material amount.

While the unique outflow has been conceptualized here as an aspect of retailing and has been estimated for the retail sector, similar statistics could be estimated for other sectors of the (local) economy, especially accommodations and food services, which are also dominated by chains.

Some caution must be used in applying the unique outflow to other communities because, as just noted, it depends on the mix of chain stores in a particular community.

The unique outflow may also be used to estimate the percentage of *total* retail sales that leaves a community, in which case the analysis will have to consider the proportion of sales going to chains and non-chains (as well as the mix of chain stores).

Finally, the negative impact of the unique outflow may be offset to some extent by the (presumed) lower prices on consumer goods associated with chain stores (Halebsky, 2009).

Non-economic considerations

Apart from strictly economic considerations, the unique outflow is important because it represents money that is not under the control of local individuals and organizations; simply put, the spread of chain stores means that local citizens lose some degree of control over various aspects of their lives and their communities. When a chain store takes the place of small merchants some portion of the local citizenry is reduced from independent business owners to employees, thus diminishing local human capital. Control over how to conduct business and what merchandise to offer is transferred from local owners to personnel at distant corporate headquarters. Moreover, the very basis on which a business is operated changes: while profit may be only one of several goals for an independent retailer, it is the only goal for a large corporate chain. This singlemindedness is a combined result of corporate law, which compels a corporation to focus on the interests of its shareholders, and the forces of supply and demand, which enforce this orientation by penalizing unprofitable firms with falling stock prices, less favorable credit ratings, and possible demise via bankruptcy, merger or acquisition (Fligstein, 1990; Reich, 2007, Ch. 5).[9]

The dominance of chains has implications for social capital and other forms of community capital (Green & Haines, 2008; Flora & Flora, 2008). Social capital, understood as the "social relationships and networks" that are crucial for a community's well-being (Green & Haines, 2002, p. 101), declines as small merchants, who are traditionally heavily involved in community affairs, become less numerous and less prosperous (Tolbert, 2005). Social capital is also undermined as a result of the tendency of chains to locate on the outskirts of town, often in malls or as part of a "power center" (a shopping center composed entirely of freestanding big box stores). This tendency often leads to the deterioration of Main Street as a commercial center, which is often associated with

its decline as a civic center, a function not taken up by the chains. Main Street helps to sustain social relationships and networks by serving as a community center (literally and figuratively), as a venue for community events, as a public space where citizens can interact with each other, and as the site for "third places" (Oldenburg, 1991) where citizens can meet each other outside of work and home. The peripheral placement of chain stores also contributes to sprawl and its attendant problems (Beaumont, 1994; Gillham, 2002). An environment characterized by low density commercial development, lack of street life, and auto-centered transportation undermines social capital by frustrating the frequent and intimate social interaction that is necessary to develop and sustain it. As the present research illustrates, the chains are quite consistent in their avoidance of downtown locations; it is not just Wal-Mart, Kmart, and a few other general merchandisers that pursue this siting strategy.

A related issue is the effect chain stores have on the local built environment. Most chains construct buildings that are out of scale and incongruous with local architectural styles; and chain stores, by their very nature, are homogeneous in appearance and operation. As they displace more and more independent merchants and take up more and more physical space in a community, local uniqueness and sense of place are undermined (Halebsky, 2009). As the physical features of a town or city become less special, local residents may identify less strongly with it and eventually invest less—financially, socially, and otherwise.

Political capital, conceived as "influence over major development projects and other issues affecting the quality of life of residents" (Green & Haines, 2008, p. 197), may also be affected by a growing preponderance of chain stores. To be specific, the political capital of local citizens may decline relative to that of non-local corporate chains. As chains come to account for a larger and larger share of the local economy—including, most decisively, jobs—their potential influence on local affairs increases correspondingly (Blanchard & Matthews, 2006). That influence, however, may remain unexercised because chains are often relatively uninterested in local affairs as long as their establishments remain profitable (Logan & Molotch, 1987).[10] From the perspective of community development, the problem with too much political capital accruing to corporate retailers is that they have no intrinsic interest in local welfare other than as it relates to the narrow goal of profitability, often evaluated on a short-term basis.

In conclusion, Cortland County has been used as a proxy to investigate what happens when retail trade in a small community becomes dominated by chain stores. The analysis suggests that their positive impact on a local economy can be unimpressive, a result, in part, of the fact that their profits and that portion of sales represented by non-local business services leave the area. There are also significant non-economic consequences for social capital and other forms of capital crucial for community development. A reversal of current trends does not appear imminent. Insofar as price competition is concerned, small merchants remain at a perpetual disadvantage because they cannot match the economies of scale and scope of the big chains. And, lastly, there is the issue of consumer preferences—as long as consumers perceive the benefits to outweigh the costs, chains will be popular.

Notes

1. The benefits of any particular export establishment must be set against any associated costs such as possible pollution in the case of a manufacturing facility or demand for financial incentives.
2. See Hustedde et al. (2005) and Shaffer et al. (2004) for an extended discussion of the multiplier. See Miller (2004) for a lucid introduction.
3. Economic Census data on operating expenses (which includes business services) are given at the national level and thus include both chains and independent retailers. Because retailing is dominated by chains these data reflect most accurately the situation for chains and thus should be appropriate for present purposes. Likewise in regard to net income as a percentage of sales: the Fortune 500 retailers are the chains that dominate retailing, so these data should be appropriate.
4. The use of midpoints is not ideal, especially when each successive sales range is larger (wider) than the previous one, which could tend to skew estimates upwards. However, exact sales data for individual establishments are proprietary information and are simply not available. In the present case the bias in the estimate of total chain sales appears slight because the only subsectors with a material volume of sales (relative to total sales) are gas stations, food/beverage, and general merchandise (see Table 4). The gas station subsector consists almost exclusively of chains (22 out of 23, or 96%), and the estimate using midpoints yields a total for the chains of $46,250,000, which is 92% of the whole subsector—a result that provides at least a partial validation for using midpoints. The other two subsectors, as noted, are so thoroughly dominated by chains that we can assume the total for the chains is the same or nearly the same as the total for all stores.
5. The pull factor was calculated as trade area capture divided by county population, or (county sales / (state sales per capita * (county per capita income/ state per capita income))) / county population. See Hustedde et al., 2005. Data were taken from the 2002

Economic Census and the 2000 Census of Population.

6. The pull factors for the seven counties that border Cortland are. 61 (Tioga), 1.05 (Madison), 1.06 (Cayuga), 1.06 (Chenango), 1.06 (Tompkins), 1.36 Onandaga, and 1.44 (Broome).

7. This may somewhat overstate the unique outflow as a dollar amount because some portion of the sales at chain stores would not have occurred at all if those stores were not present in the county. That is, in the absence of the chain stores it is possible that fewer shoppers from other counties would come to Cortland. The pull factor for Cortland (1.41) suggests that the county is attracting shoppers from other counties. This does not mean, however, that all those shoppers would not have come to the county anyway. Also, this effect is bound to diminish over time as chain stores become ubiquitous.

8. These data are taken from County Business Patterns and differ slightly from the Economic Census.

9. R.W. Hamilton (2000), author of a recent text on corporate law, writes that "at the end of the Twentieth Century, it seems that the social responsibility debate has ended. Laissez faire and the goal of profit maximization appear to have carried the day" (p. 72).

10. By contrast, some corporations are very involved in the affairs of the communities where their headquarters are located (Guthrie, 2004).

Acknowledgments

The author would like to thank Jerry Hembd and Bill Ryan for their helpful comments.

References

Albrecht, D.E., & Murdock, S.H. (1990). *The sociology of US agriculture: An ecological perspective*. Ames, IA: Iowa State University Press.

Basker, E. (2005). Job creation or destruction? Labor market effects of Wal-Mart expansion. *Review of Economics and Statistics*, 87(1), 174–183.

Beaumont, C. (1994). *How superstore sprawl can harm communities, and what citizens can do about it*. Washington, DC: National Trust for Historic Preservation.

Beaumont, C. (1997). *Better models for superstores: Alternatives to big-box sprawl*. Washington, DC: National Trust for Historic Preservation.

Bernstein, J., & Bivens, L.J. (2006). *The Wal-Mart debate: A false choice between prices and wages*. Washington, DC: Economic Policy Institute.

Bernstein, J., Bivens, L.J., & Dube, A. (2006). *Wrestling with Wal-Mart: Trade-offs between profits, prices, and wages*. Washington, DC: Economic Policy Institute.

Blakely, E., & Bradshaw, T.K. (2002). *Planning local economic development: Theory and practice* (3rd edition). Thousand Oaks, CA: Sage.

Blanchard, T., Irwin, M., Tolbert, C., & Nucci, A. (2003). Suburban sprawl, regional diffusion, and the fate of small retailers in a large retail environment, 1977–1996. *Sociological Focus*, 36(4), 313–331.

Blanchard, T., & Matthews, T.L. (2006). The configuration of local economic power and civic participation in the global economy. *Social Forces*, 84(4), 2241–2257.

Bluestone, B., Hanna, P., Kuhn, S., & Moore, L. (1981). *The retail revolution*. Boston, MA: Auburn House.

Bureau of Labor Statistics. (2007). *Local area unemployment statistics*. Washington, DC: Department of Labor. Retrieved January 29, 2009, from http://www.bls.gov/lau/

Chandler, A.D. Jr. (1990). *Scale and scope*. Cambridge, MA: Harvard University Press.

Davidson, O.G. (1990). *Broken heartland: The rise of America's rural ghetto*. New York: Free Press.

Dickman Directory, Cortland County 2006. (2006). Lewis Center, OH: Dickman Directories, Inc.

Dixon, T.J. (2005). The role of retailing in urban regeneration. *Local Economy*, 20(2), 168–182.

Falk, W.W., & Lobao, L.M. (2003). Who benefits from economic restructuring? In D.L. Brown & L.E. Swanson (Eds.), *Challenges for rural America in the twenty-first century* (pp. 152–165). University Park, PA: Pennsylvania State University Press.

Fligstein, Neil (1990). *The transformation of corporate control*. Cambridge, MA: Harvard University Press.

Flora, C.B., & Flora, J.L. (2008). *Rural communities: Legacy and change* (3rd edition). Boulder, CO: Westview.

Fortune magazine. (2008). Fortune 500. May 5, 2008.

Foster, L., Haltiwanger, J., & Krizan, C.J. (2006). Market selection, reallocation, and restructuring in the US retail trade sector in the 1990s. *Review of Economics and Statistics, 88*(4), 748–758.

Gillham, O. (2002). *The limitless city: A primer on the urban sprawl debate.* Washington, DC: Island Press.

Global Insight. (2005). *The economic impact of Wal-Mart.* Waltham, MA: Global Insight, Inc.

Goetz, S., & Swaminathan, H. (2006). Wal-Mart and county-wide poverty. *Social Science Quarterly, 87*(2), 211–226.

Gottdiener, M. (2001). *The theming of America: American dreams, media fantasies, and themed environments* (2nd edition). Boulder, CO: Westview.

Green, G., & Haines, A. (2002). *Asset building and community development.* Thousand Oaks, CA: Sage.

Green, G., & Haines, A. (2008). *Asset building and community development* (2nd edition). Thousand Oaks, CA: Sage.

Gruidl, J., & Kline, S. (1992). What happens when a large discount store comes to town. *Small Town*, March–April, 20–25.

Guthrie, Doug (2004). *Corporate-community relations study.* New York: Social Science Research Council.

Halebsky, S. (2004). Superstores and the politics of retail development. *City & Community, 3*(2), 115–134.

Halebsky, S. (2009). *Small towns and big business: Challenging Wal-Mart superstores.* Lanham, MD: Lexington Books.

Hamilton, R.W. (2000). *The law of corporations in a nutshell* (5th edition). St. Paul, MN: West Group.

Hustedde, R.J., Shaffer, R., & Pulver, G. (2005). *Community economic analysis: A how to manual* (revised edition). Ames, IA: North Central Regional Center for Rural Development, Iowa State University Press.

InfoUSA. (2007). *Sales estimates for 83 chain stores in Cortland County.* New York.

Jarmin, R.S., Klimek, S.D., & Miranda, J. (2005). *The role of retail chains: National, regional, and industry results.* (CES 05-30). Washington, DC: Center for Economic Studies, Bureau of the Census.

Karjanen, D., & Baxamusa, M. (2003). *Subsidizing Wal-Mart: A case study of the college grove redevelopment project.* San Diego, CA: Center on Policy Initiatives.

Kayani, N. (2002). *Food deserts: A practical guide.* London: Chadwick House Publishing.

Kraakman, R., & Hansmann, H. (2004). What is corporate law? In R. Kraakman, P. Davies, H. Hansmann, G. Hertig, H. Klaus, H. Kanda, & E. Rock (Eds.), *The anatomy of corporate law* (pp. 1–19). New York: Oxford University Press.

Kunstler, J.H. (1993). *The geography of nowhere: The rise and decline of America's man-made landscape.* New York: Simon & Schuster.

Lexis-Nexis Corporate Affiliations. (2006). New Providence, NJ: Lexis-Nexis.

Logan, J., & Molotch, H. (1987). *Urban Fortunes.* Berkeley, CA: University of California Press.

Lowe, M. & Wrigley, N., (Eds.). (1996). *Retailing, consumption and capital: Towards the new retail geography.* London: Longman.

Manning's Cortland Directory 1976–77. (1977). Bellows Falls, VT: H.A. Manning Co.

Mattera, P., & Purinton, A. (2004). *Shopping for subsidies: How Wal-Mart uses taxpayer money to finance its never-ending growth.* Washington, DC: Good Jobs First.

Miller, W.P. (2004). *Economic multipliers: How communities can use them for planning.* Little Rock, AR: University of Arkansas, Division of Agriculture, Cooperative Extension Service.

Million Dollar Directory 2006. (2006). Bethlehem, PA: Dun & Bradstreet.

Moe, R., & Wilkie, C. (1997). *Changing places: Rebuilding community in the age of sprawl.* New York: Henry Holt.

Muller, T., & Humstone, E. (1996). *What happened when Wal-Mart came to town? A report on three Iowa communities with a statistical analysis of seven Iowa counties.* Washington, DC: National Trust for Historic Preservation.

Neumark, D., Zhang, J., & Ciccarella, S. (2007). The effects of Wal-Mart on local labor markets. Discussion paper number 2545. Bonn: Institute for the Study of Labor.

Oldenburg, R. (1991). *The great good place.* New York: Paragon House.

Peterson, M., & McGee, J.E. (2000). Survivors of 'W-Day': An assessment of the impact of Wal-Mart's invasion of small town retailing communities. *International Journal of Retail & Distribution Management, 28*(4/5), 170–180.

Pittman, R.H., & Culp, R.P. (1995). When does retail count as economic development? *Economic Development Review, 13*(2), 4–6.

Reich, R.B. (2007). *Supercapitalism.* New York: Alfred A. Knopf.

Rockne, J., & Milchen, J. (2003). Local ownership pays off for communities. Retrieved July 14, 2007, from http://reclaimdemocracy.org/

S&P Register of Corporations, Directors and Executives, 2007. (2007). Charlottesville, VA: McGraw-Hill.

Shaffer, R., Deller, S., & Marcouiller, D. (2004). *Community economics: Linking theory and practice* (2nd edition). Ames, AI: Blackwell.

Shaffer, S. (2002). Firm size and economic growth. *Economics Letters, 76,* 195–203.

Shaffer, S. (2006). Establishment size by sector and county-level economic growth. *Small Business Economics, 26,* 145–154.

Stone, K. (1995). *Competing with the retail giants: How to survive in the new retail landscape.* New York: John Wiley.

Stone, K., Artz, G., & Myles, A. (2002). *The economic impact of Wal-Mart supercenters on existing businesses in Mississippi.* Starkville, MS: Mississippi State University Extension Service.

Tolbert, C.M. (2005). Minding our own business: Local retail establishments and the future of Southern civic community. *Social Forces, 83*(4), 1309–1328.

Tracy, J.A. (1994). *How to read a financial report* (4th edition). New York: John Wiley & Sons.

US Census. (1977). *County business patterns, New York,* Table 2. Washington, DC: United States Bureau of the Census.

US Census. (1977). *County and city data book.* Washington, DC: United States Bureau of the Census.

US Census. (1996). *The population of states and counties of the United States: 1790 to 1990.* Washington, DC: United States Bureau of the Census. Retrieved January 29, 2009, from http://www.census.gov/population/www/censusdata/cencounts/files/ny190090.txt

US Census. (2000). *County and city data book.* Washington, DC: United States Bureau of the Census.

US Census. (2002). *Census of governments, local government employment and payroll in individual county areas.* Washington, DC: United States Bureau of the Census. Retrieved February 1, 2009, from http://www.census.gov/

US Census. (2002). *County business patterns, New York,* Table 6. Washington, DC: United States Bureau of the Census.

US Census. (2002). *Economic census, geographic area series.* Washington, DC: United States Bureau of the Census. Retrieved January 31, 2009, from http://factfinder.census.gov/

US Census. (2002). *Economic census, retail trade.* Washington, DC: United States Bureau of the Census. Retrieved February 7, 2009, from http://factfinder.census.gov/

US Census. (2002). *Economic census, retail trade, establishment and firm size.* Washington, DC: United States Bureau of the Census. Retrieved January 4, 2008, from http://factfinder.census.gov/

US Census. (2002). *Economic census, retail trade, sales and operating expenses by type and kind of business.* Washington, DC: United States Bureau of the Census. Retrieved December 19, 2008, from http://www.census.gov/

US Census. (2007). *Population estimates.* Washington, DC: United States Bureau of the Census. Retrieved February 7, 2009, from http://factfinder.census.gov/

US Census. (2007). *Small area income and poverty estimates.* Washington, DC: United States Bureau of the Census. Retrieved January 29, 2009, from http://www.census.gov/did/www/saipe/data/statecounty/

US Department of Agriculture, National Agricultural Statistics Service. (2002). *County summary highlights.* Washington, DC: United States Department of Agriculture. Retrieved January 31, 2009, from http://www.nass.usda.gov/

Urry, J. (1995). *Consuming places.* London: Routledge.

Vias, A.C. (2004). Bigger stores, more stores, or no stores: Paths of retail restructuring in rural America. *Journal of Rural Studies, 20,* 303–318.

Vidich, A.J., & Bensman, J. (1958). *Small town in mass society.* Princeton, NJ: Princeton University Press.

Worpole, K. (1992). *Towns for people: Transforming urban life*. Buckingham, England: Open University Press.

Wrigley, N., & Lowe, M. (1999). New landscapes of consumption. In J. Bryson, N. Henry, D. Keeble, & R. Martin (Eds.), *The economic geography reader* (pp. 311–314). Chichester, England: John Wiley and Sons.

Zukin, S. (1998). Urban lifestyles: Diversity and standardization in spaces of consumption. *Urban Studies, 35*(5/6), 825–839.

MICRO BUSINESSES AS AN ECONOMIC DEVELOPMENT TOOL: WHAT THEY BRING AND WHAT THEY NEED

By Glenn Muske and Michael Woods

ABSTRACT

Micro businesses, defined as having ten employees or less, represent a substantial sub-segment of all small businesses. As such, they are credited as a significant contributor to economic growth of a community. This research focused on understanding the micro business owner, their contribution to the local economy in terms of profits, jobs, and their ability to bring outside dollars into a local economy. As the major economic engine in many areas, especially in rural areas, the success of the micro business is important to a local community's development and progress. The research also evaluated the support needs of the micro business owner during start-up and on-going operation. Most often, the business owners expressed a need for help with marketing and financing. The research also analyzed what agencies these micro business owners have turned to for help. The study supports the idea that a local economic development strategy must include development of the micro business segment and suggests ways to tailor such assistance efforts and programs.

INTRODUCTION

A key element in the development of a healthy community rests on the strength and diversity of its local economy (Kettering Foundation, 2000). When tied to other building blocks such as human capital including strong, local leaders, an involved citizen population, and youth development programs; infrastructure including not only roads and bridges but high speed communications access; and available capital, day care, educational programs and networks, the local economy becomes poised to provide a community with sustained economic development and growth. Such growth will be shared among all the citizens thus increasing overall quality of life (Beaulieu, 2002; Woods, 2000).

One key to a strong local economy is the micro business owner. This segment has been an important part of the small business engine that drove the United States' economic boom of the 1990s. Today, the micro business owner again is being asked to pull the economy out of its recent slowdown. For rural states, the importance of the small business has been even more dramatic. In Oklahoma, a past Executive Director for the Oklahoma Department of Commerce wrote that the small business entrepreneur has "become the building block in Oklahoma's growth and development" (Presley, 1997).

Glenn Muske, Department of Design, Housing and Merchandising, Oklahoma State University. Michael Woods, Department of Agricultural Economics, Division of Agricultural Sciences and Natural Resources, Oklahoma State University.

The purpose of this study is to examine how the micro business sector of a rural state, Oklahoma, supports economic growth and how the expansion of that segment can be supported in its growth. The study will focus on what micro businesses provide in terms of profits, jobs, and the ability to draw "new" dollars (dollars from consumers located outside the local area) into a local economy. While a local economy benefits from all economic activity, it is the new dollars, those coming from outside the system, that allow for the greatest growth opportunities and creation of new wealth (Fruth, 1999).

SUPPORTING LITERATURE

Community Development and Economic Development

Community development overall "entails the enrichment of material and social well-being as measured in the flow of money and goods over time; increases in a jurisdiction's quality and quantity of public goods (clean air and water, freedom from crime, better schools, etc.); and access to good jobs" (Beaulieu, 2002; Woods, 2000). Pigg (1999) defines community development as a "process of building the capacity of community residents to create, maintain, and enhance generalized structures. Development also includes such activities such as leadership, infrastructure, citizen involvement, and sustainability. Hill (1998) recognized this when he wrote, "Community development is a much broader area" yet "community is...shaped, or influenced by the economy" (Teitz, 1989).

Yet mention community development to many people and they will define it as expanding the economic opportunities within the community. For them, community development is synonymous with economic development or increasing the flow of money, goods, and jobs (Woods & Sanders, 1989). Today these are likely to be comprehensive and include recruitment not only of "smokestack" industries but a variety of small and big, service and product, high-tech and low-tech businesses. This differs from earlier economic development activities when the focus was on the attempted recruitment of large manufacturing firms into an area. Economic developers have realized that industry recruitment had a low probability of success, at best reaching only a 1 percent success rate, and even that success still left a community dependent upon a single employer (Flora & Johnson, 1991; Shapero, 1987).

Today community economic development plans, while varying in goals, objectives, and strategies (Eisinger, 1988; Flora, Flora, Green, & Schmidt, 1991; Rowley, Sears, Nelson, Reid, & Yetley, 1996; Sharp & Flora, 1999), focus on four complementary strategies. These comprehensive plans, or "third wave," economic development efforts support business development through information, leadership, and brokering (Bradshaw & Blakely, 1999; Bradshaw & Winn, 2000). Such plans increase the probability of success and offer the diversification necessary for a healthy economy (Leistritz & Sell, 2001; Rupasingha, Wojan, & Freshwater, 1999; Sharp & Flora, 1999).

Typically a community's economic development plan today includes the expansion and retention of existing businesses or a community's existing assets (Woods, Frye, & Ralstin, 1999). In addition, it is common that an economic development plan will include "self-development" or business creation (Rupasingha, Wojan, & Freshwater, 1999; Sharp & Flora, 1999; Woods, Frye, & Ralstin, 1999). Creation focuses on entrepreneurship and self-employment building on a community's human capital (Bartsch, 1989; Hayden, Kruse, & Williams, 1985; Pulver, 1988; Whatmore, Lowe, & Marsden, 1991). Finally, the plan will retain an effort to attract new businesses.

To achieve all four development activities, creation, attraction, retention, and expansion (Kettering Foundation, 2000; Woods, Frye, & Ralstin, 1999), the plan will contain, for new businesses, the development of strong infrastructures, financing packages, various tax breaks and incentives, and business-friendly regulations and laws. For existing businesses, again infrastructure improvement, financing and tax benefits, and beneficial regulations and laws are important as well as the creation of networking opportunities and educational and one-on-one support systems. For the creation of new businesses through entrepreneurship, an entrepreneurial-friendly environment through reduced taxes and regulations and a system of education, nurturing, and coordination is required. Also, the creation of risk-capital with reduced loan criteria and incubators where space, support services, and management help are available at no- or low-cost (Kettering Foundation, 2000; Scudder & Rettig, 1989; Woods & Rushing, 1995; Woods, Williams, Allen, & Frye, 1994). Finally, for creation of entrepreneurs, long-term mentoring and assistance as opposed to simple one-time educational programs are important (Lichtenstein & Lyons, 2001).

Micro Businesses in the Literature

For three of the four primary economic development activities, creation, retention, and expansion, the target audience often is the small business owner, defined by the Small Business Administration as a business with "fewer than 500 employees" (Devins, 1999; U.S. Small Business Administration, 2001). In the United States, over 99 percent of businesses are considered small. These businesses employ 51 percent of the workforce, produced over 80 percent of all new jobs, and 52 percent of the gross domestic product (Henderson, 1997; U. S. SBA, 2000; U. S. Census, 2001).

Yet, for most people this definition of "small" far exceeds their personal view in which businesses with 50 to 100 employees are considered "big" business. This working definition is especially true in rural areas. A common solution to the "small" category is to divide it into various subcategories. One such category is that of the "micro" business or firms that employ less ten people (Devins, 1999). Micro businesses form a dynamic, integral part of the market economy providing goods and services and a gateway by which millions enter the economic and social mainstream of American society (Sexton, 1999; U.S.

SBA, 1998). Micro businesses account for, in the United States, 94 percent of all firms and 84 percent of employer firms. They employ up to 25 percent of all individuals or over 11 percent of all employees within employer-only firms (Family Economics and Nutrition Review, 2001; U. S. Census, 2001). For Oklahoma, 77 percent of firms are micro in size, and they employ 13 percent of all workers (U.S. SBA, 2000).

So how do micro businesses contribute? Most importantly, they provide the owner the ability to build assets and create wealth (Lichtenstein & Lyons, 2001). For the community, micro businesses contribute in three primary ways. First, micro businesses contribute through the income and profits they generate, 13 percent overall with that number becoming much higher in rural areas (Family Economics and Nutrition Review, 2001; U.S. Census, 2001). Those receipts often remain in the community and become multiplied thus creating a stronger local economy. A multiplier is what occurs, according to economists, when a portion of a dollar spent flows back into the economy to buy raw materials, supplies, or pay for wages. As this process occurs over and over, the single dollar initially spent becomes perhaps $2 or $3 in total economic growth (U. S. Dept. of Commerce, 1992).

The second contribution of the micro business to the local economy comes in the creation of jobs (Halstead & Deller, 1997). During the 1990's, 69 percent of all new jobs were created by start-up businesses with the largest percentage of jobs added by companies with four or fewer employees. These companies had an overall job growth rate of 213 percent during that time (Chun & Griffin, 1996; Sexton, 1999).

Third, micro businesses owners are often involved in community activities and take on leadership roles (Miller, 1998; Sharp & Flora, 1999). It has been argued that micro businesses, because they are often controlled and operated by local owners, are more often and more deeply involved in civic activities. Whether this is done selfishly in order to build up the business or from an idealistic perspective, the micro business owner becomes a great deal more than just a provider of goods and services (Miller, 1998; Tolbert, Blanchard, Irwin, Lyson & Nucci, 2001).

For many rural areas, the contributions of micro businesses become even more important as this segment is the primary, and perhaps only, business segment. Since the 1980's, many rural states have struggled and have seen their economic fortunes become stagnant or decline (Barkley, 1993; Bastow-Shoop, Leistritz, Jolly, Kean, Gaskill, Jasper, & Sternquist, 1995; Leistritz & Hamm, 1994; Miller, 1998). With 40 percent of the population living in non-metropolitan counties, Oklahoma can be considered one such rural state (Woods & Sanders, 1989). For rural areas with a declining agriculture sector and little other major industry, the consequences have been harsh with increased out-migration, a reduction in schools, health services, public transportation, and other services in general along with a reduction in retail activity and a general deterioration in the rural quality of life (Rowe, Haynes, & Stafford, 1999; U.S. Bureau of the Census, 2000, Tables 727 & 759; Wiley, 1997).

To combat this decline, rural states and others have attempted to stabilize and enhance those traditional economic bases through economic diversity by building on local assets, entrepreneurs, and small businesses (Bartsch, 1989; Bradshaw & Blakely, 1999; Bradshaw & Winn, 2000; Flora & Johnson, 1991; Ghelfi & Parker, 1996; Goodall, Kafadar, & Tukey, 1998; Hayden, Kruse, & Williams, 1985; Leistritz & Sell, 2001; Pulver, 1988; Shapero, 1987; Whatmore, Lowe, & Marsden, 1991). Rural business owners, according to estimates, have accounted for 80 percent of the economic growth (U.S. Chamber of Commerce, 1994; Woods et al., 1994).

Yet efforts to support rural micro businesses face the rural realities of a small and undiversified market, a limited skilled and even unskilled labor pool if workers are available at all, and limited or inadequate support services that make start-up and on-going success difficult (Buss & Lin, 1990; Osborne, 1988; Reid, 1987). In addition, little research has focused on how this subgroup might be strengthened and enhanced (Devins, 1999; Fitzsimmons, 2002; Lichenstein & Lyons, 2001). The purpose of this study is to examine the micro business sector of one rural state's economy. The study will focus on: (1) the general demographic make-up of that sector; (2) an analysis of what these businesses provide to the local community in terms of profits, jobs, drawing new dollars from consumers outside of the local economy; and allowing the owner the time to commit to community leadership activities; and (3) developing an understanding of the support and assistance needs of the business owner in developing a successful enterprise as well as examining what agencies the owners have turned to in the past for help. Businesses will be categorized on whether or not the business is considered an exporter (makes the majority of sales outside the local area) or if it depends primarily on local sales.

METHODOLOGY

The sampling frame was developed through combining lists of existing businesses from the Oklahoma State University Food and Agricultural Products Center, the Oklahoma Department of Agriculture, the Oklahoma Tax Commission, and the Oklahoma Cooperative Extension Service Home/Micro Business program. Because of rural interest of the study, these agencies were approached in order to increase the likelihood of locating rural businesses. The lists were merged into one master list and duplicate names were eliminated.

In August of 2000, all the businesses on the list were contacted by letter explaining the study. The letter explained that they may be contacted and interviewed by telephone, by the OSU Bureau of Social Research. The Bureau, through its staff of trained interviewers and using its computer-based questionnaire, was able to take respondents answers quickly and accurately. Being computer-based allows the interviewer to be directed to the next appropriate question if that is an option. It also allows the data to be entered immediately and to be initially screened to ensure that the answer inserted is a valid answer to the question. The computer-based questionnaire for the study was developed and pre-tested for accuracy and completeness.

Respondents were contacted during the fall based on random-digit dialing. A screening question asked about the business size in terms of number of employees. Only micro business owners, defined here as owners employing ten employees or less, were interviewed. The employees could work either full or part-time. These interviews lasted between 20-30 minutes. If there was no answer to the telephone call, three additional contacts were attempted at other times and days. Seventy percent of the 274 owners contacted, or 193 owners, responded to the survey.

Several of the questions including business type, support needs both at start-up and currently, and reason for starting the business were asked as open-ended questions. Those questions were later divided into categories.

The results are divided into categories: general demographics about the owner and business; business success in terms of profit, number of employees, ability not to work at multiple jobs, and if the business is an exporter, defined as generating 51 percent or more of sales from an area outside of a 50-mile radius from the primary business location, as opposed to having primarily local sales; and an evaluation of the support and assistance needs of the owner. Frequencies and percentages were calculated for the various questions. Chi-square analysis, ANOVA and T-tests, based on data type, were used to determine variable significance.

RESULTS

Micro Businesses: Who They Are

Overall, 37 percent of the respondents operated food-based businesses, 29 percent operated a product business, and 34 percent operated some other type of business. Forty-eight percent of the businesses were rural with an additional 20 percent located in small towns and the rest in cities. The majority of businesses, 44 percent, were structured as sole proprietorships with an additional 33 percent incorporated and the rest operating under some other business structure. The typical owner was male (54 percent), age 45-60 (54 percent), and had started the business for control and independence reasons (52 percent) (See Table 1).

The demographics of the businesses were evaluated based on whether or not the business made the majority of sales within 50 miles of the business location (a local sales business) or outside that geographical area (an exporter). Only for business type was there a significant difference for the demographic variables based on this categorization ($x^2(15, N =193) = 15.826, p = .000$). Businesses with local sales were more likely to operate a food-based business (48 percent) as opposed to exporters with 22 percent running a food business. This data can be seen as logical for two reasons, the difficulty in transferring food products and the problem of spoilage

Table 1. General Demographics

	All Businesses (n=193) %	Exporters (n=82) %	Local Sales (n=111) %
Business product or service*			
Food	37	22	48
Product	29	40	20
Other (service, retail, misc)	34	28	32
Business location			
Farm/Rural, non farm	48	46	50
Town - Up to 25,000	20	23	17
City 25,001 and up	32	31	33
Business structure			
Sole Proprietorship	44	36	51
Corporation	33	37	30
Other	23	30	19
Gender of business manager			
Male	54	54	53
Female	46	46	47
Age of business manager			
< 45	28	27	28
45 - 60	54	57	53
61+	18	16	19
Reason to start business			
Control/Independence	52	58	47
Financial	18	15	21
Creativity	12	12	11
Other	18	15	21

* Significant differences (p=.05) between exporting businesses and businesses with primarily local sales.

Although exporting and local sale businesses were not significantly different on other variables, there are some interesting differences. Exporters were substantially more likely to be found in towns (23 percent) as opposed to cities (17 percent) and operated a business structure other than a sole proprietorship (67 percent vs. 49 percent). Owners of export businesses were more likely to have started the business for control and/or independence (58 percent vs. 47 percent) and less likely to have done so for financial or other reasons (15 percent vs. 21 percent).

Micro Businesses: What They Offer

As noted in the review of literature, micro businesses often form the economic backbone of a community by providing a cash flow stream, much of which will pass through the community multiple times, and profits, which for local-owned businesses are typically invested in local financial institutions. Generally, the businesses in the survey reported small profits with 50 percent reporting yearly profits of $5000 or less. An additional 18 percent indicated that their profits were between $5001 and $25,000. Over 70 percent of these businesses do provide the owner with some level of profit. The businesses in this study reported an estimated average profit of over $35,000. Overall, these businesses brought nearly $6 million dollars of profit into the local economy (See Table 2). On average, 48 percent of all sales were generated from exports (data not shown).

Table 2. Business/Community Returns

	All Businesses (n=193) %	Exporters (n=82) %	Local Sales (n=111) %
Profit*			
Less than $5000	50	53	48
$5001 – 25,000	18	21	15
> $25,000	32	16	27
Number of employees			
1 - Self only	38	38	38
2 - 3	30	32	30
4+	32	30	32
Owner works another job			
Yes	31	27	33
Spouse works another job			
Yes	46	50	43
% of sales			
Local - Majority of sales are within 50 miles	54	18	79
Exporter - Majority of sales are outside of 50 miles	46	82	21

* Significant differences (p=.10) between exporting businesses and businesses with primarily local sales.

Micro businesses also brought jobs to the local community. While 38 of the businesses only employed the owner, the other 62 businesses had one or more additional people on the payroll. Overall, business owners reported 582 employees on the payroll. This number represents an average of three people employed per business.

Businesses can also strengthen the local community by allowing the owner financial freedom to offer his or her time as a community leader. Only 31 of the 193 business owners reported having to work another job. The idea that owners who do not work another job are in businesses that are more financial stable is supported by the finding that "working outside the business" was significant, in a negative relationship, with owners working outside the business earning smaller profits ($x^2(8, N=165) = 5.938, p = .051$). Although not significant, an interesting note was that although exporting businesses were more likely to allow the business owner to forego working another job, it was more likely that the exporter's spouse was working another job.

Finally, businesses support the local community by drawing new money into the local economy. Overall 54 percent of the businesses indicated that the majority of their sales were local or within 50 miles of the business location. This meant 111 of the 193 firms interviewed were classified as "local sales" businesses. These businesses on average generated 79 percent of their sales locally. Exporter businesses, or businesses that generated the majority of their sales from outside a 50-mile radius, represented 82 businesses. These businesses generated 82 percent of their sales from exports and only 18 percent from local sales. One unexpected result was the finding that exporting businesses reported a lower level of profits ($F(1, 193) = 3.152, p = .077$).

Micro Businesses: What They Need

A third area of questions focused on gathering information that can be used to enhance the existing support programs for the micro business owner. The most often expressed start-up need was for financial help (29 percent). Because this answer represents the coding of an open-ended question, it is important to understand the breadth of what the owners were requesting. Requests for help included everything from the need for additional capital to help in understanding financial statements to locating financial assistance programs. Only 11 percent of business owners (21 of the 193 respondents) indicated they had ever received government aid or a tax incentive. In examining the support business owners currently wanted, help in marketing (38 percent) and financial assistance (22 percent) ranked highest (See Table 3).

Interestingly, there was a significant difference in level of profitability by the type of help currently requested ($x^2(4, N=165) = 10.855, p = .028$). Business owners indicating a need for help with either marketing or finances were more likely to report lower profits than people reporting needing other types of help. Also, the type of help currently needed varied by whether or not the business was an exporter or relied on local sales ($x^2 (4, N=193) = 10.185, p = .037$) with business owners who exported reporting less need for marketing assistance but a greater need for financial help. This result somewhat matched the start-up needs of these two groups with exporting businesses indicating a higher need for financial assistance.

These results are also supported by business owners' comments that marketing was a major problem (31 percent), second only to employee issues at 39 percent. When the major issues were compared between exporting and local sale businesses, some substantial, although not significant differences, were found in pricing (12 percent vs. 8 percent), understanding, and complying with government regulations (22 percent vs. 15 percent), record keeping (17 percent

vs. 3 percent), and developing a business plan (19 percent vs. 13 percent). Only for employee motivation (19 percent vs. 9 percent) and developing marketing strategies (33 percent vs. 27 percent) did business owners relying on local sales indicate through higher response rates that these issues were major problems.

Looking at exporters as opposed to local sale businesses, exporters indicated a significantly higher need for help with financial record keeping and financial reports ($x^2(1, N =193) = 5.793, p = .016$ and $(x^2(1, N =193) = 3.739, p = .053$ respectively). Owners who exported indicated a substantially higher need for help with regulations, business planning, pricing, and quality control help.

Owners were asked in what geographical region, within 50 miles of the business, within the state, in surrounding states, in the United States, or international, they would most like to increase sales. Typically, owners wanted to increase sales in the area where they already made the majority of their sales ($x^2(5, N =193) = 24.040, p = .000$). This finding is of concern for owners who already depend on local sales. These owners face smaller markets that will more easily reach the saturation point and the mature product stage. This makes if difficult to help the local sales business owner who wants more help with marketing (44 percent) but is not considering going outside the local area. As might be anticipated, businesses dependent on local sales were also less likely to be using the Web as a sales outlet (22 percent vs. 32 percent).

Before leaving the support and assistance needs of business owner, business owners were asked where they had most often received help from five Oklahoma agencies, the Oklahoma Department of Agriculture (ODOA), the Oklahoma State University Food and Agricultural Products Center (FAPC), the Oklahoma Cooperative Extension Services (OCES), the Small Business Development Centers (SBDCs) and the local Vo-Tech Centers (Vo-Tech). ODOA and FAPC were mentioned most frequently in general and certainly by food-based businesses. Only the difference in the use of FAPC by food-based businesses was significant ($x^2(1, N =193) = 8.719, p = .003$) with food-based businesses more often using the Center.

When exploring the relationship between type of help used and profitability, the assistance provided by the FAPC did translate into the business being more likely to have greater profits ($x^2(2, N =193) = 7.882, p = .019$). This finding supports Lichtenstein and Lyons (2001) comments suggesting that effective entrepreneurial support programs must move from providing services and one-time programs to developing entrepreneurs. The FAPC offers a complete set of support from product idea refinement through business plan development and on into production, pricing, and marketing. Not only is such support offered during start-up, but also the Center stands ready to provide on-going management and operational support. The idea is that the entrepreneur, to be successful, must have sustained contact, support, and mentoring and that the entity providing such support must look at development as a process and competency gained over time.

Table 3. Assistance Needed

	All Businesses (n=193) %	Exporters (n=82) %	Local Sales (n=111) %
At Start-Up			
Marketing	18	18	17
Financial	29	32	26
General Business Training	20	18	22
Tax/ Regulations/Legal	6	5	7
Other	27	27	28
Current Needs*			
Marketing	38	28	44
Financial	22	27	19
General Business Training	5	7	4
Tax/ Regulations/Legal	4	1	6
Other	31	37	27
Have received government aid or tax incentives*			
Yes	11	16	4
Issue is major business problem (Multiple answers accepted)			
Employees	39	40	39
Marketing	31	27	33
Workers Compensation	19	19	19
Regulations	18	22	15
Family/Business Conflict	17	17	16
Business Plan	15	19	13
Motivation	12	9	14
Financial Reports*	12	17	8
Record Keeping*	11	17	6
Pricing	10	12	8
Benefits	9	9	10
Customer Needs	6	6	5
Quality Evaluation	3	6	2
Where would you most like to increase sales?*			
Within 50 mile radius	25	15	32
Oklahoma	19	12	25
Surrounding States	17	16	18
Rest of U.S.	35	52	21
International	4	5	1
Do you conduct web sales?			
Yes	26	32	22
Have received help from - multiple answers allowed			
OSU Food & Ag Products*	42	29	51
OK Coop. Ext. Service	27	26	28
OK Dept. of Ag	62	60	64
SBDC's	21	23	19
Vo-Tech Centers	25	24	25

* Significant differences (p=.10) between exporting businesses and businesses with primarily local sales.

DISCUSSION AND IMPLICATIONS

Micro businesses are a significant segment of any state's economy and in particular a rural state such as Oklahoma. With a $6 million profit found among the respondent firms and if one assumes an estimated 10 percent return on investment, this means these firms generated $60 million in revenues. Certainly a large number of owners earned $5000 or less but there are several possible reasons for this including being early in the start-up process, or perhaps the business is only a means to generate an enhanced revenue stream such as from a value-added enterprise. In addition, the business focus may be to generate a small amount of money to meet the needs or goals of the family or used to start and/or maintain another business. Whatever the reason, potential success of these owners has significant implications for local economic diversification and future community development.

Requested Help

Marketing. One often stated support need was for marketing assistance, a priority need for micro business owners. Ranking second among start-up owners, it grows substantially, a 20-point shift from 18 percent to 38 percent, as a current need of business owners. Some owners requested specific marketing programs to get their product or service in front of the consumer. Other owners were trying to determine if their idea, developed from a passion, an opportunity, or from a need to use their skills in a creative way, had a market and if that market was willing to pay the price that the owner wants. Once in business, owners were looking for an outlet for the product and/or service. Requested help might include group marketing efforts and cooperative sales opportunities or arranging for a sales representative to represent a group of products similar in nature or from a specific region.

One marketing aspect that must be encouraged is the expansion of the owner's geographical marketing horizon. Fifty-four percent of owners indicated that one-half of their sales came from within a 50-mile radius of the business. While positive, a limited population potentially limits these businesses as the market quickly becomes saturated without a continuous flow of new products. Companies doing business locally also are more susceptible to local slowdowns, have fewer and smaller growth opportunities, and the dollars they generate are not new money but instead reflect a recycling of existing market resources.

Yet changing the owner's view of his or her potential market will be difficult as owners were most interested in expanding in the area where they already make the majority of sales. While growth is not impossible without an expansion of the market base, it is certainly more difficult. By building a geographically broader market base, a business can bring new dollars into the local economy. Such businesses are less affected by local conditions.

One reason why the owner may not consider new markets may be a lack of information on how to approach marketing in an unknown area. Entering a new market may require the owner to develop new outlets, shipping, return policies, etc. In addition, the owners may already be selling everything they produce. Thus, production expansion may be necessary before any additional marketing is needed.

One possible solution to reaching new markets might be through e-commerce. Yet one of the difficulties in making e-commerce an effective outlet for products and services is creating an awareness of a business and its website. To do this requires a focused marketing program. Also, certain products, such as some food products or services, may not lend themselves to being offered a substantial distance away from the home office of the business, although there are many examples in Oklahoma alone where e-commerce works very well for a food-based business.

For the existing business owner who already relies on export sales, marketing support takes on a different meaning. Marketing support for them may mean the identification of new market areas. These owners were already more likely to use websites so the help they need may come in the form of focused advertising and promotion campaigns to get their site recognized. It also may come from efforts such as the Oklahoma Department of Agriculture's website where multiple business owners can be found simply by going to the "Made in Oklahoma" site.

Financial. A second area of help requested by business owners was for financial assistance. This may be helping to locate existing funds but probably means looking for grant programs or perhaps loans. This need also included help with record keeping and analysis of the financial data they had collected. Along those same lines, pricing, although also a marketing issue, might be an area where business owners are not able to determine what price to charge in order to make a certain profit level.

Other. Business owners also indicated that government regulations and record keeping were major problems. This finding might reflect the increase in local, state, and even international rules and procedures that face an owner as he or she tries to sell goods and services to a wider geographical market. It may also reflect the burden that some owners feel in staying aware of relevant regulations and then doing the necessary paperwork needed to comply with them.

Local Community Support Ideas

Often state and federal policies are considered key elements in effective community development. While state and federal policies are certainly important, there is reason to believe that local policies and support provide the greatest assistance to the micro business owner. Today, entrepreneurship and encouragement of micro businesses is becoming an increasingly important strategy in local planning. The question arises: "What policies at the local level can make a difference?" Recent work by several authors offers potential policy actions. For instance, Nolan (2003) notes entrepreneurship-centered efforts are not a "cure-all" but rather offer hope in the long run. Nolan cites several policy innovations including business networks to enhance cooperation, information sharing and peer support among fledgling entrepreneurs. Building a network of business angels to possibly provide critical venture capital is also cited by Nolan, and policy efforts are often local in scope and implementation. Nolan also notes there are many sources of assistance available often what micro businesses and entrepreneurs need is visible access to these programs. Many times an emerging entrepreneur simply does not know where to go for help. Local community developers can provide important assistance by building network and making sources of information more accessible.

Small communities have additional development challenges not faced by larger urban areas. There is no critical mass and a sparse population limits options for markets and input suppliers. Lyons (2003) discusses the policy challenges in building an entrepreneurial region. He notes there are four skill sets required of successful entrepreneurs: technical, managerial, entrepreneurial, and personal. Providing support to enhance these skills is a large local policy undertaking. A regional coalition with multiple players and partners makes much sense. Lyons advises regional efforts to include "players" from the private, public, and non-profit sectors and to be sure any regional coalition is representative of all who may contribute.

Koven and Lyons (2003) note an important distinction between entrepreneurship and self-employment. They argue the distinction revolves around the existence of an innovative business concept or idea. Entrepreneurs are attempting to develop something new while people who are self-employed are typically selling labor to perform a specific set of routine tasks (Koven & Lyons, p. 116). Barriers to entrepreneurship identified by Koven and Lyons include lack of financial capital, lack of industry and markets, lack of training and education, lack of information, lack of transportation, and community resistance to business development. Local policies targeted to address these barriers would enhance the potential for entrepreneurial growth. Nolan (2003) also supports the notion of overcoming community resistance when he suggests using a variety of media to promote public awareness and influence local attitudes.

According to some authors, learning, leveraging, linking, and leadership become the bedrock upon which local economic, and therefore community, development can be built (Bradshaw & Blakely, 1999; Hill, 1998; National Academy of Public Information, 1996). And while development efforts need to start with educational programs, such efforts cannot end there but must be continuous through mentoring, alliances, and entrepreneurial clusters working in similar businesses (Bradshaw & Blakely, 1999; Lichtenstein & Lyons, 2001). Key in developing these linkages are agencies such as the Cooperative Extension Service, Small Business Development Centers, Service Corp of Retired Executives, and vocational and technology programs as well as through the linkages the owner can form through mentoring programs and support efforts of his or her local Chamber of Commerce. These agencies need to increase their visibility to the owner as well as evaluate their programmatic efforts in order to provide more sustained help similar to that currently being undertaken by OCES through its "Initiative for Rural Oklahoma" program. This Initiative provides targeted leadership training for rural communities as well as technical assistance when local leaders identify specific projects. The Initiative website (ifro.okstate.edu) provides additional background.

Devin (1999) suggests that micro business owners need to have business advisors ready to help and respond. His recommendations also included a local presence and networking. Where these elements were missing, he noted a loss in momentum in building the micro business segment.

All of the above occurs because of leadership and that leadership occurs at the local level. Someone must take charge of bringing the players together and building the necessary support network/s if results are to be achieved. While consultants and state officials can assist and provide some of the tools for the process, an effective development process begins in the local area. Small steps such as networking, mentoring, encouragement of local trading, local events, and providing local training are all examples of key parts to an economic, and thereby a community, development plan.

Perhaps the most important element is that the support effort must be focused and on-going. Already these business owners recognize that they must continually change if they are to be successful in the marketplace. This fact means that their needs will be on-going. Although not earlier reported, at least 54 percent of all business owners had tried a new marketing method, a new product or a new means of customer service and support (the highest category with over 70 percent of owners acknowledging they had made a change in this category).

It is important to note that one concept of sustainability for a local economy has emphasized local-owned businesses in contrast with larger corporate businesses. The argument presented is that local businesses tend to spend more in the local economy and extract fewer profits to be sent to distant corporate offices. Micro businesses certainly fit this concept of sustainability. Yet, this concept may be somewhat of a dilemma. When first emerging, micro businesses tend to sell to local markets. Growth often implies an expansion of the market area, first statewide, then nationwide, and for some worldwide. If exports/sales to the outside world grow a local economy, then encouraging growth of exports supports the notion of links (economically) to the outside world. The more a micro business grows, the more likely it will become a large business (someday maybe even publicly owned). The more successful the micro business is, the more it competes with micro businesses in other localities. Thus, a successful growing micro business may ultimately threaten sustainability in some other area.

SUMMARY

The purpose of this study was to examine the micro business sector of one rural state's economy (Oklahoma) and to determine (1) what these businesses provide to the local community in terms of profits, jobs, and drawing new dollars from outside consumers into a local economy, and (2) what support and assistance needs do these micro business owners identify. The findings of over $6 million dollars of annual profits, the employment of on average three employees per firm or nearly 200 people and the fact that nearly one half of the businesses make over 82 percent of sales outside of their local area and thus bring new wealth into a community offer significant reasons for the support of micro businesses and their owners.

Beyond current returns to the owner and local community, the micro business segment forms the base from which the majority of large firms and "gazelles," defined by Chun and Griffin (1996) as rapidly growing firms, begin. The micro businesses also form the basic "critical mass" that can attract other businesses as well as help retain existing businesses. Before things such as the business clusters identified by Bradshaw and Blakely (1999) can begin, there must first be a solid business base that forms an interlocking network of basic support for each other, for other entrepreneurs and for the local community. A strong micro business segment offers diversity, that business base and is a key ingredient to a healthy economy.

This paper suggests that local support is an important key in developing the micro business community. Based on what the owners requested, local communities can provide help with:

- Market understanding, development and assistance such as cooperative marketing programs and e-commerce education and support.

- Finance: access to but also the development and understanding of financial reports

- Record keeping and government regulations.

Other ways the local community can support the micro business owner include:

- Assistance in forming supportive networks and coalitions.

- An ombudsman or mentor who knows what support is available and can guide the owner through the process.

- Developing a program to build the micro business owner's technical, managerial, entrepreneurial, and personal skill set.

- Ensuring that the necessary infrastructure exists.

- Building community support for local business development.

- Listening and responding to the needs of business owners.

- Developing local leaders who are prepared for their role in the development process.

REFERENCES

Barkema, A. D., M. Drabenstott, & J. Stanley. 1990. Processing food in farm states: An economic development strategy for the 1990s. *Economic Review* (Federal Reserve Bank of Kansas City) 75(4): 5-23.

Barkley, D. L. (ed.). 1993. *Economic adaptation: Alternatives for nonmetropolitan areas.* Boulder, CO: Westview Press. :

Bartsch, C. 1989. Government and neighborhoods: Programs promoting community development. *Economic Development Quarterly* 3: 157-168.

Bastow-Shoop, H., F. L. Leistritz, L. Jolly, R. Kean, L. Gaskill, C. Jasper, & B. Sternquist. 1995. Factors affecting the financial viability of rural retail businesses. *Journal of the Community Development Society* 26(2): 169-185.

Beaulieu, L. J. 2002. *Creating vibrant communities & economies in rural America.* Mississippi State, MS: Southern Rural Development Center.

Bradshaw, T. K., & E. J. Blakely. 1999. What are third wave state economic development efforts? From incentives to industrial policy. *Economic Development Quarterly* 13(3): 229-244.

Bradshaw, T. K., & K. Winn. 2000. Gleaners, do-gooders and balers: Options for linking sustainability and economic development. *Journal of the Community Development Society* 31(1): 112-129.

Buss, T. F., & X. Lin. 1990. Business survival in rural America: A three-state study. *Growth and Change* 21(3): 1-8.

Chun, J. & C. E Griffin. 1996. The mouse that roared. *Entrepreneur* September: 118-122.

Devins, D. 1999. Supporting established micro businesses: Policy issues emerging from an evaluation. *International Small Business Journal* 18(1): 86-97.

Duke, C. R. 1996, Fall. Exploring student interest in entrepreneurship courses. *Journal of Marketing Education* 18: 35-45.

Eisinger, P. K. 1988. The rise of the entrepreneurial state: State and local economic development policy in the United States. Madison, WI: The University of Wisconsin Press.

Fallin, M. February, 1998. *Business forum report.* Oklahoma City, Oklahoma: Office of the Lieutenant Governor.

Family Economics and Nutrition Review. 2001. Small business: Evidence from the 1998 survey of small business finances. *Family Economics and Nutrition Review 14*(1), 84-85.

Fitzsimmons, E. L. 2002, April. Small cities abuzz with business in Nebraska. *Business in Nebraska 57*(666) 1-3. Bureau of Business Research.

Flora, C. B., J. L. Flora, G. P Green, & F. E. Schmidt. 1991. Rural economic development through local self-development strategies. *Annals of the American Academy of Political and Social Science* 529: 48-58.

Flora, J. L., & G. T. Johnson. 1991. Small business. Pp. 47-59 in C. B. Flora & J. A. Christenson (eds.), *Rural policies for the 1990s.* Boulder, CO: Westview.

Fruth, W. H. 1999. The flow of money and its impact on local economies. *Annual Conference of the National Association of Industrial and Office Properties.*

Ghelfi, L. & T. Parker. 1996. Urban influence. *Rural Development Perspectives* 12(2): 32-41.

Goodall, C. R., K. Kafadar, & J. W. Tukey. 1998. Computing and using rural versus urban measures in statistical applications. *The American Statistician* 52(1): 101-111.

Halstead, J. M., & S. C. Deller. 1997. Public infrastructure in economic development and growth: Evidence from rural manufacturers. *Journal of the Community Development Society* 28(2): 149-169.

Hanham, A. C., S. Loveridge, & B. Richardson. 1999. A national school-based entrepreneurship program offers promise. *Journal of the Community Development Society* 30(2): 115-130.

Hayden, F. G., D. C. Kruse, & S. C. Williams. 1985. Industrial policy at the state level in the United States. *Journal of Economic Issues* 19(2): 383-397.

Henderson, J. 1997. How important are small businesses in the 10th district? *Regional Economic Digest* 8(3): 9-14.

Hill, E. W. 1998. Principles for rethinking the federal government's role in economic development. *Economic Development Quarterly* 12(4): 299-312.

Kettering Foundation. 2000. *Creating a health (sustainable) economy for our community.* Dayton, OH: Kettering Foundation.

Koven, S. G., & T. S. Lyons. 2003. *Economic Development: Strategies for State and Local Practice.* International City/County Management Association, Washington D.C.

Leistritz, F. L., & R. R. Hamm. 1994. *Rural Economic Development, 1975-1993: An Annotated Bibliography.* Westport, CT: Greenwood Publishing Group.

Leistritz, F. L., & R. S. Sell. 2001. Socioeconomic impacts of agricultural processing plants. *Journal of the Community Development Society* 32(1): 130-159.

Lichenstein, G. A & T. S. Lyons. 2001. The entrepreneurial development system: Transforming business talent and community economics. *Economic Development Quarterly* 15(1): 3-20.

Lyons, T. S. 2003. Policies for Creating an Entrepreneurial Region. Pp. 97-105 in *Main Streets of Tomorrow: Growing and Financing Rural Entrepreneurs.* Center for the Study of Rural America, Federal Reserve Bank of Kansas City.

Miller, N. 1998. Local consumer spending: A reflection of rural community social and economic exchange. *Journal of the Community Development Society* 29(2): 166-185.

National Association of Public Administration. 1996. *A path to smarter economic development: Reassessing the federal role.* Washington, D.C.: National Academy of Public Administration.

Nolan, A. 2003. Entrepreneurship and Local Economic Development: Policy Innovations in Industrial Countries. Pp77-90 in *Main Streets of Tomorrow: Growing and Financing Rural Entrepreneurs.* Center for the Study of Rural America, Federal Reserve Bank of Kansas City.

Osborne, D. 1988. *Laboratories of Democracy.* Boston, MA: Harvard Business School Press.

Perry, S. C. 2001. The relationship between written business plans and the failure of small businesses. *Journal of Small Business Management* 39(3): 201-209.

Pigg, K. E. 1999. Community leadership and community theory: A practical synthesis. *Journal of the Community Development Society* 30(2): 196-212.

Presley, R. 1997, March. Entrepreneurial development: Key building block in Commerce economic development model. *Commerce Folio* (Oklahoma Department of Commerce) 5(6): 3.

Pulver, G. 1988. Community economic analysis. Pp. 3-25 in *Revitalizing Rural America: Getting Down to Business.* Corvallis, OR: Western Rural Development Center.

Reid, N. J. 1987. *Entrepreneurship as a Community Development Strategy for the Rural South.* Washington, DC: Economic Research Service, U. S. Dept. of Agriculture.

Rowe, B. R., G. W. Haynes, & K. Stafford. 1999. The contribution of home-based business income to rural and urban economies. *Economic Development Quarterly* 13(1): 66-77.

Rowley, T. D., D. W. Sears, G. L. Nelson, J. N. Reid, & M. J. Yetley (Eds.) 1996. *Rural Development Research: A Foundation for Policy.* Westport, CT: Greenwood Press.

Rupasingha, A., T. R. Wojan, & D. Freshwater. 1999. Self-organization and community-based development initiatives. *Journal of the Community Development Society* 30(1): 66-82.

Scudder, J. N. & L. S. Rettig. 1989. Recruitment strategies for new industry. *Public Relations Review* 15(8): 25-38.

Sexton, L A. 1999. Small business is good business. *Arkansas Business and Economic Review* 32(3): 18-19.

Shapero, A. 1987. Entrepreneurship. Pp. 115-135 in *Proceedings of the Community Economic Development Strategies Conference.* Ames, IA: Iowa State University, North Central Regional Center for Rural Development.

Sharp, J. S. & J. L Flora. 1999. Entrepreneurial social infrastructure and growth machine characteristics associated with industrial-recruitment and self-development in nonmetropolitan communities. *Journal of the Community Development Society* 30(2): 131-153.

Stanforth, N. & G. Muske. 1999. Family and consumer sciences students' interest in entrepreneurship education. *Journal of Family and Consumer Sciences* 91(4): 34-39.

Teitz, M. 1989. Neighborhood economics: Local communities and regional labor markets. *Economic Development Quarterly* 3(2): 111-122.

Tolbert, C. M., & T. C. Blanchard, Mi D. Irwin, T. A. Lyson, & A. R. Nucci. 2001, Fall. Engaging business: Civic engagement and locally oriented firms. *Southern Perspectives* 5(2): 1-2.

U. S. Bureau of Census. 2001. *Statistics about Business Size.* www.Census.gov/epcd. www/smallbus.html.

U. S. Bureau of the Census. 2001. *Statistics of U. S. Businesses: 1998.* www.census.gov/epcd/susb/1998/us/US—.htm.

U.S. Bureau of the Census. 2000. *Statistical Abstract of the United States: 1994* (120th ed.). Washington, DC: U. S. Dept. of Commerce

U. S. Chamber of Commerce. 1994. *Studies in Organizational Management.* Washington, DC: Industrial Development Institute Dept.

U. S. Department of Commerce, Bureau of Economic Analysis. 1992. *Regional Multipliers: A User's Handbook for the Regional Input-Output Modeling System (RIMS II)* (2nd ed.). Washington, DC: Government Printing Office.

U. S. Small Business Administration. 2002, February. New reports on small business share of GDP; Small business economic indicators. *The Small Business Advocate* 21(2): 2.

U. S. Small Business Administration. 2001. *Statistics of U. S. Businesses: Firm Size Data.* http://www.sbaonline.sba.gov/advo/stats/data.html.

U. S. Small Business Administration. 2000. *Employer Firms, Establishments, Employment and Annual Payroll by Firm Size and State.* Washington, DC: Small Business Administration. www.sba.gov/advo/stats/st.pdf.

Whatmore, S., P. L. Lowe, & T. Marsden. 1991. *Rural Enterprise: Shifting Perspectives on Small-Scale Production.* London: David Fulton.

Wiley, J. 1997. *Rural Sustainability in America.* London: Chichester.

Wilkinson, K. P. 1991. *The Community in Rural America.* New York: Greenwood Press.

Woods, M. D., V. J. Frye, & S. R. Ralstin. 1999. *Blueprints for Your Community's Future: Creating A Strategic Plan for Economic Development* (Fact sheet # WF-916). Stillwater, OK: Oklahoma Cooperative Extension Service.

Woods, M. D. & R. Rushing. 1995. Oklahoma's small business incubator network: An economic development tool. *Oklahoma Current Farm Economics* 68(3).

Woods, M. D. 2000. Diversifying the rural economy: Tourism develpment. In *The rural South: Preparing for the Challenges of the 21st Century, #10.* Mississippi State, MS: Southern Rural Development Center.

Woods, M. D. & L. Sanders. 1989. *Economic development for rural Oklahoma* (Fact sheet #858). Stillwater, OK: Oklahoma Cooperative Extension Service.

Woods, M. D. & L. Sanders. 1989. Rural development: A critical Oklahoma issue. *Current Farm Economic,* 62(3): 3-16.

Woods, M. D., N. Williams, C. Allan, & J. Frye. 1994. *Retention and expansion: A local economic development strategy* (Circular E-128). Stillwater, OK: Oklahoma Cooperative Extension Service.

Woodworth, W. P. 2000. Third World economic empowerment in the new millennium: Microenterprise, microentrepreneurship, and microfinance. *S. A. M. Advanced Management Journal* 65(4): 19-28.

CITIZEN PARTICIPATION IN NONPROFIT ECONOMIC DEVELOPMENT ORGANIZATIONS

By Daniel Monroe Sullivan

ABSTRACT

Citizen participation in community development, including economic development, is vital for a viable democratic society to flourish. As more U.S. cities shift some or all of their economic development efforts from the city government to nonprofit economic development organizations (NEDOs) – which use resources from both the public and business sector to promote local economic growth – it is important to examine what implications this shift has on citizen participation. Some researchers highlight the advantages of NEDOs, portraying them as high-performing organizations that facilitate cooperation between city government and the local business community. But are there any disadvantages to promoting development via NEDOs in terms of citizen participation? Using survey data from nearly 500 NEDOs, this study finds that the local business community and city government are heavily involved in NEDOs, including founding them and contributing board members, money, and policy advice. However, in most NEDOs, citizens who are not part of local business organizations do not participate directly, but they participate indirectly through their public officials. Community development practitioners should work towards increasing direct citizen participation in NEDOs, especially when NEDOs use significant public resources.

INTRODUCTION

Researchers and practitioners alike have long asserted the importance of citizen involvement in the community development decision-making process (Daley & Marsiglia, 2001; Gaunt, 1998), including the promotion of economic development (Sharp & Flora, 1999). Citizen involvement is essential for genuine local and representative democracy to develop. In addition, citizens can help identify community needs, articulate development goals to meet these needs, and contribute their knowledge and skills.

Starting in the 1970s, city governments began to promote economic development actively by engaging in an array of activities such as operating industrial parks, running small business incubators, and orchestrating downtown revitalization programs (Clarke & Gaile, 1998). More recently, cities have created nonprofit economic development organizations (NEDOs) to help promote

This material is based upon work supported by the Cooperative State Research, Education and Extension Service, U.S. Department of Agriculture, National Research Initiative, under agreement no. 97-35401-4353. Any opinion, finding, conclusions, or recommendations expressed in this publication are those of the author and do not necessarily reflect the view of the U.S. Department of Agriculture.

development (Clarke, 1998; Humphrey & Erickson, 1997; Sullivan, 1998). NEDOs are nonprofit organizations that use resources from both the public and business sector to promote economic growth in a city or region; they are often called industrial development corporations or economic development corporations.

Given the importance of citizen involvement in promoting economic development, coupled with the rise in popularity of NEDOs, the main goal of this paper is to examine the extent to which citizens participate in NEDOs. For example, are citizens allowed to attend meetings? Do they elect the boards of directors? Do citizens' organizations have regular contact with NEDOs?

Despite the growing popularity of NEDOs, there is still a dearth of knowledge about them. Although there have been some case studies of NEDOs, primarily in large cities, there have been few national studies and even fewer that have examined case studies in small and mid-sized cities. I address these shortcomings by using survey data from nearly 500 NEDOs in cities of all sizes from throughout the United States.

Nonprofit Economic Development Organizations

NEDOs are nonprofit organizations that straddle the public-private divide. In certain respects, NEDOs are similar to government economic development agencies. Most NEDOs have access to public funding (Humphrey & Erickson, 1997), typically in the form of city government bonds, and they have exclusive access to specific local tax revenue streams (e.g., a hotel tax) or development funds from the county, state, or federal government that pass through the city government to them. NEDOs may have access to such public resources as government office space, office equipment, and staff support. City governments may transfer public authorities to them, including eminent domain, zoning, and authorization to lend public money to businesses. Some NEDOs that lack formal control over these public authorities can still use them through their city government with minimal oversight.

In other respects, NEDOs look like private business organizations. Many receive part of their funding from private sources, for example, from membership dues or donations (Humphrey & Erickson, 1997). In addition, NEDOs often coordinate their activities with business organizations such as the chambers of commerce, and many of their board members come from the business community.

Rise in Popularity

NEDOs started to become popular during the 1980s, and they have been growing in popularity ever since. The 1998 *Local Government Economic Development Survey* conducted by the author reports that 89 percent of cities have at least one NEDO, either operating in their city (64 percent) or in their county (83 percent). They are the most active promoter of economic development in 19 percent of the cities.

There are several reasons that explain their popularity. Starting in the 1970s, a series of events negatively affected many local economies. Companies were going out of business or moving to lower-wage areas such as developing countries. Furthermore, at a time when cities needed additional assistance from the federal government to combat these economic troubles, federal support was declining (Fainstein & Fainstein, 1989). As a result, large cities, followed by smaller ones, became more aggressive in attempts to stimulate their local economy.

Entrepreneurial city governments often promote development with assistance from their local business community. They form public-private partnerships, many of which are institutionalized in the form of NEDOs (Walzer & Jacobs, 1998). Case studies have shown that the main benefit of these public-private partnerships is that city government and business organizations have unique resources and expertise that complement one another (Premus & Blair, 1991). City governments, for their part, often have planners and economic developers in their agencies, possess vital public powers such as eminent domain and zoning, and have exclusive access to public funding – both local funding and development funds from the county, state, and federal governments.

Business leaders have a set of skills that complement those of the city government, including marketing, accounting, negotiating with businesses, writing contracts, and performing cost-benefit analyses (Austin & McCaffrey, 2002; Premus & Blair, 1991). In addition, operating NEDOs tend to improve communication and build strong bonds of trust between government officials and business leaders, who facilitate cross-sector cooperation and minimize conflict.

Citizen Involvement in NEDOs

Despite the popularity of NEDOs, some researchers and community leaders are critical of them. Their main criticism is that NEDOs use public resources but are not accountable to the public. Community developers should be concerned because critics argue that many NEDOs are undemocratic organizations that give local business leaders easy access to their decision-making process, while citizens who are not business leaders are largely marginalized.

For example, local business leaders have an easier time influencing NEDOs than city governments (Humphrey & Erickson, 1997). Many NEDO board members themselves come from the business community, bringing with them a general pro-business, pro-growth agenda (Brown et al., 2000). These board members are heavily embedded in the local business community, facilitating strong inter-organizational relations between NEDOs and local business organizations such as chambers of commerce. In these ways, NEDOs are in tune with the local business community: they share similar goals and define problems and solutions in similar ways.

In addition, citizens tend to not be involved in NEDOs. It is very difficult for citizens to get on NEDO boards of directors because few board members are publicly elected (Kantor, 1995). Instead, some board members are chosen because of their official position in the business community; for example, slots may be designated for the presidents of the chambers of commerce or utility companies.

Others are nominated by NEDO members, who are themselves from the business community and tend to favor electing other business leaders. To be considered for nomination one may already have to be a member of the organization, which can involve making substantial financial contributions that many citizens cannot afford.

Citizens may be uninvolved for several other reasons. Some NEDOs do not open their meetings to the public and do not publicly advertise them. In addition, public funding for NEDOs is often not exposed to annual city government budgetary scrutiny. Instead, off-budget allocations – either pass-through grants from the state and federal government, or local off-budget allocations (e.g., sales tax revenues) – allow public money to be automatically channeled to NEDOs with no public debate and often with little public knowledge (Kantor, 1995; Squires, 1996).

Potential Benefits of Citizen Involvement

Many community development researchers and practitioners assert that citizen participation in city government decision-making is an essential element of genuine democracy. Gaunt (1998) asserts that there should be an open "communication process" whereby citizens are involved in a "mutual exchange of information, reaction, and dialogue for the purpose of influencing decision making" (p. 277). Berry et al. (1993) agree that there needs to be citizen involvement and further argue that their involvement should be "structured," thus enabling citizens to have a routine voice in the policy-making process. Given that NEDOs rather than government development agencies are becoming an increasing popular type of organization to promote economic development, it follows from the above argument that citizen participation in NEDOs could be similarly important.

Gaunt (1998), building on the work of Warner (1971), posits that there are three general ways in which citizens can participate. (1) *Informational participation* means that citizens receive information from NEDOs, for example information about upcoming development projects and the amount of public money that will be used. Although this level of participation is the least influential of the three, it does allow citizens to serve as "watchdogs" (Burke, 1983), and it may lead to more active citizen participation in the future. (2) *Review participation* refers to citizens not only obtaining information about development projects but also commenting on the proposed projects before they are implemented. This level of participation allows citizens to express their needs and interests, which may be different from those of business leaders (Abatena, 1997; Daley & Marsiglia, 2001), and to evaluate whether the project will satisfy those needs. The limitation of review participation is that citizen participation is merely reactive; they are not involved in designing the development projects. (3) The third and highest level is *interactive participation* whereby citizens are involved in development projects from the early stages. They help define the problems and needs of the community and participate in designing projects that can meet these needs.

Repercussions of Citizen Involvement. Advocates of citizen participation argue that when citizens are left out of the decision-making process, development projects tend to focus exclusively on growth and pay little attention to equality or benefiting non-elite residents. In larger cities, this exclusive focus on growth may be manifested in developers benefiting disproportionately from such projects as downtown office buildings, retail centers, performing arts centers, and sports stadiums (Cummings, 1988; Eisinger, 2000; Squires, 1989). These projects rarely benefit neighborhood residents, especially those who are low-income, because they are often not hired, or are hired for low-wage, low-skill jobs in the service sector. Funding large downtown projects may also lead to cities having less money for municipal services that are vital to neighborhood residents, such as policing, street maintenance, public education, and parks. In smaller cities and rural areas this may be manifested in recruiting manufacturers or meatpacking plants that tend to hire in-migrants and pay low wages, which do not benefit local residents (Davidson, 1991; Summers, et al. 1976).

In contrast, citizen involvement can lead to more progressive development policies. Research has shown that city governments influenced by citizens implement policies that make explicit attempts to ensure that residents benefit more from development. Elkins (1995) finds that neighborhood group activism increases the likelihood that cities require developers to create low- and middle-income housing in new development projects. Goetz (1994) finds that neighborhood group activism has a positive impact on the number of progressive policies adopted, including requiring the participation of women- and minority-owned businesses. Other researchers have documented citizen and neighborhood groups advocating rent control (Clavel, 1986), living wages (Pollin & Luce, 1998), and local banks contributing to community reinvestment funds (Squires, 1992). In rural areas, Flora et al. (1991) identify over 100 "self-development" projects that involve a diverse array of local residents. Sharp and Flora (1999) find that when this diversity of local actors is absent, more traditional business organizations tend to favor industrial recruitment.

In this paper, I examine the extent to which citizens are involved in NEDOs. A major weakness of previous NEDO studies is that most only examine one or a few NEDOs, and usually only those operating in large cities. Therefore, it is difficult to know whether their findings are generalizable to other NEDOs, especially those in small and mid-sized cities. To address these shortcomings I use survey data to examine nearly 500 NEDOs that are located in cities of all sizes.

METHODOLOGY

Data come from the 1999 *National Economic Development Organization Survey.* One of the obstacles to collecting information on NEDOs is that there is no comprehensive list. To develop the list, I first conducted a mail survey in 1998 of all municipalities with a population greater than 2,500. City government officials familiar with economic development identified all NEDOs operating in their municipality or region. The resulting list of NEDOs was then expanded through an extensive search on the Internet.

In total, 1,306 NEDOs were identified and sent surveys. A total of 666 NEDOs responded, resulting in a 51 percent response rate. Of these, 204 are excluded because they are either purely public or purely private organizations. Purely public organizations are those whose entire budget comes from public sources, and they have either no board of director or one composed of only public officials. Purely private organizations are those whose entire budgets come from private sources, that have a board of directors composed of only private sector persons, and that have no direct authority to use public powers (zoning, eminent domain, ability to give public subsidies). Overall, 462 cases are included in this study. Table 1 shows that about half of NEDOs operate in metropolitan counties and half in nonmetropolitan counties. Many of the NEDOs are in smaller cities (2,500 to 25,000 residents), and there are more from the Midwest and South than from the Northeast and West.

Table 1. Characteristics of Cities that Have Nonprofit Economic Development Organizations

	N	percent
Metropolitan county	220	48%
Nonmetropolitan county	237	52%
Population size	237	52%
2,500 - 9,999	263	58%
10,000 - 24,999	111	24%
25,000 - 49,999	49	11%
50,000 - 99,999	18	4%
100,000 +	5	1%
Region		
Northeast	67	15%
Midwest	137	30%
South	167	36%
West	91	20%

N = 462

Indicators

The main goal of this paper is to examine how citizens are involved in NEDOs. The term "citizen" is difficult to define. Technically all residents of a city are citizens. However, for this paper, I use the term "citizen" to refer to residents who are not involved in a business organization (e.g., chamber of commerce, utility company, developer) or some other leadership position (e.g., city or county government official or economic development expert affiliated with higher education institution or Extension). The term "citizen/neighborhood organization" refers to such non-business and non-governmental organizations as neighborhood associations, citizen advisory boards, and church groups (that deal with economic development issues). Although it is possible that members of citizen and neighborhood organizations are also local business leaders (or government officials or experts affiliated with a higher education institution or Extension), they are not formally serving in those roles while they are participating in citizen or neighborhood organizations.

Citizen involvement can be measured directly (through citizen participation) and indirectly (through the participation of public officials). Citizen involvement in NEDOs is measured six ways: participation in founding NEDOs, funding NEDOs, electing their board of directors, NEDOs opening their meetings to the public, NEDOs notifying the public of their meetings, and NEDOs maintaining routine relations with citizen/neighborhood organizations and public agencies.

In regards to this last way of measuring citizen involvement – relations with other organizations – I compare NEDO relations to city government relations. In particular, I pay close attention to whether, on the one hand, city officials have closer ties to citizen and neighborhood organizations (citizen advisory boards, neighborhood associations, and church groups) and public organizations (county, state and federal government, regional planning commission, universities, technical and community colleges, and Extension) while, on the other hand, NEDOs have closer ties to business organizations (chambers of commerce, utilities, and developers). In this section of the analysis, I only examine local NEDOs, – i.e., NEDOs that operate within the same geographical boundaries as their city governments – to compare their relations to city governments more fairly. NEDOs are excluded from this part of the analysis if they span several cities or an entire county, or if they operate only in one part of a city.

Inter-organizational relations are measured three ways: interaction, policy coordination, and participation in developing strategies. Interaction is measured by asking local NEDOs and city governments how frequently they interact with other actors specifically regarding economic development. There are three levels of interaction: at least yearly, at least monthly, and at least weekly. Policy coordination is measured by how frequently local NEDOs and city governments coordinate specific policy activities with other organizations: never, sometimes, usually, and always. If NEDOs coordinate at least sometimes, they identify with which specific organizations they coordinate. Participation is measured by asking whether NEDOs allow other organizations to participate in developing their economic development strategies. If they answer "yes" to that question, they indicate all of the organizations that participate and which of these is the most influential.

FINDINGS

Overall, the survey findings show that business organizations and city and county governments are heavily involved in NEDOs, but citizens are not. In the majority of cases, citizens are only involved indirectly through their government officials. In terms of founding NEDOs, at least one public institution is involved in founding 82 percent of them, while at least one business organization is involved in creating 71 percent of them. Table 2 illustrates that city governments are by far the most frequently involved in establishing NEDOs, in terms of having any involvement (71 percent of NEDOs) and being the most involved (23 percent). One other public institution – county government – and two types of business actors – chamber of commerce and "other business persons" – are also involved in a substantial number of cases. In contrast, citizen and neighborhood organizations are rarely involved in any capacity.

The mean 1999 budget for NEDOs is $359,162 (median $155,000). Sixty-two percent of their funding come from public sources and 33 percent come from private sources (5 percent come from other sources). The most common sources of public funding are city government revenues (69 percent of NEDOs receive them) and county government revenues (58 percent). The most common private sources are contributions from individual businesses (47 percent) and chambers of commerce (38 percent), and NEDO membership dues (34 percent).

Table 2. Organizations Involved in Founding NEDOs

	Any Involvement	Most Involved
City government	71%	23%
County government	48%	21%
Chamber of commerce	44%	17%
Other business persons	44%	16%
Utility company	26%	4%
Developers	17%	3%
County NEDO	15%	2%
State government	13%	2%
Higher education institution	13%	2%
Citizen/neighborhood organization	13%	1%
Private consultant	8%	0%
Federal government	5%	0%

N = 462

Overall, NEDOs have less citizen involvement than do city governments. For example, although city government meetings must be open to the public by law, there is wide variation in public access to NEDO meetings. On one extreme, 48 percent of NEDOs always open their meetings to the public, while on the other extreme, 17 percent of NEDOs never allow the public to attend. The remaining 35 percent sometimes or usually open their meetings to the public. When they close their meetings to the public, they often discuss their dealings with particular businesses, including negotiating with specific firms (73 percent) or discussing financial incentives to offer to firms (54 percent). Fewer NEDOs notify the public of their meetings. Forty-three percent always notify, but 30 percent never do so. The remaining 28 percent sometimes or usually notify the public of their meetings. Not surprising, those NEDOs that open more of their meetings to the public also tend to notify the public more often of upcoming meetings (Spearman's rho = 0.659).

In terms of selecting NEDO board of directors, over half are elected without any public involvement. Forty-four percent are elected by NEDO members, and a small percentage are appointed because of their position in a business organization like the chamber of commerce (7 percent) or because they contribute financially to their NEDO (3 percent). Of those appointments that involve public input, most are indirect because they are appointed by city and county governments (33 percent). A small percentage of members are public officials themselves (6 percent) and, most significantly, very few are elected directly by voters (4 percent).

Local NEDO Relations with Other Organizations

In this section, I examine only local NEDOs – i.e., NEDOs that operate within the same geographical boundaries as their city governments. Overall, the survey findings indicate that local NEDOs tend to interact most frequently with city officials and local business organizations, especially the chambers of commerce, and they rarely interact with citizen and neighborhood organizations. In terms of weekly interaction, Table 3 illustrates that 57 percent interact with city officials and 43 percent interact with their chambers. Some also interact weekly with several other business actors – developers, banks, utilities, – and their county governments. Few local NEDOs interact with citizen and neighborhood organizations, higher education institutions, or state and federal government agencies.

Table 4 shows that most local NEDOs (97 percent) coordinate their development projects at least sometimes with one or more development organizations. Many local NEDOs coordinate with city government (81 percent) and chamber of commerce (68 percent), and some coordinate with developers, utilities, county NEDOs, and county government. Few coordinate with citizen and neighborhood organizations.

Sixty-three percent of local NEDOs allow one or more organizations to participate in developing their economic development strategies. City government is by far the most frequent participant (54 percent), followed by a number of business organizations – chambers (33 percent), utilities (28 percent), and developers (22 percent) – and their county government (21 percent) (see Table 5). Only 11 percent of local NEDOs allow citizen and neighborhood organizations to be involved.

Local NEDOs that cite at least one organization participating in developing their strategies are then asked to name the one organization that is most influential. Local NEDOs report that city government is most often the most influential participant (61 percent); sixteen percent identify their chamber of commerce or county NEDO. All other organizations are rarely or never the most influential, including citizen and neighborhood organizations.

Table 3. Comparing Local NEDOs and City Governments, by Interaction with Other Development Organizations

	Yearly Interaction			Monthly Interaction			Weekly Interaction		
	Local NEDO	City Gov't	t-stat	Local NEDO	City Gov't	t-stat	Local NEDO	City Gov't	t-stat
City government (118)	95%	—	—	—	87%	—	—	57%	—
Local NEDO (107)	—	97%	—	—	81%	—	—	44%	—
Chamber of commerce (114)	90%	96%	1.965**	83%	86%	-0.726	43%	50%	1.302
County government (112)	89%	88%	-0.425	63%	51%	2.254**	18%	24%	1.406
Developers (106)	87%	84%	-0.687	58%	63%	-0.948	20%	22%	0.598
State government (115)	86%	90%	0.815	39%	35%	0.761	7%	12%	1.420
Financial institution (113)	83%	81%	-0.352	62%	51%	1.645*	16%	7%	-2.742***
Utility (115)	81%	89%	1.818*	55%	59%	-0.799	17%	23%	1.352
County NEDO (91)	66%	71%	0.799	45%	56%	-1.683*	10%	10%	0.000
Community college (81)	62%	54%	-1.521	26%	31%	-0.754	5%	4%	-0.332
Consultants (92)	61%	65%	0.616	23%	35%	-2.000	8%	11%	0.894
Regional planning commission (96)	61%	69%	1.553	22%	48%	-4.117****	4%	6%	1.000
Federal government (110)	56%	60%	0.744	6%	15%	-1.990***	0%	2%	1.421
University/college (65)	50%	42%	-1.488	20%	31%	-1.473	4%	4%	0.000
Citizen advisory board (60)	39%	46%	1.421	27%	58%	-4.113****	2%	9%	2.596****
Extension (67)	33%	37%	0.665	13%	19%	-1.000	3%	3%	0.000
Church group (99)	25%	31%	1.136	7%	9%	-0.533	2%	1%	-0.575
Neighborhood association (60)	25%	31%	1.061	2%	27%	-4.086****	1%	5%	1.646*

*p<.10, **p<.05, ***p<.01, ****p<.001

Comparing Local NEDOs and City Governments

Table 3 indicates that local NEDOs and city officials have in some respects similar levels of interaction with other development organizations, including business organizations, supra-local government agencies, and higher educational institutions. However, there are several notable exceptions. More local NEDOs meet monthly or weekly with financial institutions, and more city governments meet at least yearly with chambers of commerce and utilities. City governments are also more likely to meet monthly with two regional institutions: county NEDOs and regional planning commissions. In addition, city governments are far more likely to interact with citizen advisory boards and neighborhood associations regarding economic development issues. For example, more than twice as many city governments than local NEDOs interact at least monthly with citizen advisory boards (58 percent vs. 27 percent), and while 27 percent of city governments meet at least monthly with neighborhood associations, only 2 percent of local NEDOs do so.

Local NEDOs and their city governments also exhibit similar levels of overall policy coordination with other development organizations (see Table 4). They also tend to coordinate with the same organizations. Over 80 percent of local NEDOs and city governments coordinate with each other, and many coordinate with their chamber, county NEDO, county government, utility, and developers. Local NEDOs and city governments rarely coordinate with citizen and neighborhood organizations.

Table 4. Comparing Local NEDOs and City Governments, by Policy Coordination

	Local NEDO	City Government	t-statistic
Does your organization coordinate its economic development activities with another organization(s)?			
Always	27%	31%	0.821
Usually	35%	39%	0.564
Sometimes	34%	28%	-1.338
Never	3%	3%	-0.377
With which organization(s) does your organization coordinate?			
City government	81%	—	—
Local NEDO	—	86%	—
Chamber of commerce	68%	72%	0.665
County NEDO	44%	54%	1.615
County government	42%	34%	-1.346
Utility company	39%	37%	-0.427
Developers	36%	27%	-1.482
Citizen/neighborhood org.	9%	12%	0.687

N = 117

The biggest difference between local NEDOs and city governments is apparent in terms of allowing other organizations to help develop their own economic development strategies. Eighty-three percent of city governments allow one or more organizations to participate, compared to only 63 percent of local

NEDOs. Table 5 illustrates that city governments allow a higher percentage of all types of organizations to participate, including business organizations, supra-local government agencies, higher educational institutions, and citizen and neighborhood organizations. City governments are especially more likely to allow the participation of supra-local organizations: county NEDOs, state government, and federal government. In terms of the most influential organization, it is not surprising that many local NEDOs are most influenced by their city government (61 percent), and that many city governments are most influenced by local NEDOs (63 percent). Eight to ten percent of local NEDOs and city governments report that chambers of commerce and county governments are the most influential organizations. Almost no other public or private sector organization is the most influential, including citizen and neighborhood organizations.

Table 5. Comparing Local NEDOs and City Governments, by Other Development Organizations Involvement in Developing Economic Development Strategies

	Local NEDO	City Government	t-statistic
Any Involvement[1]			
City government	54%	—	—
Local NEDO	—	73%	—
Chamber of commerce	33%	65%	5.046****
Utility company	28%	38%	1.871*
Developers	22%	37%	2.596***
County government	21%	38%	3.126***
County NEDO	16%	45%	5.345****
Higher education institution	13%	22%	2.071**
Citizen/neighborhood org.	11%	20%	1.986**
Private consultant	11%	22%	2.561**
State government	9%	26%	3.349****
Federal government	2%	8%	2.143**
Most influential[2]			
City government	61%	—	
Local NEDO	—	63%	
Chamber of commerce	8%	9%	
County NEDO	8%	10%	
County government	3%	1%	
Higher education institution	3%	1%	
Utility company	3%	0%	
Citizen/neighborhood org.	1%	5%	
Developers	0%	0%	
State government	0%	4%	
Private consultant	0%	5%	
Federal government	0%	0%	

Notes: Local NEDOs operate only in one city. For most influential, "other" = 12 percent for NEDOs and 1 percent for city governments.

1: N = 117; 2: N = 71 for local EDOs, and N = 92 for city governments. Because they have different number of cases, I could not perform a paired t-test.

* p<.10, **p<.05, ***p<.01, ****p<.001

DISCUSSION

Given that more cities are putting public resources into NEDOs to promote economic development, the goal of this paper is to examine the extent to which citizens are involved in the NEDO decision-making process.

My findings indicate that citizens are more likely to be indirectly involved through their public officials than directly involved in NEDOs. City and county governments are often involved in creating NEDOs, and they tend to be the biggest financial contributors. In addition, NEDOs have more contact with city officials than with any business organization, and they have some contact with other public institutions such as county governments and higher educational institutions. Therefore, overall, *if* government officials involved in NEDOs represent the interests of non-business citizens, then we can say that, indirectly, citizens have some influence over NEDOs.

However, citizens are less involved directly in NEDOs, and this may be a point of concern for community development practitioners. For example, although city and county government meetings must be publicly announced and open to the public by law, NEDOs are not obligated to announce or hold public meetings. As a result, some NEDOs do not notify the public of their meetings or allow the public to attend. Thus, even the weakest form of citizen participation – informational participation – is not available in all NEDOs. In addition, it is difficult for citizens who are not business leaders to become members of their boards of directors because few board members are publicly elected. Rather, most are voted in by NEDO members or appointed by government officials. Moreover, citizen and neighborhood organizations that are interested in economic development rarely have contact with NEDOs, in terms of interaction, policy coordination, or assistance in developing NEDO strategies. Although it is true that many citizen and neighborhood groups do not have relations with their city government about economic development issues, even fewer have relations with their NEDOs. These findings suggest that the two strongest forms of citizen participation – review and interactive participation – are not available in many NEDOs.

Overall, these findings suggest that community development practitioners should examine their community NEDOs to determine how many public resources they use and how much opportunity there is for citizen involvement. Citizen involvement is not only important for infusing democracy into local economic development, but it is also vital for representing the diversity of community interests and perspectives. Greater diversity can translate into identifying and developing solutions for a wider array of needs and problems so that development projects do not only reflect the interests of the business community.

In cities that already have NEDOs, community development practitioners should work towards increasing direct citizen access to NEDO decision-making, especially when NEDOs use substantial public resources. In cities that are contemplating founding NEDOs, community development practitioners should encourage NEDOs to allow citizen participation, ideally institutionalizing their participation in the NEDO charter. In terms of specific recommendations, at the very least NEDO meetings should be open to the public and advertised in the local newspaper, and NEDOs (and government officials) should be forthright about the amount of public resources they use. In addition, to represent a more diverse array of community perspectives, NEDOs should consider allowing citizens who are not business leaders to become members and to sit on their boards of directors.

REFERENCES

Abatena, H. 1997. The significance of planned community participation in problem solving and developing a stable community capability. *Journal of Community Practice* 4(2): 13-34.

Austin, J. & A. McCaffrey. 2002. Business leadership coalitions and public-private partnerships in American cities. *Journal of Urban Affairs* 24(1): 35-54.

Berry, J. M., K. E. Portney, & K. Thompson. 1993. *The Rebirth of Urban Democracy*. Washington D. C.: The Brookings Institution.

Brown, R., A. B. Nylander III, B. G. King, & B. Lough. 2000. Growth machine attitudes and community development in two racially diverse rural Mississippi Delta communities. *Journal of the Community Development Society* 31(2): 173-195.

Burke, E. M. 1983. Citizen participation. Pp. 105-127 in R. M. Kramer & H. Specht (eds.), *Readings in Community Organization Practice* (3rd ed.). Englewood Cliffs, NJ: Prentice Hall.

Clarke, S. E. 1998. Economic development roles in American cities. Pp. 19-45 in N. Walzer & B. D. Jacobs (eds.), *Public-Private Partnerships for Local Economic Development*. Westport, CT: Praeger.

Clarke, S. E. & G. L. Gaile. 1998. *The Work of Cities*. Minneapolis: University of Minnesota Press.

Clavel, P. 1986. *The Progressive City*. New Brunswick, NJ: Rutgers University Press.

Cummings, S. (ed.) 1988. *Business Elites and Urban Development*. New York: SUNY Press.

Daley, J. M. & F. F. Marsiglia. 2001. Social diversity within nonprofit boards. *Journal of the Community Development Society* 32(2): 290-309.

Davidson, O. G. 1991. *Broken Heartland*. New York: Anchor Books.

Eisinger, P. 2000. The politics of bread and circuses. *Urban Affairs Review* 35(3): 316-333.

Elkins, D. R. 1995. Testing competing explanations for the adoption of type II policies. *Urban Affairs Review* 30: 809-839.

Fainstein, S. S. & N. Fainstein. 1989. The ambivalent state. *Urban Affairs Quarterly* 25: 41-62.

Flora, J. L., J. L. Chriss, E. Gale, G. P. Green, F. E. Schmidt, & C. Flora. 1991. *From the Grassroots*. Washington D.C.: USDA, Economic Research Service.

Goetz, E. G. 1994. Expanding possibilities in local development policy. *Political Research Quarterly* 47: 85-109.

Gaunt, T. P. 1998. Communication, social networks, and influence in citizen participation. *Journal of the Community Development Society* 29(2): 276-297.

Humphrey, C. R. & R. A. Erickson. 1997. Public accountability in nonprofit industrial development organizations. *Voluntas* 8(1): 39-63.

Kantor, P. 1995. *The Dependent City Revisited*. Boulder: Westview Press.

Pollin, R. & S. Luce. 1998. *The Living Wage*. New York: New Press.

Premus, R. & J. P. Blair. 1991. Economic development planning as a relay. *Policy Studies Review* 10(2-3): 99-108.

Sharp, J. S. & J. L. Flora. 1999. Entrepreneurial social infrastructure and growth machine characteristics associated with industrial-recruitment and self-development strategies in nonmetropolitan communities. *Journal of the Community Development Society* 30: 131-153.

Squires, G. D. (ed.). 1989. *Unequal Partnerships*. London: Rutgers University Press.

Squires, G. D. (ed.). 1992. *From Redlining to Reinvestment*. Philadelphia: Temple University Press.

Squires, G. D. 1996. Partnership and the pursuit of the private city. Pp. 266-290 in S. S. Fainstein & S. Campbell (eds.), *Readings in Urban Theory*. Blackwell Publishers.

Sullivan, D. 1998. Local economic development organizations in small- and middle-sized communities. *Research in Community Sociology* 8: 143-157.

Summers, G. F., S. Evans, E. Clemente, & J. Minkoff. 1976. *Industrial Invasion of Nonmetropolitan America*. New York: Praeger.

Warner, K. P. 1971. *Public Participation in Water Resource Planning*. Arlington, VA: National Water Commission.

Walzer, N. & B. D. Jacobs. 1998. *Public-Private Partnerships for Local Economic Development*. Westport, CT: Praeger.

Community Development Corporations as Vehicles of Community Economic Development: The Case of Rural Manitoba

Kenneth C. Bessant

Researchers and practitioners routinely discuss the impact of urbanization, globalization, fiscal retrenchment, and service devolution on rural livelihoods. These wide-scale transformations have prompted the search for alternative modes and mechanisms of community development. Over the past decade, interest in community economic development (CED) has grown significantly in various parts of rural Canada. CED constitutes a comprehensive, integrated approach to economic and social revitalization that calls upon local residents, leaders, and organizations to assume more active roles in all aspects of the development process. In Manitoba, government and community representatives view community development corporations (CDCs) as important vehicles of CED, particularly through the enhancement of community capacity. The present paper examines the degree of interconnectedness between core aspects of the CED framework and the emergent role(s) of CDCs. This goal is addressed through the discussion of relevant literature and questionnaire data gathered from representatives of 55 rural Manitoba CDCs. The results of the study indicate that CDC mandates and activities reflect CED principles such as multi-sectoral initiatives, community involvement, strategic planning, and inter-organizational partnerships. And, although there is growing recognition of the social development agenda, CDC functions are heavily focused on business and economic development. The CDC model offers important opportunities to integrate economic renewal with other types of community capacity building: leadership development, collective action, and inter-organizational relations.

The future of rural communities in Canada and the United States has been the subject of basic and applied research for a good portion of the last century. Social scientists, practitioners, and policy analysts routinely discuss the challenges associated with building sustainable rural communities in the "arena society" (Fuller, 1994) or the "information age" (Allen & Dillman, 1994). Urbanization, globalization, fiscal retrenchment, and service devolution are commonly identified as factors impacting rural adjustment. Shragge (2003, p. 110) remarks that economic restructuring has led "the state and other social actors [to] attribute greater importance to the community sector as the source of social provision through the community development model." A variety of community-based organizations (CBOs) have emerged in response to the unique conditions and constraints affecting rural livelihoods. Chaland and Downing (2003, p. 13) estimate that there are "well over 3,000 community organizations or initiatives engaged in community economic development [CED] in Canada." CED, in general, refers to an integrated, multifaceted

Kenneth C. Bessant, Associate Professor, Department of Rural Development, Brandon University
The author gratefully acknowledges the contributions of Erasmus D. Monu (Brandon University),
Ted K. Bradshaw (Journal Editor), and the anonymous reviewers. Support for this research project was provided by
The Rural Development Institute, Brandon University, Brandon, Manitoba, CANADA.

approach to community improvement that includes but is not limited to generating economic opportunities and ameliorating social conditions.

The CED perspective has garnered extensive theoretical and practical interest; however, less attention has been focused explicitly on the interplay between CED principles and the functions (or activities) of CBOs. Community development corporations (CDCs) represent one facet of a broad movement toward increased local control over and participation in rural planning and development processes. CDCs are self-help organizations whose primary mandate is to mobilize the resources needed to effect economic and social revitalization. Perry (1989, p. 3) defines the term CDC as "a coalition organization of local residents to carry out their own comprehensive program[s] of community renewal activities." He makes direct linkages between the CDC model and fundamental aspects of the CED approach, for example, community participation and leadership, local control, cross-sector alliances, resource mobilization, and integrated social and economic goals. It is argued here that CDCs in rural Manitoba are becoming increasingly aligned with the CED approach to enhancing community capacity, local assets, economic self-reliance, civic involvement, and quality of life dimensions. The paper establishes a context for examining this thesis by first providing a brief overview of the emergence of the CDC model, followed by a comparative overview of several core CED principles and the CDC concept in rural Manitoba. The supporting analysis integrates existing literature with the results of a survey (i.e., mail-out questionnaire) of 55 Manitoba CDCs.

The Community Development Corporation (CDC) Model: Origins and Aspects

CBOs represent important sources of leadership, innovation, input, and collaboration around community development. Local development organizations (LDOs), and more specifically CDCs, "arose in the United States during the 1960s, a period of intense social activism, especially in the area of civil rights" (Brodhead, Lamontagne, & Peirce, 1990, p. 2). Blakely and Bradshaw (2002, p. 283) trace the initial concept of the CDC to the *War on Poverty* (1966) and a subsequent amendment to the *Economic Opportunity Act*. Over time, the initial focus on inner-city renewal expanded to include a wide range of community contexts and concerns, for example, rural issues such as economic deterioration, unemployment, and inadequate services. Brodhead et al. (1990, pp. 3–5) identify three phases of the CDC movement in the United States: (a) "advocacy and political action," (b) economic development activities based on partnerships with private and public sectors and, (c) beginning in the 1990s, a more entrepreneurial focus, that is, "an increasingly strong market orientation and . . . sharply focussed approach to business development." There was a parallel evolution of CDCs in Canada and, much like the United States experience, Manitoba CDCs (and their close counterparts, Regional Development Corporations [RDCs]) were established in response to the problems of economically and socially disadvantaged communities and areas. The CDC represents one particular type of CBO that focuses on long-term community revitalization. The emergence of CBOs in Canada is perhaps best understood in terms of the tradition of "community self-help" embodied in the cooperative movement that began in the early twentieth century (Brodhead et al., 1990, p. 6). Although CBOs are quite variable in nature, they commonly embrace both economic and social goals, for example, housing, community loan funds, business development, and local training initiatives.

Deaton (1975, p. 31) contends that the growing disenchantment with traditional, externally controlled economic development has generated "a new thrust" that "is best exemplified by grass-roots pressures to redefine through democratic means the economic destiny of community and either to maintain or to gain additional local decision-making power over the political and economic realm of the community." He and other authors describe CDCs as alternative mechanisms of rural development and "community self-determination" (Deaton, 1975, p. 32). The term community development corporation refers to a broad category of not-for-profit organizations designed to carry out a range of functions aimed at promoting economic and social development. MacLeod (1986, p. 55) refers to the CDC as "a new and emerging model," one whose "basic goal is community development and improvement through the use of economic resources." He suggests that CDCs are similar to cooperatives in that they attempt to "combine social purpose with economic realities" (MacLeod, 1986, p. 56). The CDC can take the form of an umbrella-like organization that addresses a variety of economic, social, cultural, and environmental issues. Some general features of the CDC model include:

- community-based, -oriented, and -controlled development,
- integrated economic, social, and cultural goals (e.g., business and economic development, employment, training, and affordable housing),
- reliance on volunteer time and resources (e.g., board members, committee work, administrative support, and local leadership and expertise),
- multiple sources of funding,
- reinvestment in the community,
- networks, partnerships, and collaborations with private and public institutions, and
- short- and long-term community capacity-building strategies such as capital projects and asset development.

Although a considerable amount of research has examined the effectiveness of CDCs in urban milieux (e.g., affordable housing initiatives), comparatively little attention has been focused on their presence within the rural community development arena.

The Manitoba Context: CDCs and CED

The history of CDCs, in Manitoba, spans a period of approximately five decades. Of the 92 CDCs incorporated as of 2002, 14 date back to the late-1950s and 1960s while nearly three-quarters (i.e., 67) of these organizations have been established since the mid-1990s. This recent expansion is relevant to the present paper for two reasons. First, a CDC, as defined by Part XXI of *The Corporations Act* (Province of Manitoba, 1987, p. 198), is a company established for the purpose of "fostering the social and economic development of a municipality or other local area." The *Act* refers to CDCs as corporations "with share capital" (i.e., for profit); other types of CBOs have the option of incorporating as entities "without share capital" (i.e., not-for-profit) under Part XXII of the *Act*. Second, the Province of Manitoba invested $12.5 million in the Community Works Loan Program (CWLP) in October 1995. CWLP is termed a "revolving loan pool" of capital that can be used to finance initiatives "seen to be of community value" (Manitoba Rural Development, 1995, pp. 1–3). Under CWLP, CDCs are eligible to apply for (and then administer) provincial funding at a ratio of two dollars for every dollar raised locally. Although the initial loan is limited to a maximum of $50,000, a second allotment of matching funds is also available, on a one-to-one basis (again, up to $50,000), to assist CDCs' efforts to stimulate economic opportunities (e.g., business development). The financial resources advanced to CDCs by the Province take the form of an unsecured (interest-free) five-year loan. The language and intent of *The Corporations Act* (1987), in combination with the creation of CWLP (1995), place CDCs firmly within the local development arena (e.g., micro-financing) and the broader CED focus on social and economic revitalization. Hill, Cole, and Rounds (1998, p. 2) suggest that the following "mission statement" encapsulates the diverse goals of Manitoba CDCs: "To provide an environment in which planned business and community economic development is fostered, guided, and encouraged in order to help improve the quality of community life."

The specific attributes of a CDC's structure and functioning are defined in the articles of incorporation, which, among other things, specify geographical boundaries, voting procedures, distribution of assets, directors and officers, meetings, and a host of other details. A local steering committee typically delineates the basic purpose, objectives, by-laws, and other administrative and financial aspects of the proposed entity. Only one CDC is permitted to represent a municipality or some portion thereof, although many (approximately 40 percent) comprise two or more municipalities. Also, the municipal council(s) must pass a resolution approving the formation of a CDC prior to filing an application for incorporation under the *Act*. At the present time, no core funding arrangement exists to support the administration of CDCs in Manitoba. Depending on the type of incorporation (i.e., with or without share capital) and the financial structure of the organization, revenues can be generated through a variety of means: federal and provincial funding, municipal government grants, service clubs, investors or stakeholders, philanthropists and charities, fee-for-service consulting services, real estate transactions, loan interest and repayments, and business ventures (Manitoba Rural Development and the Manitoba Community Development Corporations Association, 1998, pp. 10–11).

In addition to CDCs, the Manitoba (rural) community development scene comprises a variety of CBOs or groups with somewhat overlapping mandates, for example, RDCs, Community Futures Development Corporations (CFDCs), and Community and Regional Round Tables. All of these entities have emerged in one way or another as mechanisms for harnessing and managing the resources needed to undertake rural renewal, but they also compete for a limited pool of human, social, and financial capital. There is little coordination among these organizations with regard to issues such as local versus regional planning, cooperative linkages, and leadership roles. And, although CDCs have received some organizational and financial resources (e.g., CWLP) from the provincial government, "they are primarily funded through municipal grants and programs and most struggle to operate on very limited budgets" (Mealy, 2003, p. 7). In spite of such limitations, CDCs are vying for a leading role in community development. The Manitoba Community Development Corporations Association (MCDCA) is working to place CDCs at the center of the CED movement by strengthening organizational capacities (e.g., board and staff training) and inter-organizational networks. This endeavor is not surprising given that CED principles and CDC mandates share a common interest in ameliorating social and economic conditions in rural communities.

Notwithstanding changes in partisan politics, various provincial and federal governments have elaborated rural and community development policies, programs, and funding frameworks. There has been a notable philosophical and fiscal movement away from the regional focus of the 1960s and 1970s (e.g., growth-pole or central place models) toward a community-based approach. Over the past ten years, CED has become increasingly prominent at the provincial policy level and in the goals and activities of Manitoba CDCs. Indeed, the Province of Manitoba (2001, p. 1) has developed a CED Policy Framework intended to foster a "more inclusive, equitable and sustainable" economy. Infanti (2003, p. 83) has conducted an inventory of governmental support for CED in Canada and remarks that Manitoba "has made a strong commitment to an integrated strategy for the revitalization and renewal of community economies and social and environmental health."

There is a substantial and growing body of literature on CED (see Douglas, 1994a), but much of the terminology lacks definitional consensus. One of the core issues in CED theory and practice concerns the relative emphasis placed on business development as compared to community empowerment. Fontan (1993, p. 7) makes a related point in the process of differentiating "liberal" and "progressive" forms of CED:

> There are...important nuances between liberal local and community initiatives, designed simply to generate local entrepreneurship and some economic growth, and progressive local and community initiatives, designed to change the approach to development in order to bring about a vital, equitable, safe, quality socioeconomic environment that fosters the empowerment of the individual and the community.

This basic tension in the field of CED parallels a distinction commonly made between development-*in*- versus development-*of*-the-community. Shaffer and Summers (1989, pp. 173–174) argue that CED is a "clear example" of the former orientation in that it stresses job creation, efficient use of productive resources, and adaptability to internal and external (e.g., market) conditions. In contrast, Shragge (1997, pp. 1–2) refers to CED as a mode of intervention "that links social and economic development with a wider political strategy of social change and community empowerment." He considers CED an instrument of social transformation that includes efforts to build institutions that can more effectively respond to the needs, conditions, and concerns of community residents. Boothroyd and Davis (1993, p. 230) have endeavored to clarify discourse on CED by distinguishing three approaches based on: (a) "growth promotion" (**cEd**) – employment, income, and business development through planning, opportunity identification, incentives, improved infrastructure, and training, (b) "structural change" (**ceD**) – local control, economic diversification, stability, and sustainability, and (c) "communalization" (**Ced**) – social and emotional aspects of community well-being, social equity, and social justice. The definition of CED presented in a CDC resource manual prepared jointly by the Manitoba Department of Rural Development and the Manitoba Community Development Corporations Association (1998, pp. 3–4) proposes a combination of dimensions:

> CED is a form of self-help that seeks to marry strategies of social and economic development through building capacity within the community. This process can be achieved only through local initiative. Community needs and opportunities are determined by individual and collective input, which reflect local attitudes and values that are of focus and interest to everyone. Community involvement is sparked when community members recognize a need or opportunity and proceed to take action to address the situation, using appropriate and available resources.

There is a growing trend in Manitoba toward describing CDCs as 'CED' organizations at both the policy and the grass-roots levels. CDCs (and other CBOs) can and do vary in terms of the relative emphasis placed on CED strategies. These differences in approach can be attributed to a host of factors such as local leadership, board and staff orientations, familiarity with CED principles, and community development ideologies, agendas, plans, and priorities. Although CDCs commonly focus on business development, retention, and attraction, some pursue a broad spectrum of activities including housing projects, job skills training, as well as commercial and business ventures. Swack and Mason (1994, p. 16) remark that there is a need to conduct research on the effectiveness and appropriateness of the CDC structure for combining diverse CED practices. Table 1 outlines seven basic points of comparison between general CED principles and the CDC model (e.g., organizational structure and functioning). The contents of the table are illustrative rather than exhaustive in their treatment of CED and CDC attributes. The remainder of the paper explores the extent to which core aspects of the CED approach are reflected in the goals, operations, and activities of Manitoba CDCs.

Table 1. Comparison of Core CED Principles and CDC Characteristics[a]

Comparative Element	CED Principles and Practices	CDC Mandates and Characteristics
Community Capacity Building	concerned with enhancing diverse types of community resources (e.g., financial, human, technical, social, physical, and organizational).	focus on strengthening community capacity via business and economic initiatives, infrastructure upgrades, training, planning,...
Multi-sectoral Approach to Development	"multi-functional, comprehensive strategy or development system" (Bruce, 2001, p. 70). integration of economic, social, cultural, and environmental dimensions.	flexible structure for addressing a wide range of economic and socio-cultural goals (e.g., business development, affordable housing, and local facilities and services).
Civic Participation and Engagement	grass-roots, 'bottom-up' approach. broadly based, inclusive participation.	involve residents, groups, and organizations in processes of community revitalization.
Community Organizing, Organization, and Leadership	stress the importance of local input, leadership, organizations, and action in solving problems. employ "a core-organization format that is non-profit, independent, and non-governmental" (Bruce, 2001, p. 71).	rely on local citizens and leaders to carry out voluntary board functions, committee work, and other administrative duties. can operate as a vehicle for building community consensus, agendas, and action.
Partnerships, Collaboration, and Networks	emphasize the importance of building networks among various groups, associations, and organizations to strategize, fund, and accomplish development goals.	encourage collaboration with multi-level groups or organizations (i.e., local, regional, provincial, and/or federal), in the pursuit of development initiatives.
Program Planning, Implementation, and Review	closely aligned with strategic planning models, that is, visioning, assessing situation, setting goals, and devising, implementing and evaluating plans.	include efforts to build "the community's capacity to plan, design, control, implement, and assess its own future" (Brodhead et al., 1990, p. 12).
Community Building	comprehensive approach to building local capacities, capital, involvement, and action.	pursue a community-based, -oriented, and -controlled development agenda.

[a] Comparative elements adapted from Bruce (2001) and Roseland (1998).

METHOD

Sample and Data Collection

A survey of CDCs operating in rural Manitoba was conducted in the summer and fall of 2002 (Bessant & Annis, 2004). Information was collected on various topics including organizational goals, board characteristics, staffing arrangements, training needs, and planning processes. A working group comprising representatives of the Manitoba Community Development Corporations Association (MCDCA), the Community Futures Partners of Manitoba, the Manitoba Department of Intergovernmental Affairs, and the Rural Development Institute collaborated on various aspects of the research project. The primary method of data collection was a mail-out questionnaire, which was distributed to the (then) current list of 92 CDCs (i.e., share capital corporations) in August 2002. The cover letter, which was addressed to the Chair of the CDC, outlined the nature of the study goals and issues pertaining to research ethics. A reminder card was sent out in November 2002 to encourage additional replies and to thank those who had already returned surveys. Representatives from 55 of the 92 CDCs (59.8 percent) completed questionnaires, and the regional distribution of these cases proved highly comparable to that of the original mailing list. It should also be noted that the number of valid responses for some survey questions fluctuates because of missing values and, unless otherwise noted, study findings are based on the total sample.

RESULTS

The mail-out questionnaire covered a range of issues; however, the findings presented below have been restricted to information deemed most pertinent to the seven comparative elements outlined in Table 1. Each of these points is discussed in terms of related literature in the field and the results of relevant survey questions. The goal of the paper is to understand the role of CDCs as vehicles of community development, in general, and their reliance on CED strategies in pursuing local initiatives.

Community Capacity Building

Community capacity building is the first item listed in Table 1 because it constitutes a major theme underlying various CED principles and CDC functions. The concept of capacity building has become a euphemism for catalyzing people, resources, and action around community transformation. Much like other terminology in the development field, community capacity building is multidimensional in nature and, as such, lacks clear and concise meaning. For the purposes of the following discussion, community capacity refers to *"the interaction of human capital, organizational resources, and social capital existing within a given community that can be leveraged to solve collective problems and improve or maintain the well-being of that community"* (Chaskin, Brown, Venkatesh, & Vidal, 2001, p. 7). To the extent that community capacity has become a prominent aspect of both theoretical and practical discussions of development, it has made inroads into the research on CBOs. Chaskin et al.'s definition is well-suited to the comparative analysis of CED and CDC attributes insofar as it highlights local access to resources, community-based problem-solving, and collective action.

CDCs may be viewed as mechanisms of capacity building through their efforts to organize the community around common goals, to enhance diverse forms of community capital, to forge linkages with other organizations, as well as to design and implement strategic plans. However, it is important to distinguish between the broad concept of community capacity and a CDC's organizational capacity (e.g., financial resources, leadership, and expertise) to carry out its mandate. The mail-out survey asked representatives to provide capacity ratings for four basic CDC functions. The vast majority of the respondents described CDC capacity as either "Low" or "Moderate" in the areas of opportunity identification (84.6 percent [n=52]), proposal development (84.9 percent [n=53]), and project implementation (82.4 percent [n=51]), whereas the loan management function garnered a notable proportion of "High" capacity ratings (44.4 percent [n=54]). On a related theme, the survey participants responded as follows when prompted to evaluate the overall effectiveness of their CDCs: 18.2 percent – "Low," 70.9 percent – "Moderate," and 10.9 percent – "High." Further, a large proportion of the representatives (86.3 percent [n=51]) indicated a need for additional resources to enhance CDC capacity and effectiveness, most notably increased staffing, funding, and training opportunities.

Multi-Sectoral Approach to Community Development

CED is frequently described as a multifaceted approach to community development that combines economic, social, environmental, and other considerations. This principle reflects the recent focus on devising holistic approaches to community development, for example, Rogers and Ryan's (2001, p. 281) "triple bottom line" conception of "empowerment, human capacity building and environmental sustainability as the foundations for economic prosperity." A CED-based agenda is typically defined as one that addresses diverse aspects of development through a series of community-based initiatives. The recent emphasis on integrated development mirrors a general shift away from narrowly defined economic growth toward more comprehensive approaches to building sustainable (rural) communities. Perry (1999, p. 21) suggests that CED is "most effective" when, among other things, it assumes a "multi-functional" form and "merges social and economic goals in order to make a more powerful impact for community change and revitalization." A comprehensive CED program, then, would not focus solely on enhancing the local economy or any other single sector; rather, it would incorporate a wide range of community issues and inputs: local interests and needs, opportunity identification, impact assessment, skill development, resource management, and short- and long-term planning.

CDCs, in rural Manitoba, have been given a broad mandate to carry out social and economic development and, increasingly, they are adopting CED principles and strategies to fulfill these responsibilities. One of the goals of the study was to investigate the sectoral diversity of CDC initiatives. Representatives were queried about their CDCs' involvements in a variety of domains. Survey data concerning seven core functions were combined to generate an additive index of Multi-sectoral Activities (see Appendix A). This composite variable comprises the following items (listed in descending order of the percentage of CDCs active in each area): business development (92.7 percent), capital projects (74.5 percent), housing initiatives (50.9 percent), community facilities (47.3 percent), social or recreational projects (45.5 percent), youth development (36.4 percent), and environmental considerations (32.7 percent). An examination of the value ranges for the multi-functional index and its component items revealed that over one-half of the CDCs (30 or 54.5 percent) were engaged in four or more sectors, which is suggestive of multi-pronged CED agendas. Further, 40 representatives (72.7 percent) indicated some form of involvement in both business development and capital project initiatives, while only three CDCs were active in neither area. Clearly, a sizeable proportion of Manitoba's CDCs are making efforts to enhance business, economic, and physical assets in order to build attractive environments for prospective (and current) entrepreneurs, investors, and residents. These results are consistent with Roseland's (1998, p. 161) contention that "Development of local, small businesses has been a common goal of many CED initiatives, along with job training and provision of affordable housing."

Civic Participation and Engagement

One of the central tenets of CED is citizen participation, which is closely linked to matters of social equity, social justice, self-reliance, and empowerment. Indeed, the CED perspective is aligned with broadly based democratic principles of decision-making, governance, openness, respect for diversity, and inclusiveness. Haughton (1998, p. 874) contends that "productive community engagement can foster a sense of local ownership and bring about important insights into how initiatives can build from an area's existing strengths." Civic engagement is foundational to the 'bottom-up' nature of the CED approach and its focus on local involvement in and control over all aspects of community development, for example, visioning, planning, implementation, and evaluation (Prokopy & Castelloe, 1999). Brown (1997, p. 70, 68) suggests that "locally rooted, democratic community organizations" are more amenable to CED than traditional, bureaucratized structures (e.g., municipal governments) because they (the former) "can be more fluid, participatory, innovative, and responsive." On this point, a number of the more recently established CDCs in Manitoba emerged out of a 1991 provincial initiative (i.e., the *Community Choices Program*) designed to generate "an active approach to community development" that is based on "local participation, local leadership and local ownership of the process" (Manitoba Rural Development, no date, p. 1, 2). Through this program, Community Round Tables were organized to solicit input from community groups concerning social and economic development goals and action plans. In several instances, these provisional agendas were used to rationalize the formation of and later to provide direction for local CDCs.

This study explored some of the ways in which CDCs present opportunities for civic engagement and thereby contribute to participatory (community) development. The institutional structure of Manitoba CDCs includes a volunteer board of directors comprising various configurations of local government officials, entrepreneurs, and residents. Fifty-three survey respondents provided details concerning the various groups (e.g., organizational affiliations) represented on their CDC boards; the four most frequently mentioned categories were (a) town or municipal councillors (92.5 percent), (b) chamber of commerce members (45.3 percent), (c) business people (34.0 percent), and (d) citizens at large (32.1 percent). This information was used to generate a variable pertaining to the *Number of Sectors Represented on the Board* in order to explore linkages among various aspects of the CED perspective and the CDC model (see discussion of Table 2 and Appendix A). Suffice it to say here that the range of sectoral constituents on CDC boards is broadly indicative of civic participation. With regard to overall board size, total memberships varied from 4 to 18 members ($n=49$), with slightly over one-half (i.e., 55.1 percent) concentrated in the 5 to 8 range. Further, 13 percent of the CDC boards ($n=54$) were elected, 44.4 percent were appointed (most commonly by local councils), while the remaining 42.6 percent were determined by some combination of election and appointment.

Although boards tap into local reputational and formal leadership structures, other avenues of participation are needed to ensure that CDC activities fully reflect residents' concerns. Douglas (2003, Appendix II, pp. vii–viii) has investigated local economic development in rural Ontario and concludes that "Public participation in the plan making process is largely confined to representative processes, usually involving the business community and other local organizations, and conventional information dissemination and notification processes. A minimum of proactive outreach and resident participation takes place." Residents and leaders can also become engaged in CDC operations through their involvement in working committees. Sixty percent of the surveyed CDCs made use of committees to facilitate their activities in areas such as business development, funding, housing, recreation, and local amenities.

Further, the mail-out questionnaire investigated respondents' views concerning public familiarity with CDC functions. Representatives were asked to rate the community's overall awareness and understanding of CDC goals and, in both instances, the results were heavily concentrated (i.e., 98.2 percent) in the "Low" to "Moderate" range. These rather modest estimations of residents' familiarity with CDC mandates may be related to the frequency or means of communication, but they also suggest some degree of disconnection between the organization and the wider community. Bratt and Rohe (2004) note the importance of maintaining close ties between the CDC and the wider community through newsletters, information sessions, planning processes, and resident involvement in committees. Of the 55 CDCs that participated in this study, 49.1 percent maintains some form of Web page or Website, 58.2 percent holds annual public meetings, and 70.9 percent produces regular reports. However, the current emphasis on business and economic development initiatives, among Manitoba CDCs, may have the effect of emphasizing the participation and input of municipal and entrepreneurial leaders. If CDCs are to embrace the CED model fully, it will be necessary to engage residents in a broad spectrum of development-related processes and activities.

Community Organizing, Organization, and Leadership

Researchers and practitioners share a common interest in the associational fabric of community development. Local groups and organizations are often discussed in relationship to community capacity, which Garkovich (1989, p. 197) defines as "the ability of residents to mobilize and organize local or extra-local resources in the pursuit of communally defined goals." In this sense, capacity building occurs when community leaders and residents use existing organizations or devise new ones to build shared interests. CBOs, of various types, have emerged as mechanisms for identifying, articulating, and acting on common concerns. CDCs represent one such vehicle in that they combine, to varying degrees, community leadership, participation, and capital in the pursuit of short- and long-term development goals.

Community organizing can take a variety of forms (e.g., local development or social action) and espouse diverse values; however, it can be described broadly as a process that contributes "to social change by mobilizing people to act for their own interest in an organized way" (Shragge, 2003, p. 19). Aigner, Raymond, and Smidt (2002, p. 95) discuss theoretical advances that support the relevance of "whole community organizing," such as "the increasing focus on building more authentic reciprocating social relationships across barriers" and the treatment of the community as an interactional field (Kaufman, 1959; Wilkinson, 1991). Chaskin et al. (2001, p. 93–94) suggest that community organizing promotes community capacity building by:

• bringing people together around collective action (i.e., mobilization),
• strengthening interpersonal relations and forming alliances,
• improving access to diverse assets and resources, and
• reforming governance and decision-making processes.

There is no singular method of assessing the extent to which CDCs carry out capacity-building or community-organizing functions within a CED framework. Part of the difficulty relates to an earlier distinction made between the *liberal* and *progressive* definitions of CED. With regard to the former, CDCs in rural Manitoba are heavily embedded in business and economic development strategies. Many are involved in diverse partnerships with government, business, and other community organizations in an effort to revitalize local economies (e.g., employment creation, infrastructure upgrades, and skills training). CDCs also contribute to economic renewal through business development activities (e.g., community loan funds and incentive programs). On this point, Shragge (2003, p. 140) states that CED organizations "play an important role by bringing resources and support to groups that otherwise would be much weaker in the local economic community." The second, more inclusive, interpretation of CED introduces the issue of whether CDCs act as mechanisms of social change (e.g., equity and justice). If CDCs are to fulfill this latter role, they will be obliged to focus considerable attention on building community agendas, engaging residents and leaders, mobilizing support, and generating collective action (both in economic and social terms).

Leadership issues are embedded in various aspects of capacity building, community organizing, and organizational development. Williams and Wade (2002, p. 61) note that "The challenges facing contemporary society require leaders who are adept at community-building." Leadership development has traditionally emphasized the enhancement of human capital, that is, individual knowledge, skills, and technical competencies. Community leadership education, by comparison, is concerned with building or strengthening shared interests, interaction, relationships, collaborative action, and "mutual empowerment" (Pigg, 2002, p. 116). Some years ago, Kaufman (1977, p. 400) suggested that (community) leadership should be understood "more in terms of the coordination of activity and information than of the direct exercise of power." Pigg (1999, p. 202) has elaborated on this theme through his discussion of the convergence between community field theory and leadership, most notably "the identification and development of a common purpose as the basis for relationships and interaction."

Chaskin et al. (2001) suggest that leadership development strategies among CBOs focus primarily on board members and senior staff. Formal training represents a strategy for enhancing technical skills and knowledge related to various dimensions of community-based development. This study investigated CDC representatives' perceptions of board training opportunities and needs. Survey participants were asked to review a list of 12 general training areas and then indicate whether each was *adequate*, *in need of improvement*, or *unavailable*. The following six types of training are listed in descending order of the percentage of respondents rating each item as **needing improvement**: *business attraction and development* (66.7 percent [n=51]), *opportunity identification* (66.0 percent [n=50]), *business retention* (64.7 percent [n=51]), *project design and evaluation* (55.1 percent [n=49]), *marketing and promotion* (54.9 percent [n=51]), and *strategic planning* (52.0 percent [n=50]). These training issues are closely aligned with the previously mentioned CDC focus on business development and capital projects (see "Multi-Sectoral Approach to Community Development").

In summary, community capacity and leadership development intersect with the organizational structure and functioning of Manitoba CDCs. First, CDCs are interconnected with other community organizations through board composition, for example, chambers of commerce and municipal councils. This situation can lead to interlocking directorships, over-reliance on a limited pool of volunteers and, by implication, somewhat less inclusive participatory or representational processes. It is not sufficient simply to provide opportunities for participation; some effort should also go into activating and nurturing potential leaders. Second, CDCs can be involved in highly diverse, multi-sectoral initiatives that require a wide range of organizational, technical, and leadership skills. The enhancement of leadership resources in CDCs often takes the form of board development efforts such as providing training and involving members in policy formation or project design (i.e., on-the-job) activities. Many leadership issues are related to the cultivation of 'social entrepreneurship' as a means of achieving social and economic development or catalyzing change through innovation and resourcefulness.

Partnerships, Networks, and Collaboration

Although there are varying conceptions of and approaches to community development, Bryant (1994, p. 189) suggests that "the new form of CED . . . is characterized by participation, collaboration, cooperation and partnership-building." He further suggests that partnerships generally reflect multilateral, non-hierarchical relationships among organizations and individuals who share a common interest in and sense of responsibility for achieving community-based goals. Hence, local organizations and their interrelationships are important aspects of CED insofar as they embody the patterned and yet ever-changing ways in which people relate to each other around common concerns. Recent theoretical and practical interest in community capital and capacity building has drawn attention to the role of inter-organizational networks in rural revitalization. Cigler (1992) refers to a continuum of rural partnerships ranging from loosely configured networks to long-term multi-community collaborations. "Each type...differs in complexity of purposes (information sharing vs. complicated, joint problem-solving); intensity of linkages (based on common goals, decision rules, shared tasks and resource commitments); and the formality of agreements reached (informality vs. formality of rules guiding operating structures, policies and procedures)" (Cigler, 1992, p. 54). Further, Chaskin et al. (2001, pp. 125–126) discuss three strategies for building "organizational collaboration":

1. creating "broker organizations" that "*mediate and foster relations*" among existing organizations operating within or across various communities (e.g., information sharing, resource enhancement, and problem-solving),
2. "direct, ongoing communication and collective planning and action," and
3. developing "specialized partnerships."

Proponents of CED advocate the cultivation of inter-organizational linkages as a key capacity-building strategy. This suggestion is typically premised on the view that rural revitalization is highly complex and far exceeds the skills and resources of one organization or community. Vidal and Keating (2004, p. 127) reinforce this point in stating that the accomplishments of CDCs are a function of "the combination of their effort and of the resources and support of a sizeable cadre of other organizations." However, rural communities and CBOs have not always welcomed cooperative ventures with other organizations or neighboring towns. Manitoba CDCs commonly represent the interests of a single community, although they can encompass one or more surrounding municipalities. Further, rural CDCs are only one of several CBOs that compete for a limited pool of resources (e.g., human and financial) and sometimes share overlapping development goals. This raises the issue of how often CDCs form partnerships with other CBOs both within and beyond their immediate localities.

This study explored the involvement of CDCs in community and regional development processes. Notwithstanding the diversity of development organizations, 81.8 percent of the respondents considered the local CDC to be the "*primary* development agency" in the area. A follow-up question revealed that CDCs engage in a range of inter-organizational relations with other CBOs (e.g., RDCs, CFDCs, chambers of commerce, and LDOs). The following list of CDC activities identified by representatives has been organized in terms of Cigler's (1992, pp. 54–55) continuum of partnerships: *networks* → *cooperation* → *coordination* → *collaboration*:

- communication, liaison, information or resource sharing, and client referrals,
- participation in organizational renewal processes,
- coordination of plans with other CBOs so as to avoid duplication or conflict,
- additional financing, human resources, and loan sharing,
- partnerships on special events, promotional activities, and project development (e.g., tourism), and

- collaborating with regional development groups around common interests (e.g., local industry attraction).

The above information served as a basis for constructing a variable pertaining to the intensity or complexity of CDC *Inter-organizational Partnerships* with other CBOs, which could be correlated with other CED-related attributes (see Table 2 and Appendix A).

On a related matter, 30 (54.5 percent) representatives indicated that their local CDCs were involved in regional development processes, for example, participating on RDC boards, partnering with RDCs and Regional Round Tables, or working on joint projects with surrounding municipalities. When asked whether regional development was part of their CDCs' mandates, 30 out of a total of 52 respondents (57.7 percent) answered in the affirmative. These results speak to issues of competition and cooperation that have evolved historically between communities and regions vying for limited resources. CDCs are deemed valuable mechanisms for pursuing regional ventures, especially with regard to project identification, development, and leadership. The survey findings generally illustrate the cooperative, collaborative, and promotional roles that CDCs can and do assume in local development.

Program Planning, Implementation, and Review

Blakely and Bradshaw (2002, p. 75) remark that "The planning of local economic development is a *process meant to deliver a product.*" However, the authors distinguish between economic growth (e.g., increased employment and income) and the much more complex, multifaceted goal of building community capacity. CED theorists and researchers routinely discuss planning as an element of the larger community development process. For Frank and Smith (1999, p. 6), community development constitutes "the planned evolution of all aspects of community well-being (economic, social, environmental and cultural)." However, development planning can vary in scale from specialized sector-specific initiatives to more broadly based community goals. Douglas (1994b, p. 153) attributes the diversity of CED planning processes to the inherent complexity of community contexts, the multitude of potential actors and organizations, and the ever-changing social, economic, and political landscape. Community development planning engages a number of CED principles, for example, it is multi-sectoral, "integrated," "inclusive," "community-based," and "requires resources and dedicated leadership" (Frank & Smith, 1999, p. 33). It is also noteworthy that the *Resource Manual for Community Development Corporations* (Manitoba Rural Development and the Manitoba Community Development Corporations Association, 1998, p. 35) includes explicit references to "community strategic planning," "community economic development plans," and a ten-step planning process.

Bratt and Rohe (2004, pp. 213–214) contend that strategic planning should be central to all CDCs, with regard to issues such as "optimizing organizational efficiency," strengthening capacities, assessing environmental conditions, and identifying appropriate levels of task specialization or diversification. Lamontagne (1994) notes that strategic planning is gaining increased acceptance among CED practitioners because of its focus on community control, local participation, and long-term resource management. The survey included a series of questions pertaining to CDC involvement in planning activities, that is, plan *development*, *implementation*, and *evaluation*. Nearly three-quarters of the representatives (i.e., 73.6 percent [*n*=53]) indicated that their CDCs had engaged in some form of planning. Of this group, 74.4 percent described these activities as a combination of both short- *and* long-term planning, while a much smaller proportion reported either *short-* (20.5 percent) or *long-term* (5.1 percent) planning only. Another point of interest relates to plan implementation. Representatives were asked how closely their proposed plans were being followed, to which 63.2 percent answered "Somewhat," 34.2 percent "Very Closely," and only 2.6 percent "Not Very Closely." The vast majority of the respondents (i.e., 90.2 percent) indicated that their CDCs' development plans were reviewed periodically, most often via an internal board process that was carried out on an annual or semi-annual basis. Further, 85 percent of these CDC representatives indicated that planning activities were "integrated" or "coordinated" with those of other CBOs. This latter point concerns the extent to which CDCs are open to partnerships and collaborations with other organizations, communities, or municipalities.

Community Building

Community capacity building was introduced at the outset of this analysis as a substantive theme underlying various CED principles and CDC functions (refer to Table 1). It is important to note that, although capacity building remains influential in community development theory and practice, other related concepts continue to evolve in meaning and application. One such term is community building, which Hyman (2002, p. 196) refers to as "the foundation for community-empowered change." At the most basic level, community building is concerned with strengthening residents' "sense of community" (Roseland, 1998, p. 161), hence the implication that effective community development requires pervasive levels of citizen participation, integration, solidarity, and cohesiveness. Community building has emerged recently as a broadly framed (localistic) development concept and intervention strategy that combines asset-based capacity building with the foundational principles of civic engagement, empowerment, and social action. The concept of community building and related strategies have been applied to "the problems and opportunities of both impoverished inner-city neighborhoods and rural areas" (McNeely, 1999, p. 742), for example, school improvement, housing programs, and poverty alleviation. It is mentioned here to illustrate the close linkages that are developing between CED theory and the CDC movement in rural Manitoba.

The contention by some authors that community building is a "new approach" (e.g., Hyman, 2002; McNeely, 1999) is interesting in that neither capacity nor empowerment are new to the field of community development theory or practice. Perhaps what is novel is the integration of these two critical issues within the more comprehensive notion of community building. Hyman (2002, p. 196) remarks that community building "is guided by two fundamental beliefs—that the community or neighborhood is the appropriate focus for revitalization efforts; and that enhancing the capacity of communities to engage and support residents is essential to success." In the Canadian context, both capacity building and community building represent substrates of the CED framework. This somewhat unique and timely amalgamation of community capacity, community involvement, and community action themes has found favor across a wide range of CDCs and other CBOs. The proliferation of CED organizations reflects a growing movement among communities to take ownership over their problems, to define action agendas, and to mobilize support. In many instances, rural CDCs pursue diverse aspects of community building by and through their democratically-controlled structures, participatory mechanisms, capacity-building efforts, and linkages with local and extra-local organizations.

Inter-correlations Among CED-related Attributes of Manitoba CDCs

The foregoing discussion of study findings provides insight into the relationship between the CED perspective and the role of CDCs in rural Manitoba. However, descriptive statistics alone cannot clarify the extent to which CED principles are integrated across various aspects of the CDCs' mandates and operations. Table 2 displays inter-correlations among eight variables that reflect fundamental aspects of the CED approach. These attributes are illustrative in nature; they are presented here to explore further the interplay between CED principles and CDC practices. In several instances, composite (i.e., additive) indices have been generated in order to present data patterns more parsimoniously (see Appendix A for variable descriptions and Cronbach's alpha coefficients of internal consistency). Notwithstanding the relatively modest size of the sample, over one-half of the coefficients is |0.35| or larger, while three-quarters are statistically significant at or beyond the 0.05 level.

Table 2. Pearson Correlations Among Eight CED-related Attributes of Manitoba CDCs

Variable Names*:	1	2	3	4	5	6	7	8
1. Multi-sectoral Activities	-	.46***	.38**	.36**	.54***	.31*	.63***	.57***
2. Number of Sectors Represented on Board		-	.23	.19	.28*	.43**	.31*	.51***
3. Annual Public Meeting			-	.12	.28*	.13	.28*	.25
4. Community Familiarity with CDC Goals				-	.56***	.21	.42**	.34*
5. Perceived Organizational Capacity					-	.24	.44***	.37**
6. Inter-organizational Partnerships						-	.35*	.45**
7. Involvement in (Strategic) Planning							-	.59***
8. Plan Coordination with Other CBOs								-

N sizes vary based on pairwise deletion of missing data: 37 to 40 cases for correlations involving *Inter-organizational Partnerships* and 48 to 55 cases for all others.

* See Appendix A for descriptions of single- and multi-item variables.

* $p \leq 0.05$, ** $p \leq 0.01$, *** $p \leq 0.001$

The inter-correlation matrix exhibits several prominent clusters of association among the eight CED-CDC attributes. First, cross-sector functioning is commonly identified as a core feature of the CED perspective. The uppermost row of Table 2 shows that the index of multi-sectoral initiatives is positively and significantly correlated with all of the other variables, most notably with regard to the involvement in and the (inter-organizational) coordination of planning processes, the representatives' estimations of CDC capacity, and the sectoral diversity of board memberships. A second focal point in Table 2 concerns the two planning-related variables. The incidence of both strategic planning and plan integration with other CBOs is closely related to multi-sectoral functioning, higher perceived CDC capacity, and more complex partnerships with local organizations. Third, civic participation or community engagement is pertinent to the analysis of the CED perspective and its relationship to CDC operations. In principle, annual public meetings allow local residents to become more aware of and engaged in the affairs of the CDC. The relevant variable in Table 2 exhibits positive but generally low correlations with the remaining CED-CDC attributes. On a related point, the sectoral diversity of board members provides a basic indication of the CDC's representational or participatory breadth within the community (e.g., town or municipal councils, chambers of commerce, and local residents). The correlational results suggest that broadly based CDC boards are likely to pursue a wider range of initiatives, to coordinate their plans with other CBOs, and to form inter-organizational networks that go beyond simply exchanging information or interlocking directorships. Partnerships are fundamental to CED in that they create opportunities to share resources, to build capacity, and to enhance diverse forms of capital (e.g., financial, social, and human). Clearly, multi-sectoral initiatives, planning activities, inter-organizational (e.g., regional) affiliations, and capacity building are fundamental aspects of *both* the CED perspective and the functioning of rural Manitoba CDCs.

SUMMARY AND CONCLUSIONS

The historical emergence and continued evolution of CBOs in rural Manitoba, and various parts of Canada and the United States, evidence residents' ongoing efforts to revitalize their communities. CDCs have arisen during a time of sweeping socio-economic change, fiscal retrenchment, and devolution of responsibility for community economic development. The foregoing study findings generate a temporal image of CDCs as they function within the current and highly changeable socio-eco-political context. The purpose of this research project was to explore the goals and activities of CDCs in rural Manitoba as they relate to core aspects of the CED perspective. Several points warrant brief mention concerning the interplay between CED principles and CDC activities. First, broadly based citizen involvement and inclusiveness are hallmarks of CED. Traditional avenues of participation (e.g., board memberships and committees), although important, are insufficient to foster the close linkages needed between the CDC and the wider community of concerns, interests, and support. This point is partially reflected in respondents' moderate estimations of community awareness and understanding of CDC goals, as well as CDC effectiveness.

Second, Manitoba's rural CDCs have been given a broad mandate to enhance both social and economic conditions within their respective communities. Proponents of CED likewise embrace the principle of integrated, multi-sectoral community development. However, CDCs can and do vary in terms of the relative breadth of their development agendas, plans, and initiatives. Many factors can influence these circumstances, for example, board composition, development priorities, local concerns, and available resources. Although the results of the study indicate a measure of commitment to diverse sector initiatives, business and economic development constitute the central foci of many CDCs. This emphasis has led to a related criticism that CDCs are focusing on a *supply-side* approach to development rather than working toward the social changes needed to foster more sustainable communities (Stoecker, 1997, p. 3). Clearly, situational conditions such as agricultural restructuring, population decline, business and service loss, and youth out-migration have buttressed recent efforts to generate alternative economic and employment opportunities (e.g., entrepreneurial assistance and financial support).

Third, the matter of organizational capacity constitutes a cluster of factors (e.g., leadership, finances, knowledge, and expertise) impacting how effectively CDCs are able to resolve the diverse challenges currently confronting rural communities. Many of the CDCs in rural Manitoba and elsewhere struggle to secure adequate financial resources from various sources in order to cover the costs of administration, the employment of professional staff, and the financing of local development initiatives. In lieu of the funds needed to hire trained economic development officers, CDCs are obliged to rely quite heavily on local volunteers. Although these circumstances enhance the grass-roots, participatory character of the organization, they can also influence its overall effectiveness. Given such resource limitations, it is not surprising to find CDC directors and staff making efforts to enhance capacities through inter-agency relationships with other CBOs, for example, sharing resources, coordinating activities, cooperating on short-term initiatives, or collaborating on both local and regional development projects. The integration of CED theory and practice within the structure and functioning of CDCs affords a valuable mechanism of community renewal, one based on the principles of local control, inclusiveness, empowerment, and inter-organizational cooperation.

There are noteworthy points of overlap between fundamental aspects of CED and the mandates of CDCs in rural Manitoba. Many CDCs can be characterized as "CED intermediaries," that is, "local development organizations that oversee and support CED efforts by bringing together diverse groups (business, labour, government, and community groups) to plan and co-ordinate development strategies in their communities" (Ninacs & Toye, 2002, p. 25). However, the CED framework encompasses a comprehensive set of general principles and development guidelines that are not yet fully reflected in the current CDC model. If the ultimate goal is to align CDCs more closely with the CED perspective, greater attention will need to be focused on enhancing organizational (and local) capacity, working toward more fully integrated and multi-sectoral approaches to community development, and generating increased community participation and leadership, to name only a few basic issues. Much of the relevant literature on CED and CDCs emphasizes the central role of capacity building. Nye and Glickman (2000, p. 167, 171), for example, discuss five common needs among CDCs: (a) stable, long-term funding (*"resource capacity"*), (b) board and staff training (*"organizational capacity"*), (c) linkages with other CBOs, institutions, private and public agencies (*"networking capacity"*), (d) diverse programs or services (*"programmatic capacity"*), and (e) community recognition, advocacy, and participation (*"political capacity"*). CDCs will need to enhance various forms of capacity if they are to figure prominently in the futures of urban or rural communities. Further, Glickman and Servon (1998, p. 500) suggest that recent interest in community building reflects a growing recognition of the highly "complex and intertwined" nature of community revitalization, which has in turn precipitated the search for more comprehensive approaches to identifying "integrated solutions." And, while the authors' remarks are directed primarily at urban (i.e., neighborhood) contexts, they are equally pertinent to rural community development. Both the CDC concept and the CED perspective represent important methods of addressing rural revitalization.

One final point concerns the interactional approach to community and a series of related treatments of *community leadership* (Pigg, 1999), *whole community organizing* (Aigner et al., 2002) and *sustainable community development* (Bridger & Luloff, 1999). Nearly a half-century ago, Kaufman (1959, p. 8) spoke of "the search for community" in a rapidly changing world of diffuse territorial and social boundaries and in so doing advanced the notion of an interactional community. One of Kaufman's (1959, pp. 10–11) most noteworthy contributions is that of "community field," which "consists of an organization of actions carried out by persons working through various associations or groups." This concept is closely related to the capacity for community action insofar as it comprises associational and participatory relationships that cut across more narrowly drawn social fields. "The structural interest in the community field is expressed through linking, coordinating actions, actions that identify and reinforce the commonality that permeates the differentiated special interest fields in a community" (Wilkinson, 1991, p. 90). The interactional model underscores the importance of examining how (or whether) community participants and organizations can act collectively to address local interests, needs, and problems. Given the many changes reverberating through rural society, the interactional community represents a valuable approach to studying the linkages between social organization(s) and collective action. Sharp (2001, p. 403) has applied the community field concept to "the structures, elements, and processes that generate improved capacity for community action." His research highlights the role of inter-organizational networks and the community fields that can evolve around associational nodes within communities (i.e.,

CBOs). CDCs represent important vehicles for building interactional fields purposefully as settings for collective action. Ultimately, the effectiveness of CDCs within the community development arena will depend on their capacities to formulate comprehensive programs, to enhance local awareness and participation, to represent community interests, to mobilize resources, and to coordinate actions—put simply, to operationalize the principles of CED.

Appendix A. List of CDC-CED Attributes: Variable Descriptions, Ranges, and Cronbach's Alpha Coefficients

Variable/Index	Range	α
1. **Multi-sectoral Activities**	0 to 7	0.74
CDC involvement in ('No' | 'Yes'):		
• business development	0 to 1	
• capital projects (e.g., infrastructure)	0 to 1	
• housing development	0 to 1	
• community facilities	0 to 1	
• social-recreational initiatives	0 to 1	
• youth development	0 to 1	
• environmental issues	0 to 1	
2. **Number of Sectors Represented on Board**	0 to 5	-
Board members drawn from ('No' | 'Yes'):		
• local municipal or town councils	0 to 1	
• chambers of commerce	0 to 1	
• local businesses	0 to 1	
• community at large	0 to 1	
• other local CBOs	0 to 1	
3. **Annual Public Meetings ('No' | 'Yes')**	0 to 1	-
4. **Community Familiarity with CDC Goals**	2 to 6	0.76
• Rating of community's awareness of CDC goals ('Low' | 'Moderate' | 'High')	1 to 3	
• Rating of community's understanding of CDC goals ('Low' | 'Moderate' | 'High')	1 to 3	
5. **Perceived Organizational Capacity**	4 to 12	0.82
How would you rate ('Low' | 'Moderate' | 'High') your CDC's:		
• capacity for opportunity identification	1 to 3	
• capacity for proposal development	1 to 3	
• capacity for project implementation	1 to 3	
• overall effectiveness	1 to 3	
6. **Inter-organizational Partnerships**	0 to 3	-
• no relationship	0	
• exchange of ideas, information, reports…	1	
• cooperation on joint projects	2	
• more extensive coordination or collaboration (e.g., planning and resource sharing)	3	
7. **Involvement in (Strategic) Planning ('No' | 'Yes')**	0 to 1	-
8. **Plan Coordination with Other CBOs ('No' | 'Yes')**	0 to 1	-

REFERENCES

Aigner, S. M., Raymond, V. J., & Smidt, L. J. (2002). "Whole community organizing" for the 21st century. *Journal of the Community Development Society*, 33(1), 86–106.

Allen, J. C., & Dillman, D. A. (1994). *Against All Odds: Rural Community in the Information Age*. Boulder, CO: Westview Press, Inc.

Bessant, K. C., & Annis, R. C. (2004). *Report on the Strengths, Challenges, and Opportunities of Community Development Corporations in Manitoba*. Brandon, MB: Rural Development Institute, Brandon University.

Blakely, E. J., & Bradshaw, T. K. (2002). *Planning Local Economic Development: Theory and Practice*. (3rd ed.). Thousand Oaks, CA: Sage Publications, Inc.

Boothroyd, P., & Davis, H. C. (1993). Community economic development: Three approaches. *Journal of Planning Education and Research*, 12, 230–240.

Bratt, R. G., & Rohe, W. M. (2004). Organizational changes among CDCs: Assessing the impacts and navigating the challenges. *Journal of Urban Affairs*, 26(2), 197–220.

Bridger, J. C., & Luloff, A. E. (1999). Toward an interactional approach to sustainable community development. *Journal of Rural Studies*, 15(4), 377–387.

Brodhead, D., Lamontagne, F., & Peirce, J. (1990). *The Local Development Organization: A Canadian Perspective*. Local Development Paper No. 19. Ottawa, ON: Economic Council of Canada.

Brown, L. H. (1997). Organizations for the 21st century? Co-operatives and "new" forms of organization. *Canadian Journal of Sociology*, 22(1), 65–93.

Bruce, D. W. (2001). Building a CED movement in Canada: A policy framework to scale up CED in Canada. In: D. Bruce & G. Lister (Eds.), *Rising Tide: Community Development Tools, Models, and Processes*, pp. 69–82. Sackville, NB: Rural and Small Town Programme, Mount Allison University.

Bryant, C. R. (1994). The corporate and voluntary sectors as partners in community economic development. In: B. Galaway & J. Hudson (Eds.), *Community Economic Development: Perspectives on Research and Policy*, pp. 187–194. Toronto, ON: Thompson Educational Publishing.

Chaland, N. & Downing, R. (2003). *Profile of Community Economic Development in Canada: Results of a Survey of Community Economic Development Across Canada*. Victoria, BC: The Canadian CED Network. Retrieved October 7, 2004, from http://www.ccednet-rcdec.ca/en/docs/pubs/Profile_CED_Oct_2003.pdf

Chaskin, R. J., Brown, P., Venkatesh, S., & Vidal, A. (2001). *Building Community Capacity*. Hawthorne, NY: Walter de Gruyter, Inc.

Cigler, B. A. (1992). Pre-conditions for multicommunity collaboration. In: P. F. Korsching, T. O. Borich, & J. Stewart (Eds.), *Multicommunity Collaboration: An Evolving Rural Revitalization Strategy*, pp. 53–74. Ames, IA: North Central Regional Center for Rural Development, Iowa State University.

Deaton, B. J. (1975). CDCs: A development alternative for rural America. *Growth and Change*, 6(1), 31–37.

Douglas, D. J. A. (1994a). Community economic development in Canada: Issues, scope, definitions and directions. In: D. J. A. Douglas, *Community Economic Development in Canada*, pp. 1–64. Toronto, ON: McGraw-Hill Ryerson.

Douglas, D. J. A. (1994b). Planning and implementing community economic development: Some generalizations on process and practice in Canada. In: D. J. A. Douglas, *Community Economic Development in Canada*, pp. 119–160. Toronto, ON: McGraw-Hill Ryerson.

Douglas, D. J. A. (2003). *Towards More Effective Rural Economic Development in Ontario: An Applied Research Project. Final Report*. Guelph, ON: School of Environmental Design and Rural Development, University of Guelph.

Fontan, J-M. (1993). *A Critical Review of Canadian, American, and European Community Economic Development Literature*. Vernon, BC: Centre for Community Enterprise, Westcoast Publications.

Frank, F., & Smith, A. (1999). *The Community Development Handbook: A Tool to Build Community Capacity*. Ottawa, ON: Minister of Public Works and Government Services. Retrieved January 7, 2005, from http://www.hrsdc.gc.ca/asp/gateway.asp?hr=en/epb/sid/cia/comm_deve/handbook.shtml&hs=cyd

Fuller, T. (1994). Sustainable rural communities in the arena society. In: J. M. Bryden (Ed.), *Towards Sustainable Rural Communities: The Guelph Seminar Series*, pp. 133–139. Guelph, ON: University of Guelph.

Garkovich, L. E. (1989). Local organizations and leadership in community development. In: J. A. Christenson & J. W. Robinson, Jr. (Eds.), *Community Development in Perspective*, pp. 196–218. Ames, IA: Iowa State University Press.

Glickman, N. J., & Servon, L. J. (1998). More than bricks and sticks: Five components of community development corporation capacity. *Housing Policy Debate*, 9(3), 497–539.

Haughton, G. (1998). Principles and practice of community economic development. *Regional Studies*, 32(9), 872–877.

Hill, M., Cole, W., & Rounds, R. (1998). *Stimulating Rural Investment Ways and Means: Community Development Corporations*. Brandon, MB: Rural Development Institute, Brandon University.

Hyman, J. B. (2002). Exploring social capital and civic engagement to create a framework for community building. *Applied Developmental Science*, 6(4), 196–202.

Infanti, J. (2003). *An Inventory of Provincial and Territorial Government Support to Community Economic Development in Canada*. Victoria, BC: The Canadian CED Network. Retrieved January 7, 2005, from http://www.ccednet-rcdec.ca/en/docs/pubs/Cednet%20prov%20inv%20Eng.pdf

Kaufman, H. F. (1977). Community influentials: Power figures or leaders? In: R. L. Warren (Ed.), *New Perspectives on the American Community: A Book of Readings* (3rd ed.), pp. 399–407. Chicago, IL: Rand McNally College Publishing Co.

Kaufman, H. F. (1959). Toward an interactional conception of community. *Social Forces*, 38(1), 8–17.

Lamontagne, F. (1994). Development indicators and development planning: A case study. In: B. Galaway & J. Hudson (Eds.), *Community Economic Development: Perspectives on Research and Policy*, pp. 208–222. Toronto, ON: Thompson Educational Publishing.

MacLeod, G. (1986). *New Age Business: Community Corporations That Work*. Ottawa, ON: Canadian Council on Social Development.

Manitoba Rural Development. (no date). *Community Choices: A Sustainable Communities Program for Manitoba*. Winnipeg, MB: Manitoba Rural Development.

Manitoba Rural Development. (1995). *Community Works Loan Program: Resource Handbook*. Winnipeg, MB: Manitoba Rural Development.

Manitoba Rural Development and the Manitoba Community Development Corporations Association. (1998). *A Resource Manual for Community Development Corporations*.

McNeely, J. (1999). Community building. *Journal of Community Psychology*, 27(6), 741–750.

Mealy, R. (2003). Who are the main players in CED in Manitoba responding to community challenges? *The Motivator*, 4(1), 7.

Ninacs, W. A., & Toye, M. (2002). *A Review of the Theory and Practice of Social Economy/Economie Sociale in Canada*. SRDC Working Paper Series 02-02. Ottawa, ON: Social Research and Demonstration Corporation.

Nye, N., & Glickman, N. J. (2000). Working together: Building capacity for community development. *Housing Policy Debate*, 11(1), 163–198.

Perry, S. E. (1989). *The Community as a Base for Regional Development*. Local Development Paper No. 11. Ottawa, ON: Economic Council of Canada.

Perry, S. E. (1999). Some terminology and definitions in the field of community economic development. *Making Waves*, 10(1), 20–23.

Pigg, K. E. (1999). Community leadership and community theory: A practical synthesis. *Journal of the Community Development Society*, 30(2), 196–212.

Pigg, K. E. (2002). Three faces of empowerment: Expanding the theory of empowerment in community development. *Journal of the Community Development Society*, 33(1), 107–123.

Prokopy, J., & Castelloe, P. (1999). Participatory development: Approaches from the global south and the United States. *Journal of the Community Development Society*, 30(2), 213–231.

Province of Manitoba. (1987). *The Corporations Act*. Winnipeg, MB: The Queen's Printer for the Province of Manitoba.

Province of Manitoba. (2001). *Community Economic Development (CED) Policy Framework*.

Rogers, M., & Ryan, R. (2001). The triple bottom line for sustainable community development. *Local Environment*, 6(3), 279–289.

Roseland, M. (1998). *Toward Sustainable Communities: Resources for Citizens and their Governments*. Gabriola Island, BC: New Society Publishers.

Shaffer, R., & Summers, G. F. (1989). Community economic development. In: J. A. Christenson & J. W. Robinson, Jr. (Eds.), *Community Development in Perspective*, pp. 173–195. Ames, IA: Iowa State University Press.

Sharp, J. S. (2001). Locating the community field: A study of interorganizational network structure and capacity for community action. *Rural Sociology*, 66(3), 403–424.

Shragge, E. (1997). *Community Economic Development: In Search of Empowerment*. Montréal, QC: Black Rose Books.

Shragge, E. (2003). *Activism and Social Change: Lessons for Community and Local Organizing*. Peterborough, ON: Broadview Press.

Stoecker, R. (1997). The CDC model of urban redevelopment: A critique and an alternative. *Journal of Urban Affairs*, 19(1), 1–22.

Swack, M., & Mason, D. (1994). Community economic development: An overview of the U.S. experience. In: B. Galaway & J. Hudson (Eds.), *Community Economic Development: Perspectives on Research and Policy*, pp. 13–21. Toronto, ON: Thompson Educational Publishing.

Vidal, A. C., & Keating, W. D. (2004). Community development: Current issues and emerging challenges. *Journal of Urban Affairs*, 26(2), 125–137.

Wilkinson, K. P. (1991). *The Community in Rural America*. Westport, CT: Greenwood Press.

Williams, M. R., & Wade, V. M. (2002). Sponsorship of community leadership development programs: What constitutes an ideal partnership? *Journal of the Community Development Society*, 33(2), 61–71.

Index

Note: Page numbers in **bold** type refer to figures
Page numbers in *italic* type refer to tables
Page numbers followed by 'n' refer to notes